Ultimate Guide to
SENSORY PROCESSING
DISORDER

Ultimate Guide to

SENSORY PROCESSING DISORDER

by
ROYA OSTOVAR, PhD

All marketing and publishing rights
guaranteed to and reserved by:

Sensory World
www.thesensoryworld.com

721 W. Abram Street
Arlington, TX 76013
Toll-free: 800-489-0727
Phone: 817-277-0727
Fax: 817-277-2270
Web site: www.FHautism.com
E-mail: info@FHautism.com

Printed in Canada

Cover design: TLC Graphics
Interior design: Publication Services, Inc.

ISBN 13: 978-1-932565-62-1

DEDICATION

To my beautiful daughter Savanna

who inspires me every day, who sees the true beauty in everything and everyone, who is poised, articulate, forgiving, and mature far beyond her young age and never ceases to amaze me with her incredible capacity for love, compassion, kindness, understanding, support, and humanity.

CONTENTS

Foreword   xiii

Acknowledgments   xix

Introduction   1

What Sensory Processing Disorder Is   2

What It's Like to Have SPD   3

What We Know about SPD   4

Strategies to Help Parents   6

Chapter 1: What Is SPD?   9

Problem Child or SPD?   10

No Recognition for a Real Disorder   17

Whom SPD Affects and How   20

The Three Types of SPD   26
   Mixed Subtypes   31

What the Research Tells Us about SPD   44
   Other Research Possibilities   45

Chapter 2: What It's Like to Have SPD   49

What Causes SPD?   50

How to Step into Your Child's Shoes   51

Real Stories of Kids with SPD   53

Case Study: Samantha, Age 8—Difficulty with
   Speech, Movement, and Touch   54
Case Study: Oliver, Age 5—Difficulty with
   Speech and Movement   64

Chapter 3: Understanding SPD as a Form of Stress   75

One Reaction Does Not Fit All   77

How Stress Affects Our Bodies   81

Stressed Out and Shut Down   83

When Stress Interferes with Thinking   84

Soldiering On, Fleeing, and Fighting   84

Different Types of Stress   85

Reliving a Stressful Event Again and Again   87

What Studies Tell Us about Understanding
   Stress—and SPD   88

Three Effects of Stress on the Immune System   89

A Predisposition for Stress and SPD   90

**Chapter 4: Helping Your Child Every Day and at
Special Events**   93

Religious and Cultural Holidays   95
   Find Out the Five W's of the Event   96
   Tips for Religious and Cultural Holidays   96

Weddings and Funerals   102
   The Wedding Planner   103
   Funerals   106

Vacations   109

Grocery and Department Stores   110

Comparative Shopping   111

Sports Events   112
   At the Game   114

After the Game — 114

A Child's Birthday Party — 115
The Invitation Arrives — 115
Your Child Is at the Party — 117

Chapter 5: Assessment, Diagnosis, and Treatment—Where to Begin — 119

Step 1: Make a List of Your Concerns — 120

Step 2: Fill Out a Symptom Checklist — 121

Step 3: Get a Referral to an Occupational Therapist — 134

Step 4: Educate Yourself about SPD — 136

Step 5: Find an Occupational Therapist Trained to Assess and Treat SPD — 137

Step 6: Connect with Community, Local Organizations, Other Families — 141

The Assessment Process: What You Need to Know — 143

What a Sample Evaluation Looks Like — 144
Relevant History — 145
Behavioral Observations — 147
Recommendations — 148
Sample Occupational Therapy Sensory Evaluation — 151

What Is a Sensory Diet? — 162
Suggested Sensory Diet Activities — 164

What You Can Expect from Treatment — 167
Sensory Integration Therapy — 169

Chapter 6: How to Help Create a Sensory-Friendly Classroom — 173

The Effect of SPD on Learning and Functioning at School — 174

Creating Sensory-Friendly Classrooms   176

Convincing Schools to Help Your Child   177

Behavior as a Form of Communication   184
   Case Study: Ray—Avoiding Embarrassment
      by Acting Out   187
   Case Study: Ali's Story—Fear of Failure   190

Communicating with Your Child's School   192

Chapter 7: The Difference between SPD and
Look-Alike Disorders   211

Pervasive Developmental Disorders   212
   Autism   213
   Asperger Syndrome   215

Nonverbal Learning Disorder   217

The Learning Disorders   219

Attention-Deficit/Hyperactivity Disorder
   and Disruptive Behavior Disorders   221
   Individual Treatment for Similar Symptoms   223

Children with Bipolar Disorder   229

How Behavioral Challenges Play a Role   230
   Case Study: Emily, Age 6—Mood Instability   231

A Helpful Tool–A Developmental History Form   244

Appendix A: Typical Developmental
Stages in Children   267

Understanding Your Child's Development   268

Piaget's Developmental Theory   268
   Sensorimotor Stage   269
   Preoperational Stage   269
   The Concrete Operational Stage   270
   How an Art Project Can Act as a Sensory Feast   270
   Formal Operations   271

Appendix B: CDC Development Milestones for Children 273

Important Milestones by the End of 3 Months 273

Important Milestones by the End of 7 Months 276

Important Milestones by the End of 12 Months 278

Important Milestones by the End of 2 Years 281

Important Milestones by the End of 3 Years 283

Important Milestones by the End of 4 Years 286

Important Milestones by the End of 5 Years 289

NOTES 293

Resources 297

Books 297

Videos 299

Web Sites 300

Organizations 301

Index 303

FOREWORD

Until the 1990s, information about sensory processing disorder (SPD), also known as *sensory integration dysfunction*, was scarce for people who were not occupational therapists. One could have read Dr A. Jean Ayres' seminal books, including *Sensory Integration and the Child*, which was written in the 1970s. A search of the Internet in later years would have revealed an occasional paragraph summarizing a research article, but unless one were a dues-paying professional, the complete article was inaccessible. One might have asked an occupational therapist to sit down for several hours to explain SPD and how it affected a child or student. Otherwise, to learn the basics of SPD, one had to go to school to become an occupational therapist and take extra academic courses on the treatment of sensory disorders.

In the 1990s, something wonderful began to happen. Books and videos about SPD began to appear at bookstores. With the advent of these materials, parents, teachers, and professionals who were eager to learn about SPD were finally able to get their hands on publications that could be easily understood.

The authors of these helpful books were occupational therapists, researchers, psychologists, psychiatrists, physicians, speech-language pathologists, individuals who lived with SPD, and even teachers. Each publication broadcast the author's point of view from a particular vantage point and contributed valuable information to laypeople about the effects of SPD at home, at school, at work, at play, and out and about in the world.

Now, another voice with a unique perspective joins this swelling chorus of authors who write about SPD. Roya Ostovar, PhD, is a neuropsychologist who has worked with children with SPD since 1997. Roya and I met at a conference sponsored by Sensory Resources in 2007. She told me that she used my book, *The Out-of-Sync Child*, in her work, and that she was writing a book from a new perspective. I rejoiced at this news, as many medical and mental health professionals are still unaware of the causes and effects of sensory processing issues.

With her education, experience, compassion, and wisdom, Roya is able to spread the word about SPD not only among her colleagues, but also among the general public. She trained at the Neuropsychiatric Institute and Hospital at the University of California, Los Angeles. Today, she is a clinical instructor of psychiatry at Harvard Medical School and the director of the training and fellowship program, with direct clinical supervision of fellows, interns, residents, and other trainees interested in learning about the educational and clinical needs of children with neurodevelopmental disorders. She is also the director of the McLean Hospital's Center for Neurodevelopmental Services, or CNS, in Belmont, Massachusetts. At CNS, she runs Pathways Academy and Camp New Connections to integrate services to meet the educational, social, and developmental needs of individuals with Asperger syndrome and related learning and developmental disorders.

There's no doubt about it—Roya Ostovar knows the score!

In this book, to get the reader in sync, she sings the same tune as other authors as she reviews and confirms much of what has been written. Then she goes further and helps the reader learn that SPD must be considered a form of unmitigated stress. Roya's mission is to help us "understand what a child with SPD experiences on a daily basis, the effect of SPD on the child's body and systems, and the child's physical and emotional reactions in various situations."

To help us feel what it is like to have SPD, she reminds us what it feels like when we are under great stress:

Consider this example: Your heart beats fast, your palms are sweaty, your head hurts, and you can't think straight. You feel like your blood pressure has gone up (and it has), your skin feels clammy, you feel a bit shaky when you walk or stand up, your eyes and ears don't quite work the way you'd like them to, and even though you need a drink of water, you probably don't feel like getting one.

To be out of control is scary, and for those who have SPD, this loss of control can be a daily—and even hourly—scenario.

The stress of having SPD can lead to ailments and disorders in the body, mind, and spirit. It can affect the child's physical, immunological, psychological, social, emotional, and cognitive health and welfare. Roya's examples of children overwhelmed by SPD help the reader to hear the children's frustration and exhaustion. Complete case studies, including recommendations to parents, are interspersed throughout the book, and these are useful to show us how a neuropsychologist perceives a child's behavior.

One of the best features of this book is the hundreds of quick, smart strategies that all of us can use to provide on-the-spot intervention when a child is experiencing a stress-driven meltdown. Some strategies are ones that parents and teachers may already use from time to time; others are brilliant new ideas—and all of them work!

Before taking the child to a religious or cultural event, for example, Roya suggests that we learn the answers to these questions:

- How many people will be there?
- What is expected of everyone—singing, silence, prayer, eating, drinking, sitting, walking, standing, clapping?
- Where will the event be held?
- When will it occur?
- How will it be managed?
- Why is your family going?

During the event, she offers other practical, instantaneous tips, including:

- If you see your child struggling, don't panic! Speak calmly and use language he is used to hearing. Now is not the time to try new techniques.
- Encourage your child to use his toys, props, or objects as supports, especially if you think it will help him get through a challenging segment of the event.
- Remember, even if your child does well during "practice," the stress of the real situation could be overwhelming. Always allow for a way out.

After the event:

- Gauge how much communication your child is up for after the event. If she is exhausted or if she craves stimulation, help her address those needs . . . provide a quiet, comforting environment in your car, or go to the playground for a few minutes before driving home.
- Ask your child how she felt at the event. Your child's feedback is part of what makes her sensory diet plan or the therapeutic exercises work.

- Whatever the outcome, don't lose sight of your child's hard work. Consider each attempt to participate in events as something to celebrate (even if it does not succeed).

Another excellent feature of this book is the Developmental History Form in chapter 7. Roya has composed a lengthy questionnaire based on several others in the field of neuropsychology. Glance at this form, and you will discover that while not all questions are sensory based, all the questions *matter.* They will help you see what you may have missed or thought was unimportant in your child's development. Here are some examples:

- Did your child have a snuggly object as an infant?

- Did you ever suspect that your child could have been deaf?

- Does your child blink or protect self from a ball even when trying to catch it?

- Does your child's conversation include laughing or smiling appropriately in response to peers?

- Is your child able to generate alternative solutions to problems?

- Does your child play "pretend?"

This book will help you look at your child in a new light and bring you further along in your understanding of sensory processing difficulties. It will also guide you, the parent, teacher, or other professional who holds it in your hands, to help the child about whom you care so much.

Carol S. Kranowitz, MA
Author, *The Out-of-Sync Child*
Summer 2009

ACKNOWLEDGMENTS

This book has come to realization with the love, help, and support of many of my family members, friends, colleagues, and patients.

First and foremost, I'd like to begin by thanking my wonderful daughter, Savanna, for her endless support of my work and dreams. Her words of encouragement and reminders of the value of the book to children who live with SPD gave me the energy to keep writing, even after a long day. More importantly, I am grateful for her presence and for the incredible joy she brings to every moment of my life.

Special thanks to my family, especially my father, Akbar Ostovar, who has always believed in me with great certainty and has never held back on letting me know how much he loves me and how proud he is of me.

I wish to thank Ramin, who truly is my better half and whose love, support, encouragement, and invaluable friendship mean the world to me. His wonderful sense of humor lightens my spirit every day, makes me laugh, gets me through difficult times, and reminds me not to take life too seriously. I have gotten to know myself better and have become a much stronger person through knowing him.

My gratitude to McLean Hospital and all my friends and colleagues for their recognition of the importance of this project and for sharing of their expertise, resources, and ideas. I have benefited tremendously from the incredible wisdom of Dr Joe Gold, who has been my dear friend and mentor and whose support I can count on without hesitation.

I would like to thank my dedicated staff at the Center for Neurodevelopmental Services at McLean Hospital for sharing their experiences, providing feedback on the book, and making helpful suggestions throughout the project. In particular, I'd like to thank Laura Mead, Karen Steves, Tee Stock, Faraz Sabet, Meredith Boldon, and Kelly Madden for their invaluable help and contributions.

My heartfelt gratitude, regards, and love to my dear friend, Carol Kranowitz, who has been nothing short of an angel throughout this project. She is truly a legend and a pioneer in the field of SPD and I have been incredibly fortunate to get to know her personally and professionally. Her own remarkable book, *The Out-of-Sync Child*, educated me, and her feedback improved the quality of my work.

I am grateful for the opportunity to have collaborated on this project with the following individuals: everyone at Sensory World—in particular, the wonderful Gilpin family, including Wayne, who made me feel like I was a part of his family right from the start, and Jennifer, who has touched me with her personable approach, kindness, and capacity to give—and I thank David Brown and my wonderful editor, Heather Babiar, for her hard work and tireless attention to details.

Perhaps needless to say, I am forever indebted to and grateful for my patients, and all the children and families who have entrusted me with their care and life stories over the years. In particular, I thank those families who so generously agreed to share their experiences to add to the quality and value of the book for others. It has been a pleasure and a privilege to be a part of your team of care providers and to have made a difference in your children's lives. Thank you.

INTRODUCTION

Kaveh, age 5, was referred to me by his parents as "a difficult and inflexible child," who would have a meltdown if he didn't have everything his way. At first glance, and on the basis of his parents' chief complaint, it seemed as though he was an uncooperative child, with a volatile temperament and incessant behavioral problems.

Detailed questionnaires and an interview with his parents, however, revealed much more. Getting Kaveh dressed in the morning was a monumental task that more often than not involved several changes of clothes. Kaveh often refused to wear weather-appropriate clothes, cried, complained that his clothes were uncomfortable, and refused to wear socks, certain shoes, gloves, hats, and jackets. His mother reported that she would take Kaveh shopping to buy whatever clothes he would agree to wear. Once they found something he liked, such as a pair of pants, she would buy several pairs of the same pants. However, that approach didn't work all the time.

"What felt comfortable to him last week may not feel comfortable this week," his mother said. This daily morning struggle would set the tone for the rest of the day, resulting in Kaveh being late to school and his mother arriving late to work, feeling frustrated and upset.

In addition, Kaveh was a picky eater, needed a great deal of his parents' help to fall asleep, and raged against personal hygiene activities, such as clipping his nails, washing, and brushing his hair. He had weak muscles, tired easily, and was terrible at sports and physical activities, according to his parents.

Following the initial evaluation, Kaveh received a diagnosis of sensory processing disorder (SPD).

What Sensory Processing Disorder Is

Sensory processing disorder is, at the most basic level, an inefficiency in our central nervous system to process information, namely incoming stimuli. Our nervous system organizes the information we take in—the sights, smells, touches, tastes, and noises—and processes it for us to use in our day-to-day lives. Difficulties in the processing of this information can lead to numerous problems, such as disrupted motor coordination, sleeping, eating, paying attention, learning, and functioning socially and emotionally.

In Kaveh's case, he was referred to an occupational therapist for a sensory processing evaluation. This is a specific evaluation by a trained occupational therapist who assesses and determines the child's sensory profile, which is a list of the child's sensory issues and problems, and makes specific treatment recommendations. An example of such an evaluation is provided in chapter 7.

Kaveh's parents received an individualized set of helpful activities to implement at home and at school, including learning exercises to strengthen his fine motor skills, practicing handwriting, manipulating small objects, developing a calming bedtime routine, and using a weighted (heavy) vest to help Kaveh get the sensory input he seeks. In addition, Kaveh began occupational therapy twice a week.

Knowing the cause and reasons behind Kaveh's behavior and receiving effective and practical tools for helping him reduced the family's stress tremendously, improved Kaveh's overall functioning, and prevented this problem from becoming a larger one in the future. This is, in part, how I hope to use this book to help parents of children with SPD.

What It's Like to Have SPD

Kaveh is one of many children with SPD who, on the surface, may seem difficult, strong-willed, uncooperative, and temperamental, and whose behavior is simply confusing and does not make sense to his parents. How can Kaveh's parents, and others like them, understand their child's behaviors and what he or she may be experiencing? Consider the following analogy.

Imagine living in a home with an electrical system that is completely ineffective in processing the information sent to and from all the wiring in the house. Every time you turn on the television, the volume is on the loudest level. When you turn on any light in the house, it is either too bright, is too dim, or flickers. The heating and cooling systems force out air that is either uncomfortably hot or painfully cold, if they come on at all. The stove only works on two levels: fiery hot and barely warm. If all that isn't bad enough, there is a strong, noxious odor of burned wiring circulating in the air that you can't remove.

How would you feel living in that house? What would it be like for you? Would you feel uncomfortable, frustrated, angry, disorganized, or lost? Your inability to control the electrical system and equipment would probably lead you to behave differently than if everything worked according to your expectations. Your reactions to the extreme and unpredictable conditions might be out of your control—and loss of self-control is one of the scariest feelings to experience.

If you can think of the main electrical panel of the house as the human brain and the electrical wiring as the nervous system, the above analogy can help you to understand what it may feel like for your child to have sensory processing disorder.

What We Know about SPD

SPD is gradually gaining recognition, but many professionals in the medical field seem to be unfamiliar with this disorder and how it may manifest in children.

Encouragingly, there has been great progress in the understanding, assessment, and treatment of sensory processing disorder since SPD pioneer A. Jean Ayres, PhD, OTR, published her first book on sensory integration in 1972. Ayres, a frontrunner in the field of occupational therapy and a psychologist, was the first to identify sensory integration dysfunction, now known as SPD.

Since then, the most important development in SPD has been the increased awareness and accumulation of information that parents, teachers, and service providers can use in helping children with the disorder. However, compared to other disorders that have such a clinically significant impact on an individual's functioning, such as Asperger syndrome, which was first described in 1944, we don't have nearly as much information or as many resources as we would like. Much work lies ahead of us in this field, particularly in the area of educating those who may be in the frontlines of providing care to children, such as pediatricians, family physicians, and pediatric nurse practitioners.

I have worked with children with SPD since 1997, when I entered my postdoctoral fellowship in the field of neurodevelopmental disabilities and related disorders at the Neuropsychiatric Institute and Hospital, University of California, Los Angeles. Initially, most of the children I saw had some degree of difficulty processing sensory information as part of their diagnosis of pervasive developmental disorder, such as autism. However, more and more I began to see children who were referred to my private practice for diagnostic testing and evaluation of behavioral problems, inattention, and socialization difficulties. In many cases, they were coping with SPD.

Today, in my private practice, I almost always include at least one questionnaire about the child's sensory functioning and sensory profile as a screening tool in a broader, more comprehensive evaluation process. If there are indicators of clinically significant problems in the area of sensory functioning, I will perform additional testing, complete more specific questionnaires, observe the child during free and structured play, and recommend further evaluation by an occupational therapist who specializes in this area.

All the case examples presented in this book are of real children who came to my practice for neuropsychological evaluation or diagnostic consultation or whom I became familiar with as an expert consultant but did not treat personally. Neither the children nor their families knew much about SPD at all, at the outset. Their journey, their child's problems, the findings of the evaluation, and the treatment recommendations can help shed light on this process for any family that has a child with SPD. These families graciously agreed to share their stories so that you could benefit from their experiences (their identifying information has been deleted or changed to respect confidentiality).

As the director of the McLean Hospital's Center for Neurodevelopmental Services in Belmont, Mass, I oversee all the services provided to children and adolescents with autism spectrum disorders who attend our year-round school or summer camp. Most of the children in these programs have some degree of sensory processing difficulty. We develop an individualized and specific sensory integration treatment program for each child.

Strategies to Help Parents

In this book, I not only discuss what sensory processing disorder is, but I also focus a great deal on understanding this disorder on the basis of a stress model, which is essentially my way of helping parents understand SPD as a source of chronic stress for their child. I've tried to help parents get a feel for what it's really like to have this disorder, as well as its effect on their children's learning, behavior, and self-esteem.

This book can help parents help their children because I've provided important, practical, and helpful methods and step-by-step techniques to support and improve a child's functioning at home, at school, and in the community. There are very specific recommendations for almost every conceivable circumstance, problem, scenario, and situation. These include strategies for helping your child get more organized for school and prepare for various social situations, such as a birthday party, as well as getting your child evaluated, receiving treatment services, and helping your child be more comfortable at home. I also help walk you through several important and key processes, such as identifying the problem, describing the evaluation process, participating in a neuropsychological and occupational therapy evaluation, and talking with your child's school and teachers.

Case studies included throughout the book show how SPD is manifested in children—that is, the behavioral manifestations of SPD, how it affects a child's life, how it may occur along with other psychiatric and/or developmental disorders, what the assessment process entails, what an evaluation report looks like and what it includes, as well as some typical and helpful sample recommendations.

Reading these case examples should remove much of the mystery involved in questions such as, what is a neuropsychological evaluation? or what does a typical report look like and include? or what do you do if you suspect your child has SPD? Using clear, simple terms and language, I've addressed many of these questions and included thorough discussions of assessment, treatment, and resources.

In the end, however, all I would like you to know is that SPD is a real diagnosis and disorder that is neurobiologically based, and that children with SPD can be treated with impressive results. Treatments such as occupational therapy—more specifically, sensory integration therapy and the use of an individualized set of helpful activities called a sensory diet—can make a world of difference in improving the life of a child with SPD. An effective treatment program can help the child with SPD to better organize and modulate his or her senses and responses to various stimuli from the surrounding environment. More importantly, it can help the child to identify and reach for objects and activities that can help him or her to be more comfortable in any given situation.

Many children with SPD appear to have behavioral problems and are misunderstood and mislabeled as behaviorally challenging kids. However, if the reason for that behavior is an ongoing sensation of discomfort, or SPD, then focusing on the behavior alone does not make sense. The good news is that a very high number of children respond favorably to the specific treatments currently available for SPD, such as sensory integration therapy. Therefore, a correct diagnosis and treatment make all the difference in the prognosis of this disorder.

Although SPD may be an unfamiliar disorder to most, an impressive amount of information has been gathered on this topic in a very short period of time. Hopefully this book sheds new light on this fascinating disorder and helps families by providing general information on

SPD, including relevant research findings, various ways of understanding the disorder (such as perceiving it as a stressor on the child's body), case examples, sample neuropsychological and occupational therapy reports, and more importantly, step-by-step strategies and practical suggestions for parents to help their child.

1

WHAT IS SPD?

Omid is a 9-year-old boy with a history of wide-ranging behavioral difficulties since preschool.

"He was never an easy child," his mother says. "He seemed to require every ounce of my energy just to get through the day."

Omid, more than anything else, needed his parents' help to calm down, relax, and fall asleep. He never seemed to be able to stand or sit still, pay attention for long, or control his impulses or his disruptive behaviors.

In addition, he appeared clumsy, fell frequently, was overly active, put everything in his mouth, and had poor postural strength, poor handwriting and fine motor skills, and poor muscle tone. Omid also displayed a great deal of anxiety around performance (accomplishing any given task) and responded with disruptive and disorganized behaviors when required to perform tasks involving the use of his fine motor skills.

All of the above problems became more apparent as Omid got older, and needless to say, he became less socially acceptable. A refusal to use scissors and an outburst of crying in response to the teacher's request to do so may be an acceptable behavior at age 4, but it is considered oppositional and defiant at age 9.

Parents and teachers had tried to be as accommodating as possible with Omid, but Omid's poor response to a variety of interventions, his recent increase in behavioral problems, his older age, physical size, and the increasing frequency of his meltdowns led his family to look for an in-depth diagnostic assessment.

Omid's problems and disconcerting behaviors also included hyperactivity, a need to constantly be on the move, an inability to pay attention and focus on the task at hand, difficulty with being and remaining in a calm state, and mouthing and chewing objects. His anxiety around performance (accomplishing tasks) and using fine motor skills continues to be a problem.

Problem Child or SPD?

Omid received a diagnosis of sensory processing disorder (SPD), a neurological dysfunction whereby the brain is unable to accurately and efficiently process the incoming sensory information from the senses.

As a result, the child can experience difficulty with sensory modulation—that is, he or she may be overresponsive (have an exaggerated response to touch, for instance) or underresponsive (have no reaction to being scratched) to sensory stimuli or just crave and seek sensory stimulation (needing to crash into things).

The child may also have difficulty with sensory discrimination (not knowing where a sensation comes from). Lastly, the child may have sensory-based motor problems, such as difficulties with his postural strength or weak muscle tone.

These problems can affect all the familiar senses— touch, hearing, taste, sight, and smell. SPD can interfere with another sense, the vestibular sense, which lets us know where our body is in space. For example, a child may have a fear of heights or falling, dislike being tipped upside down, or become distressed when his or her feet leave the ground.

SPD can also affect the proprioceptive sense, which gives us information about what position our body is in. For example, the child may walk, push, bang, or write too hard, bump into objects, or trip and fall frequently.

SPD can also hinder our emotional, internal, and regulatory senses, hampering our ability to calm down to fall asleep or handle anxiety.

WHAT SENSORY PROCESSING MEANS

Simply put, sensory processing is the neurological process of organizing our sensations so that we can successfully maneuver in the world. Sensory processing is an unconscious process—it occurs without us having to think about it.

Most importantly, it helps us sort through all the incoming sensory information and focus on a specific activity. This aspect of sensory processing is the bedrock of all forms of learning—academic, daily living skills, social skills, and more subtle phenomena like empathy.

What we see, hear, smell, touch, and taste translates into our day-to-day, moment-to-moment experience of living. In addition, two other senses include information about our bodies and environment. One sense, referred to as the vestibular system, involves balance and movement. The other sense, called the proprioceptive sense, involves input from our muscles, joints, and body parts. Like a symphony, our senses all need to be in tune to deliver their "notes" in a coherent, predictable manner. Our brain, like a symphony conductor, directs our sensory input and brings together the music of our senses in a harmonious, seemingly effortless manner.

Using Our Senses

Here's another image to keep in mind as we talk about our senses—eating freshly baked bread. Picture this: You're sitting in the living room, and you smell bread baking, and walk toward the kitchen.

You stop, put on a pair of oven mitts, open the oven, slide out the bread, and set it down. You carefully cut a piece of bread, pick the bread up and bring it to your mouth, and bite down. You chew and experience the sound and sensation of the first crunch. You taste the delicious bread, and swallow. You then accidentally drop a piece of bread on the floor and bend down to pick it up to throw away later. You cut another slice, take a bite, taste, chew, and swallow, until the piece of bread is gone.

While this bread-eating scene sounds very ordinary, there is a complex neurological process constantly working to help you make functional meaning of your environment.

How the Seven (Not Five) Senses Work

Let's take a look at each of the senses, and as we do so, keep in mind that all of your senses are part of a large system of sensory input, processing, interpretation, and behavior. Much of the "work" of the sensory system is unconsciously accomplished by our nervous system and brain.[1]

Taste

Our tongue drives the gustatory sense or taste sense. Whenever food or another substance enters the mouth, the tongue immediately acts as a filter for the type of tastes we experience. There are four main types of tastes: sweet, sour, salty, and bitter. It was previously believed that everyone more or less experienced taste in the same manner, with some variations. However, recent research[2] suggests that genetic variations in a specific taste gene, combined with a vast array of cultural influences, are associated with differences in sensitivity to bitter tastes and preferences for sweet-tasting foods.

Similarly, within the world of food science and chemistry, there has been controversy over the physiology of sour taste perception. However, recent scientific evidence suggests that there is at least one sour taste receptor associated with one piece of genetic code.[3] Combined together, these research outcomes, as well as other research results, show us that taste is not simply a question of subjective judgment. Rather, taste has a genetic component. Variations in the way in which the genetic piece interacts with cultural or environmental factors contribute to differences in how individuals experience taste. The important piece of information to remember about taste is that there can be variations in how any one individual responds to a specific taste.

Touch

Touch, referred to as the tactile sense, is the largest sensory system in our bodies, and it plays a pivotal role in the development of a balanced nervous system. It's the first sensory system to develop in utero (in the womb), and serves as a launching pad for further neural development.

Think of your skin as a giant switchboard with millions of receptors. Those receptors that are below your neck send impulses to the spinal cord, and then onward to the brain stem. The receptors above your neck send their messages (impulses) directly to the brain stem. The brain stem, acting as a clearinghouse of sorts, sends information about touch to different regions of your brain. Interestingly, the brain stem can tell us when something is hot, cold, painful, or pleasurable, but specific details about the tactile experience—the shape, size, or location of the source of the touch—is actually processed in the more complex sensory processing areas in the cerebral cortex.

Hearing

Our inner ear acts as the initial point for sound waves to enter our sensory processing system. Along with the vestibular system and sensory input from our eyes and muscles, auditory impulses integrate with other sensory information via the brain stem, and then travel to different parts of the cerebral hemispheres. Without integration with other sensory information, we would not be able to interpret sounds that are meaningful, such as speech.

Interestingly, a recent study about the effects of noise pollution[4] reported that adults who were exposed to airport noise overnight experienced an increase in blood pressure. There were several outcomes and recommendations that came out of this study, and one outcome that is pertinent to our discussion. Namely, the adults in the study were clearly processing auditory sensory information while they were asleep. This type of research shows us that your brain works 24/7 to process and integrate sensory input.

Smell

The olfactory sense, otherwise known as your ability to smell, begins with odor molecules in the air traveling through your nose and being absorbed into the porous lining of the nasal passages. There, the molecules bind to olfaction sensory neurons and travel to the limbic system. Unlike the other senses, smell does not detour through the brain stem before reaching the cerebral hemispheres. This unique sensory path means that our olfactory experiences can more directly link to our emotional experiences, as illustrated in the beautifully detailed accounts of memories and feelings associated with the scent of delicious food in the 19th century book *Remembrance of Things Past*, by Marcel Proust.[5]

Sight

The visual sense, or what we "see," starts with our eyes. Light waves in our environment enter our visual processing system through our retinas, and then travel to the brain stem. As mentioned during our description of auditory sensory processing, visual information mixes in with other types of sensory input in the brain stem, and then moves on to the cerebral hemispheres. The more complex, detail-oriented visual information is processed in the cerebral cortex. Unlike auditory sensory input, we can't passively receive visual input while we sleep, but dreams are a wonderful example of how images we "see" while we sleep are not available for direct sensory input after we wake up.

The Vestibular System

This important sensory system coordinates movement and balance, and helps us recover when we trip or stumble. Vestibular information enters our body through our middle ear, and then travels to the brain stem in a steady stream of sensory input.

This sensory system is unique because its main purpose is to help our bodies exist in relation to gravity. This means that for our entire life on earth, our vestibular sensory receptors will send information to a specific part of the brain stem designed to keep us upright. We are reminded of this process whenever we have a middle ear infection and feel dizzy or imbalanced. Inner ear infections make the vestibular system work harder and much less efficiently. Similarly, if you spin yourself around in circles for a minute or so, you'll have a tough time keeping your balance. Again, this is because your vestibular system is momentarily impaired.

The Proprioceptive System

This often-overlooked sensory system is responsible for registering the sensations (most of which are unconscious) that our muscles and joints emit when moving. Even if we are completely still, our muscles and joints still send sensory information through the spinal cord to the brain stem and onward to areas of the brain that process unconscious activity. Without the proprioceptive system, we would not be able to move smoothly, effortlessly, or quickly.

Bread-Baking Reprise

Now that you have an understanding of our sensory system, let's walk through the bread-baking scene again and apply our knowledge.

You're sitting in the living room, and you smell bread baking (olfactory) and start walking toward the kitchen (proprioceptive and vestibular). You stop, put on a pair of oven mitts (tactile), open the oven, slide out the bread, and set it down (proprioceptive, vestibular, visual). You carefully cut a piece of bread, put the piece of bread in your mouth, and bite down (proprioceptive, vestibular, visual). You chew and experience the sound and sensation of the first crunch (auditory, proprioceptive, vestibular), taste the delicious bread, and swallow (proprioceptive, vestibular, taste). You then accidentally drop a piece of bread on the floor and bend down to pick it up (vestibular input) to throw away later. You cut another slice, take a bite, taste, chew, and swallow, until the piece of bread is gone. As you can see from this brief description, baking and eating bread involves all of our senses, and many regions of our brain and spinal cord.

No Recognition for a Real Disorder

The term *sensory processing disorder* is relatively new, and is not yet a diagnostic category in the fourth edition of the *Diagnostic and Statistical Manual of Mental Disorders,* a handbook for mental health professionals that lists different categories of mental disorders and their diagnostic criteria. This manual, published by the American Psychiatric Association, plays a critical role in legitimizing and promoting treatment options for individuals with mental illnesses.

Lucy Jane Miller, OT, is a leader in the research, treatment, and evaluation of SPD and founder of the Colorado-based Sensory Processing Disorder Foundation. She is also working on developing the first standardized guide for conducting SPD research.

Miller is heading up an effort to petition the American Psychiatric Association to include SPD in the fifth edition of the *Diagnostic and Statistical Manual of Mental Disorders*, due out in 2012. Because of the current lack of a diagnostic category dedicated to the specific forms of SPD, some children receive the wrong diagnosis, such as a behavioral issue, or are judged to be lazy, disinterested, or noncompliant. Prolonged misdiagnosis may contribute to the child underachieving in school, becoming socially isolated, and experiencing depression and poor self-esteem.

Although the American Psychiatric Association does not yet officially recognize SPD, it is a real disorder, which exhibits indicative symptoms and causes an individual suffering. On the basis of what the clinical and research community knows about SPD, individuals with SPD share a number of commonalities. First, it occurs in all racial, ethnic, and socioeconomic groups.

Second, certain groups of children have a higher prevalence of SPD than others. These groups include children who are born prematurely or have a stressful birth; children who are severely neurologically compromised or receive a diagnosis of a form of autistic spectrum disorder; children who are adoptees from sensory-deprived environments; and highly gifted individuals. The unifying theme among these groups of children is that a certain percentage of them are either overly responsive or under-responsive to stimuli.

In some of these cases, it can be challenging to separate out symptoms that are specific to SPD. Also, not all clinicians have been trained in discerning the symptoms of SPD, which can lead to misdiagnosis or, worse, the child being labeled as having behavioral issues. We will talk more about the differences between SPD and other look-alike diagnoses later in this book.

For children like Omid and his family, SPD is real, despite its lack of recognition and categorization. For Omid, creating a personalized program consisting of sensory activities that reduce his symptoms—called an individualized sensory diet—was the answer. One such activity was giving him appropriate objects to help with his need for oral input, such as gum or a Chewy Tube—a soft plastic tube. He also pushed and pulled heavy objects to help him calm down and experience more body awareness. He used yoga movements to build endurance and to calm him and regulate his attention and arousal state.

These and other specific activities helped Omid go from a child who was previously viewed as behaviorally troubled to one who needs small, yet critical, accommodations to function at his optimal level on a daily basis.

REIMBURSEMENT LACKING FOR "FRINGE" DISORDER

In June 2007, *The New York Times* journalist Benedict Carey detailed the plight of individuals with SPD and their struggle to obtain health care reimbursement.

Conditions such as SPD, attention deficit disorders, and developmental delays are now commonly discussed among special education teachers in public schools throughout the United States. Similarly, advocacy groups and parent self-help groups dedicated to SPD have sprung up, as well.

Unfortunately, SPD remains on the fringes of mainstream medicine and has not yet been officially recognized as a legitimate disorder. This translates into little or no health insurance coverage for treatment, and minimal, if any, funding for research into its causes, diagnosis, and treatment.

In his article, Carey underscored the fact that the medical community's resistance to accepting SPD as a legitimate diagnosis stems from concerns that integrating the diagnosis into mainstream medical practices will cause practitioners to rethink other behavioral disorders that resemble SPD. For example, there could currently be a group of children with a diagnosis of attention-deficit/hyperactivity disorder who actually have SPD.

Although there clearly are children with genetically based disorders, such as autism, who also suffer from SPD, it is less clear to the medical community how prevalent the disorder is among the general population. Put simply, many health providers would have to rethink their treatment plans and consider SPD as a possible underlying cause of specific maladaptive behaviors.

The cluster of symptoms that occupational therapists and special education professionals refer to as SPD is predominately based on anecdotal references rather than scientific evidence. Carey does mention recent research regarding auditory oversensitivity and atypical brain responses to multiple sensory inputs, as well as a study examining sensory processing therapy. There is a tremendous need for further research regarding the origins (such as genetic or neurological), diagnosis, and treatment of SPD.

Whom SPD Affects and How

Sensory integration is a complex process that weaves together distinct messages in our nervous system and translates those messages into behaviors of some sort. Whether you bite into a hamburger, ride a bicycle, or read a book, your successful completion of the activity requires processing sensory input, or "sensory integration."

SPD (formerly known as sensory integration dysfunction) is a condition that exists when sensory signals *don't* appropriately map out, so behavior is out of sync. Pioneering occupational therapist and neuroscientist A. Jean Ayres, PhD, OT, OTR, compared SPD to a "traffic jam" that prevents certain parts of the brain from receiving the information needed to interpret sensory information correctly, making appropriate behavioral and motor responses difficult.

Research by the Sensory Processing Disorder Foundation indicates the disorder is pervasive in varying degrees among children.

One in every twenty children experiences symptoms of sensory processing disorder that are significant enough to affect their ability to participate fully in everyday life. Symptoms of SPD, like those of most disorders, occur within a broad spectrum of severity. While most of us have occasional difficulties processing sensory information, for children and adults with SPD, these difficulties are chronic, *and they* disrupt *everyday life.*

Although a large proportion of SPD diagnoses occur in childhood, there are adults who have lived with SPD symptoms for many years, and may have only recently received a diagnosis of the disorder.

An individual with SPD can experience different levels of discomfort. At the sensory processing (neurological) level, an individual can find external stimulation overwhelming—sounds can be too loud, lights too bright, and textures too intense. This discomfort is magnified by the behaviors associated with the sensory disruption. For example, a child who experiences sounds too loudly may withdraw and have a difficult time playing with friends and family. This social isolation could lead to depression and low self-esteem, both of which are uncomfortable at best, and despairing at worst.

This same child could find school to be overwhelming, so he or she might have difficulty learning, which, if left unaddressed, could subvert and interfere with the child's academic achievement. Also, in this case, the child's physical development could be adversely affected because of his or her withdrawal from gross motor activities, such as organized sports, swimming, and bike riding. Children's overall development is very much dependent on interactions with their environment.

GAME TIME

Parents and teachers play a critical role in supporting the development of a child with SPD. Interactions with siblings and friends also play an important role in the social and emotional life of your child, and are critical to promoting your child's self-esteem.

A number of excellent books (see the *Resources* section) describe fun, sensory-nourishing games designed for children with SPD. Many of these games were created for you or your child's teacher to play with your child, yet you can easily adapt some of them to siblings and friends. By involving siblings and friends, you help other children develop a deeper understanding of your child's disorder, which contributes to building empathy and ultimately promotes kindness.

For example, Carol Stock Kranowitz talks about a fun and easy game that you can play with your child. Here's the game as described in her book, *The Out-of-Sync-Child Has Fun: Activities for Kids with Sensory Processing Disorder.*

Tra La Trampoline

Jumping improves rhythm and helps to regulate the nervous system. Always be nearby while your child enjoys this activity.

Developmental Age Range: 3 years old to teenage years

What You Will Need:

Mini trampoline (the kind used for exercise)

Pillows and beanbag cushions

Chalkboard and chalk, or big paper and a marker

Books or favorite songs, jump-rope chants, and poems

Optional: recordings of movie themes, rap, drum beats, etc (perhaps of the child's choosing)

Preparation

Place the pillows around the edges of the trampoline and on the floor.

Together, make a list of songs and rhymes to jump to.

To add visual cues, draw a representative symbol after each title, such as a star for "Twinkle, Twinkle, Little Star" or a watermelon for "Down by the Bay."

What You Can Do

While your child jumps, recite or sing the chosen ditty or play favorite recordings.

What Your Child Can Do

Read the title aloud or point to the picture representing the song or rhyme of his choice.

Jump to the rhythmic beat and chant or sing the words along with you.

Benefits of the Activity

Vigorous jumping (a form of oscillation) on the resistive trampoline provides strong vestibular input as the child moves up and down.

Jumping provides deep pressure to the joints and muscles to strengthen proprioception and gross motor skills.

Thinking up songs and rhymes promotes auditory memory.

Choosing a title from the chart encourages visual discrimination and early reading skills.

Jumping to the beat promotes auditory discrimination and ear-body coordination.

Jumping on a trampoline stimulates the speech and language centers of the brain. Your child may be more articulate than usual when the jumping is done.

Coping Tips

A child with poor muscle tone or gravitational insecurity may be uncomfortable jumping. Other calming experiences include standing on the trampoline and bending and straightening the knees, or sitting on it and rocking.

Adaptation

The Tra La Trampoline game can definitely be adapted to include siblings and friends. For example, they can sing along and take turns jumping on the trampoline. This normalizes the experience for your child and adds to the fun. Like any activity, it will have a shelf life, and you will need to pay attention to when any of the children have had their fill of it.

SPD VERSUS TYPICAL DEVELOPMENT

Throughout this book, you will read about three main types of SPDs. Before reviewing the three types, let's compare typical sensory processing with SPD in the chart below.

Typical Development vs SPD		
	Typical Sensory Processing	SPD
What is it?	The ability to take in information from the environment through the senses, organize the information, and use it to function in everyday life	Ineffective processing of sensory information
Where does it take place?	Occurs in the central nervous system (nerves, spinal cord, and brain), in a well-balanced, reciprocal process	Occurs in the central nervous system, when the flow between sensory input and any motor activity (either fine or gross motor activity) is disrupted
Why is it important?	Enables a person to survive, make sense of the world, and interact with the environment in meaningful ways	Ineffective connection and communication occurs between the neurons via chemicals called neurotransmitters
How does it take place?	Sensory neurons get messages from the senses and then send them to the central nervous system. Motor neurons get messages from the muscles and send them to the central nervous system for motor responses. This happens automatically as the person takes in sensations through sensory receptors in the skin, the inner ear, the muscles, and the eyes, ears, mouth, and nose	Sensory and/or motor neurons do not receive sensory and/or motor messages accurately, causing sensory and/or motor responses to be ineffective.
When does it start?	Sensory system develops before, during, and after birth and continues through adolescence.	Can develop before, during, and after birth, after illness, etc

The Three Types of SPD

As you read about each type of SPD below, keep in mind that each one can occur alone or in combination with another type or types. Also, the examples of each type are not inclusive of every possible symptom; rather, they serve as a snapshot to help you visualize each type.

1. Sensory Modulation Disorder

This category describes situations or behaviors where children have difficulty adjusting to their sensory experience. They either avoid or seek too much of a specific sensory experience.

In some cases, a child may be indifferent to incoming sights, sounds, tastes, and other sensory information. The types of modulation are understimulated, overstimulated, and sensory seeking (needing more stimulation than typically developing people require), as explained below.

a. Overresponsive Reaction

Children who are overresponsive to sensory stimulation may behave as though the contact with the stimulus is painful or frightening. They may appear to be anxious and frightened in situations that many kids would consider fun. Some examples of overresponsivity include the following.

Overresponsivity by Sensory System	
Sensory System	Overresponsivity
Taste	Is oversensitive to food textures and tastes, may spit out food, gags easily
Touch	Is very sensitive to being touched, particularly unexpectedly; even light touch, such as brushing against someone or being tapped on the shoulder, feels uncomfortable
Auditory (Hearing)	Is hyperaware of sounds; may hear sounds that others are not even aware of, such as the hum emitted by fluorescent lighting; covers ears, especially in response to loud sounds, such as vacuum cleaners, sirens, and alarms

Olfactory (Smell)	May be aware of and react to odors that most people don't even notice, such as dried beans
Visual (Sight)	Feels overwhelmed when in a space with too many things to look at or see; is sensitive to lights that most people find comfortable; prefers incandescent light to fluorescent
Vestibular (Balance and Movement)	Is fearful of falling, does not like heights (even small steps), has trouble stepping off to a different level (such as from the sidewalk to the street) and/or difficulty with balance
Proprioceptive (Position)	Does not like motor or physical activities, has problems with movement, appears rigid

b. Underresponsivity

Children who experience underresponsivity seem unaffected by or disinterested in sensory experiences. Children who are underresponsive may appear to be indifferent or "lazy." This type of judgment of the child does not address the SPD, and it will erode his or her self-esteem. Some examples of underresponsivity include the following.

Underresponsivity by Sensory System	
Sensory System	Underresponsivity
Taste	Is not aware of the intensity of various food tastes, such as too salty or too bitter
Touch	May have a cut, scratch, or injury and not be aware of it or not experience pain because of it
Auditory (Hearing)	Only responds to and is aware of very loud sounds
Olfactory (Smell)	Does not seem to be bothered by noxious and offensive odors
Visual (Sight)	Is not readily aware of changes in the environment, doesn't "see" or notice if the room décor has been changed
Vestibular (Balance and Movement)	Seems clumsy and uncoordinated to others, bumps into things, appears to have poor balance
Proprioceptive (Position)	Tires easily and, after a minimum amount of physical activity, has to take breaks frequently after walking, running, or exercising

c. Sensory-seeking Response

Children who have a sensory-seeking response often engage in what we might call thrill-seeking behaviors, or overindulgence. They generally want more of a specific sensory experience, and will seek out activities and situations to meet that need.

Children who exhibit sensory-seeking responses may mistakenly receive a diagnosis of attention-deficit/hyperactivity disorder, or ADHD, because many of the behaviors associated with sensory-seeking responses look like ADHD behaviors. We will discuss the differences between ADHD and SPD in chapter 6. Some examples of sensory-seeking behavioral responses include the following.

Sensory-seeking Response by Sensory System	
Sensory System	**Sensory-seeking Response**
Taste	Chews on "everything," even nonedible objects such as pens, ruler, or fingers; may appear like a 2-year-old who puts everything in his or her mouth; may overeat, snack frequently, prefer hard foods like crackers, and need to have something in his/her mouth all the time; loves pickle juice
Touch	Hoards items, fills up a room with too many things; fills up his or her arms with too many things; dives into substances that are satisfying to the touch, such as cake frosting
Auditory (Hearing)	Speaks too loudly, always has to be told to lower his or her voice, likes to listen to loud music and TV
Olfactory (Smell)	Smells objects not meant for smelling, such as hair; seeks or is not at all bothered by strong and even offensive odors
Visual (Sight)	Seeks out busy scenes in books (such as *Where's Waldo?* books), real life, or TV; enjoys visually busy or stimulating pictures, games, and puzzles
Vestibular (Balance and Movement)	Craves movement, moves quickly and is constantly on the go; may exhibit physical, thrill-seeking behavior, such as running down the slide fast and repeatedly
Proprioceptive (Position)	Loves hard hugs, enjoys squeezing things hard, loves to wrap self in things (such as blankets)

In some cases, an individual could display a mixture of sensory modulation responses. For example, a child could be underresponsive to touch and overresponsive to smell. This child could sustain an abrasion from falling, but is indifferent to the pain. A caring adult might attempt to clean up the abrasion with a cotton swab and alcohol, but the smell of the alcohol swab is overwhelming for the child, so he or she runs away.

2. Sensory Discrimination Disorder

This category of SPD describes individuals who have a difficult time understanding their sensory experience, or have a tough time separating out different sensory input. Learning new content is difficult for an individual with sensory discrimination disorder, and he or she often has a hard time protecting or asserting him- or herself. Some examples of the behaviors associated with sensory discrimination disorder are the following.

Sensory Discrimination Disorder by Sensory System	
Sensory System	Sensory Discrimination Disorder
Taste	Has a hard time differentiating between various tastes, such as salty and sour; may say, "it all tastes the same to me"
Touch	May not be able to "feel" the difference between different fabrics, seems messy, has difficulty learning skills of daily living
Auditory (Hearing)	Has a hard time listening and comprehending when there are competing and/or background sounds, such as understanding the teacher if there is a lawn mower outside the classroom
Olfactory (Smell)	Has difficulty distinguishing between smells that are clearly different, such as a banana and an orange
Visual (Sight)	Has a hard time reading nonverbal cues, such as facial expressions, in social communication; cannot successfully navigate around objects without bumping into things
Vestibular (Balance and Movement)	May be confused when body position or direction changes, such as when faced the other way; may not be aware that they have fallen
Proprioceptive (Position)	Seems uncoordinated and clumsy; cannot assess and adjust his or her force, as in erasing too hard and ripping the paper

You may have noticed that many of the behavioral symptoms of sensory discrimination disorder are similar to some of the symptoms associated with underresponsive disorder. Similarly, you will see that children who struggle with sensory discrimination disorder may also exhibit some of the behaviors associated with sensory-based motor disorder. Children may not always receive a diagnosis of a specific subtype of SPD. However, if they do, the diagnosis would be based on which category encompasses the majority of the symptoms affecting the child's day-to-day functioning.

3. Sensory-based Motor Disorder
This third category, called sensory-based motor disorder, includes two subtypes: postural disorder, and dyspraxia.

a. Postural Disorder
The first subtype, postural disorder, describes individuals who slouch, have trouble maintaining a stable posture when standing or sitting, and can't seem to organize their own movements. Children with this disorder lose balance easily and often cannot integrate bodily movement that requires coordination between the left and right sides of their bodies.

For example, a child may find it difficult to draw a picture with one hand because he or she cannot coordinate the sensory processes necessary to combine sensory impulses from the left and right sides of the brain. This same child may also use both hands to complete a task that would normally only require one hand (such as alternating hands when cutting with scissors).

b. Dyspraxia
The second sensory-based motor disorder subtype is known as dyspraxia. Individuals with dyspraxia have trouble planning, organizing, and carrying out new tasks. In addition to struggling with the unconscious planning

part of the activity, the child also finds it challenging to actually carry out the novel movement.

For example, a child with dyspraxia would find it difficult to learn how to jump rope or use a keyboard. This same child may appear to be clumsy and struggle to climb stairs or engage in other gross motor play activities. In terms of fine motor skills, children with dyspraxia may find it difficult to pronounce words or write them down on paper. Seemingly simple tasks, such as copying words from the blackboard onto a piece of paper, can be very challenging, as can tracking moving objects and shifting visual focus from one object to another.

British actor Daniel Radcliffe, who plays Harry Potter in the films of the same name, announced in 2008 he has a mild form of dyspraxia. The disorder manifests itself in bad handwriting and an inability to tie his shoelaces. Daniel does not let his dyspraxia get him down—he is successful because he practices very hard at doing things correctly.

Mixed Subtypes

We mentioned earlier that some children who have an underresponsive sensory experience might also exhibit symptoms of sensory discrimination disorder and appear to have postural disorder and/or dyspraxia.

For example, a child who avoids foods with a strong flavor might also have a tough time visually distinguishing objects (sensory discrimination) and may appear to be clumsy or unaware of his or her surroundings (postural disorder).

You can see that at the behavioral level, SPD is a complicated picture with many levels of detail. In the next chapter, we'll share what it's like to spend a day in the life of a child with SPD.

Viewing SPD as a Spectrum Disorder

An important concept that will guide you in understanding SPD is viewing it as a spectrum disorder. This means that there is a variation in the degree to which an individual experiences SPD. The range starts with a mildly problematic sensory response, involving one of the senses, and ends with severe, multilayered sensory integration challenges, involving multiple senses.

We previously reviewed the different types of SPDs, so now let's turn to three factors we can use to examine SPD—behavior, development milestones, and neuropsychology.

Behavioral Clues to SPD

Behavioral clues include the actions and activities a child performs, such as walking, drawing, talking, watching, throwing, and spinning. Behavior is any action that we as parents, teachers, and friends can witness or observe.

Many of the Web sites, books, clinical case studies, and reports that are written about children with SPD discuss the behavioral signs and patterns that point to a diagnosis of SPD. In some of the literature, behavior may also be referred to as functional or goal-directed activity.

The following chart is by no means exhaustive, but it offers a starting point for thinking through your child's behavioral symptoms. Here, examples of behavioral manifestations of various sensory problems are provided to highlight the fact that so many of a child's behaviors with SPD are symptomatic of a larger underlying problem. Therefore, parents, teachers, and care providers must be careful to not only address the behavior, but to look for the meaning of the behavior and what it might indicate about the child.

Behavioral Clues to SPD	
Sensory Problem	Signs or Behaviors
Oversensitivity to Touch, Movements, Sights, or Sounds	The child jumps and gets angry when touched unexpectedly; does not like hugs, kisses, or handshakes; doesn't like movement activities, slides, roller coasters, or being held upside down; covers eyes in bright lights, such as in public bathrooms; covers ears, cries, or runs out of the room when the vacuum cleaner is turned on.
Underresponsivity to Sensory Stimulation and Input	The child seeks activities that may feel rough to others, such as falling on the floor, rocking against the wall, and jumping excessively; enjoys hard massages.
Unusually High or Low Activity Level	The child is always on the go, jumping, standing, running, and climbing, or tires easily; would lie down if given the choice; is not physically strong.
Coordination and Balance Problems	The child has a hard time learning activities that require motor balance and coordination, such as riding a bicycle or walking on a balance beam; refuses participation in sports that emphasize these weaknesses.
Delays in Academic Achievement or Activities of Daily Living or Life Skills	The child exhibits delay and/or weaknesses in fine motor skills, such as those required for handwriting, using scissors, tying shoe laces, and personal hygiene tasks; can't keep up with writing tasks, making projects, and such.
Poor Organization of Behavior or Behavioral Challenges	The child may appear anxious, avoidant, and cautious; may frustrate easily, have frequent meltdowns or tantrums, and appear impulsive, inflexible, unreasonable, and demanding.
Poor Self-Perception or Low Self-Esteem	The child may seem unmotivated, as though he or she does not want to even try to learn or do a task; may be perceived as lazy, defiant, or incapable; may even appear arrogant and snobbish; may say a task is childish, stupid, and uninteresting.

Developmental Milestones You Need to Know

Each stage of child development has milestones, or highlights, that mark the child's achievement of specific motor or psychological skills. Many of the milestones are described as behavioral (eg, grasps an object from the table), but the assumption is that a developmental milestone includes the cognitive and neurological development of the child—the intangible or invisible part of human development.

Much of the literature about SPD, including case histories, educational Web sites, and books, will mention developmental milestones as a key component in recognizing an emerging pattern of SPD.

One Web site, The Sensory Processing Disorder Resource Center, at www.sensory-processing-disorder .com, offers a wealth of information for parents of children with SPD. The creator of the Web site is an occupational therapist who has worked extensively with children with SPD. She's also the parent of an adolescent daughter who has struggled with SPD since birth. Combining her expertise as an occupational therapist with her experience as a parent, she has come up with a guide to help parents identify developmental delays in their children. Keep in mind that each child's development will vary somewhat from the guidelines, and that each checklist offers a starting point, not a definitive diagnosis.

You can use the following guide from The Sensory Processing Disorder Resource Center to help decide whether your child should undergo further evaluation by an occupational therapist, developmental pediatrician, or neuropsychologist. Part of the evaluation process may include a discussion about the possibility of a referral to an early intervention program, which is a developmental support program offered by the U.S. public school system. It is available to any child with a developmental delay up to age 3.

Note: For other guides to your child's development, turn to the Resources section of this book.

Developmental Red Flags That May Warrant Early Intervention

Gross Motor Skills

If a child is...

Not rolling by 7 months of age

Not pushing up on straight arms or lifting his head and shoulders by 8 months of age

Not sitting independently by 10 months of age

Not crawling ("commando" crawling—moving across the floor on his belly) by 10 months of age

Not creeping (on all fours, what is typically called crawling) by 12 months of age

Not sitting upright in a child-sized chair by 12 months of age

Not pulling to stand by 12 months of age

Not standing alone by 14 months of age

Not walking by 18 months of age

Not jumping by 30 months of age

Not independent on stairs (up and down) by 30 months of age

...an early intervention/developmental therapy referral may be appropriate.

Other Gross Motor Red Flags

"Walking" their hands up their bodies to achieve a standing position

Only walking on their toes, not the soles of their feet

Frequently falling or tripping, for no apparent reason

Still "toeing in" (pointing toes inward) at 2 years of age

Displaying unusual creeping patterns

Has a known medical diagnosis that can be considered a red flag, such as Down syndrome, cerebral palsy, or a congenital heart condition

Fine Motor Skills

If a child is...

Frequently exhibiting both hands in a fist position after 6 months of age

Not bringing both hands to midline (center of the body) by 10 months of age

Not banging objects together by 10 months of age

Not clapping his or her hands by 12 months of age

Not deliberately and immediately releasing objects by 12 months of age

Not able to tip and hold a bottle by himself and keep it up, without lying down, by 12 months of age

Still using a fisted grasp to hold a crayon at 18 months of age

Not using a mature pincer grasp (thumb and index finger, pad to pad) by 18 months of age

Not imitating a drawing of a vertical line by 24 months of age

Not able to snip with scissors by 30 months

...an early childhood intervention or developmental therapy referral may be appropriate.

Other Fine Motor Red Flags

Using only one hand to complete tasks

Not being able to move or open one hand or arm

Drooling during small tasks that require intense concentration

Displaying uncoordinated or jerky movements when doing activities

Crayon strokes are either too heavy or too light to see

Has a known medical diagnosis that can be considered a red flag, such as Down syndrome, cerebral palsy, or a congenital heart condition

Cognition and Problem-Solving Skills

If a child is...

Not imitating body action on a doll by 15 months of age (eg, kiss the baby, feed the baby)

Not able to match two sets of objects by type by 27 months of age (eg, placing blocks in one container and people in another)

Not able to imitate a model from memory by 27 months of age (eg, shows you how she brushes her teeth)

Not able to match two sets of objects by color by 31 months of age

Having difficulty problem solving during activities in comparison to his or her peers

Unaware of changes in his or her environment and routine

...an early intervention or developmental therapy referral may be appropriate.

Sensory Skills

If a child is...

Very busy, always on the go, and has a very short attention span when faced with a task

Often lethargic or exhibits a low level of arousal (appears to be tired or is slow to respond all the time, even after a nap)

A picky eater

Not aware of getting hurt (no crying, startle response, or reaction to injury)

Afraid of swinging or movement activities; does not like to be picked up or placed upside down

Showing difficulty learning new activities (motor planning)

Having a hard time calming himself down appropriately

Constantly moving around, even while sitting

Showing poor or no eye contact

Frequently jumping and/or purposely falling to the floor or crashing into things

Seeking opportunities to fall without regard to his or her safety or that of others

Constantly touching everything they see, including other children

Hypotonic (floppy body, like a wet noodle)

Having a difficult time with transitions between activity or location

Overly upset with change in routine

Angry at bath time or grooming activities, such as tooth brushing, hair brushing, haircuts, or having nails cut

Afraid of, averse to, or avoids being messy or touching different textures, such as grass, sand, carpet, paint, or Play-Doh

...an early childhood intervention or developmental therapy referral may be appropriate.

Note: Sensory integration and processing issues should only be diagnosed by a qualified professional (primarily occupational therapists and physical therapists). Some behaviors that appear to be related to sensory issues are actually behavioral issues that occur independent of sensory needs.

Possible Visual Problems May Exist If the Child Does Not

Make eye contact with others or holds objects closer than 3–4 inches from one or both eyes

Reach for an object close by

Possible Hearing Problems May Exist If the Child Does Not

Respond to sounds or to the voices of familiar people

Attend to bells or other sound-producing objects

Respond appropriately to different levels of sound

Babble

Self-Care Skills

If a child is...

Having difficulty biting or chewing food during mealtime

Needing a prolonged period of time to chew and/or swallow

Coughing or choking during or after eating on a regular basis

Demonstrating a change in vocal quality during or after eating (eg, they sound gurgled or hoarse when speaking or making sounds)

Having noticeable difficulty transitioning between different food stages

Not feeding him- or herself finger foods by 14 months of age

Not attempting to use a spoon by 15 months of age

Not picking up and drinking from a regular open cup by 15 months of age

Not able to pull off a hat, socks, or mittens when requested by 15 months of age

Not attempting to wash own hands or face by 19 months of age

Not assisting with dressing tasks (excluding clothes fasteners) by 22 months of age

Not able to deliberately undo large buttons, snaps and shoelaces by 34 months of age

...an early intervention or developmental therapy referral may be appropriate.

Social, Emotional, and Play Skills

If a child is...

Not smiling by 4 months of age

Not making eye contact during activities and interacting with peers and/or adults

Not performing for social attention by 12 months of age

Not imitating actions and movements by 24 months of age

Not engaging in pretend play by 24 months of age

Not demonstrating appropriate play with an object (eg, instead of trying to put objects into a container, the child leaves the objects in the container and keeps flicking them with his fingers)

Fixating on objects that spin or turn (eg, music boxes, toy cars) or trying to spin things that are not normally spun

Having noticeable difficulty attending to tasks

Getting overly upset with change or transitions from activity to activity

...an early intervention or developmental therapy referral may be appropriate.

The First Line of Evaluation: A Neuropsychologist

For a variety of reasons, most families seeking help will see a neuropsychologist first, before ever knowing about or consulting with an occupational therapist.

One reason is that most insurance companies view a neuropsychological evaluation as a "medical necessity" and will mostly or fully pay for it. Also, pediatricians, more often than not, will refer their patients to neuropsychologists first to rule out any major issues of concern. Typically and historically, and due to the novelty of SPD as a disorder, only children with fine motor weaknesses have been referred to occupational therapists first.

Another reason is that many children, by the time they are identified and in need of services, have had behavioral manifestations of SPD. Some children may have already been identified as behaviorally difficult children by their parents or the school system.

Neuropsychologists can assign the initial SPD diagnosis or, if they suspect it, they can refer patients to an occupational therapist for a full diagnostic evaluation, treatment planning, and therapy services.

How a Neuropsychologist Can Help

Neuropsychology seeks to describe and explain the relationship between the brain and behavior. In terms

41

of understanding the symptoms your child exhibits, neuropsychological assessments offer a window into your child's brain and cognitive functioning.

While brain imaging technology can show a picture of how your child's brain functions, it can't show the behavioral manifestation of your child's cognition. Similarly, standard behavioral assessments would also only show us part of the puzzle.

A neuropsychological evaluation provides the link between traditional medical diagnostic modalities (such as magnetic resonance imaging, or MRI), examinations, and occupational therapy behavioral assessments. In particular, a neuropsychologist will look at what a child can and can't do with a variety of cognitive tests, and will look at how the child accomplishes or doesn't accomplish tasks by using a particular test. Here, the child's approach to any given task is crucial and provides a wealth of knowledge for the neuropsychologist. In other words, the process is just as important as the end result.

For example, many children who receive a diagnosis of a form of learning disability score substantially lower on standardized academic tests than their cognitive capabilities allow (as measured with intelligence quotient, or IQ, testing). A standard battery of neurological diagnostic tests would not uncover this disparity between performance and ability.

Another pertinent example is that of a large discrepancy between verbal and performance scores on an IQ test. This discrepancy can favor verbal abilities, a child's problem-solving abilities, or the performance score. Depending on which score is higher, there are several explanations and reasons that may be deduced that could provide invaluable information.

This information, examined along with the child's actual scores (acquired with various neuropsychological measures), can then be useful for diagnostic purposes, identification of how the child learns best, and treatment planning. When combined together, neuropsychological assessments, behavioral descriptions, and observations of developmental milestones create a more complete and comprehensive picture of your child.

THE WRONG LABEL: "A BEHAVIORAL KID"

Before a child receives a diagnosis of SPD, parents and other caregivers might worry that (1) some mistake in their parenting led to the problematic behaviors, or that (2) the child has control over his or her behaviors and is choosing to act out or be disruptive, as a way of taking control or rebelling.

As is consistent with the message throughout this book, uncovering the drivers behind your child's behavior is critical to understanding and helping your child.

If it is not clear to you or your child's teacher why your child is behaving in a particular manner, you can request a functional behavioral assessment of your child's behaviors at school. Parents can speak with their child's teacher, who can put them in touch with the school counselor and the principal. This type of assessment seeks to understand what it is your child is trying to communicate through his or her behavior. The assumption that drives a functional behavioral assessment is that a child who "misbehaves" is doing so for one or more reasons, and it's our job to figure out what he or she is telling us. We will discuss functional behavioral assessments again in chapter 2.

What the Research Tells Us about SPD

Although research specifically focused on SPD is limited within the scientific and medical communities, recent studies have added to what we already know about SPD.

In February 2008, for example, researchers in the Department of Kinesiology at the University of Wisconsin-Madison examined the effects of prenatal stress and moderate-level prenatal alcohol exposure on tactile sensitivity in 38 5- to 7-year-old rhesus monkeys. The researchers also evaluated the relationship between tactile sensitivity and dopamine function. (Dopamine is a neurotransmitter in the brain that has an important role in a variety of functions—most notably movement, emotional responses, motivation, learning, addiction, and the ability to experience pain and pleasure.)

The monkeys were divided into four groups: (1) monkeys exposed to prenatal alcohol, (2) monkeys exposed to prenatal stress, (3) monkeys exposed to prenatal alcohol and prenatal stress, and (4) monkeys exposed to sucrose (control group).

Researchers exposed each monkey to repeated tactile stimulation that included touch with a feather, a cotton ball, and a stiff brush, and then measured their dopamine levels and the extent to which each monkey withdrew from the tactile stimulation. Using neuroimaging technology, researchers found increased dopamine levels in the monkeys that withdrew the most from the tactile stimulation. Researchers noted that the group of monkeys that were exposed to prenatal stress had the highest rate of withdrawal from tactile stimulation.

This means that in this study, monkeys whose mothers were exposed to stress during pregnancy grew more disturbed by touch over time. Also, the study may have implications for women of childbearing age, in that decreasing stress before and during pregnancy may decrease sensory sensitivity in their children. This study does not explain the developmental journey of individuals with SPD, but it does offer some pieces of the puzzle and creates new data for future research.

Other Research Possibilities

What we now know about SPD is just the tip of the iceberg. There is much room for expansion, building on current research and starting new research projects to address all aspects of this complex disorder.

As with any new disorder, solid and respectable research findings will not only give the disorder validity, legitimacy, and credibility, but also create opportunities for important, much-needed funding for education, resources, and direct clinical services. The following are some research projects, topics, and findings that are relevant and good to be familiar with.

Brain Neurodevelopment. Neuroscience (the study of the brain and nervous system) offers a number of research tools, methods, and constructs for understanding the neurological functioning of the human brain. Neuroscience research is therefore a natural platform for investigating and comparing typical brain functions with disordered brain functioning (such as Alzheimer disease and schizophrenia).

In April 2008, researchers at the U.S. Child Psychiatry Branch of the National Institute of Mental Health reported a study in which brain maps based on postmortem brain tissue were compared and integrated with noninvasive time-lapse brain imaging "movies" taken in 375 typically developing children. Researchers indicated that regions of the brain with a simple structure, including the limbic area, show simpler growth patterns. Interestingly, these brain structures are similar in all mammalian brains. In contrast, sensory-rich, higher-order functioning regions of the brain presented a more complex map and an associated complex developmental path unique to primates. That is, the sensory processing function of the brain is an intricate one, involving a complex path in the brain.

The results of this neurodevelopmental study of the human brain could prove to be useful in examining the regions of the brain associated with SPD. Neurodevelopmental data could be factored into a model of SPD that could, at a minimum, include genetic, neurological, environmental, and behavioral components.

Gene Expression. At first glance, genetic research offers a seemingly simple or single-variable explanation for the development of disease, the endgame of pathology. This, of course, is an oversimplification. The number of diseases and disorders that can be 100% attributed to genetic factors is small in comparison to the multitude of disorders in which many factors (such as environment and nutrition) contribute. The basic premise of genetic research is that the human genome contains the map of human development, as well as many clues to the triggers and predispositions to specific diseases.

In July 2008, researchers at Children's Hospital Boston and the departments of Neurology and Neurobiology at Harvard Medical School published an article in which they described the genetic component of neuronal synaptic development (how neurons grow). Specific neuronal activity appears to regulate a process of gene expression that is key to aspects of neuronal development, including dendrite growth, synapse development, and synapse elimination. Researchers suggested that genetic mutations in this process could promote neurological disorders. That is, damage to genes could be involved in the development of neurological disorders.

Further neuronal gene expression studies could contribute to scientists uncovering the matrix of genetic mutations that potentially contribute to the development of SPD.

Brain Architecture. Similar to brain neurodevelopment, research involving detailed and differentiated images of the human brain offers a high-resolution blueprint of the neural networks and pathways that are essential to brain functioning.

In July 2008, collaboration between researchers at the University of Lausanne in Switzerland, Harvard Medical School, and Indiana University produced a map of the "wiring" of the human brain. Previous imaging studies produced functional images, or pictures of activity within each region of the brain. The goal of this study was to uncover a detailed map of the neural wiring of the brain, and match the wiring to functional regions of the brain. Combined together, images of the structure and function of the brain could provide much-needed insight into the way in which sensory information and other higher-order cognitive activities are orchestrated.

After analyzing the data, researchers discovered that there are neural pathways in the cortex region of the brain that are highly connected and centralized, forming a core to the structure of the brain. This core region is an area of the brain that is highly active at rest, when the brain is not involved in complex, specialized tasks. Interestingly, researchers also found that patterns of activity in the core region of the brain were highly correlated (co-occurred) with the structural connection patterns. This suggested that the structural core of the brain might play a critical role in integrating information from different regions of the brain.

The insights from this study could provide a useful starting point for analyzing the neural pathways (structure) and patterns of sensory processing (function) within the core of the human brain that are associated within typical sensory processing and disordered sensory processing.

Clearly, SPD is a phenomenon that scientists and clinicians are only just beginning to understand. Future research on the mechanisms that cause and sustain SPD is critical to the development of effective clinical treatment, and will ultimately contribute to the mitigation of human suffering.

2

WHAT IT'S LIKE TO HAVE SPD

For those of us who do not have SPD, it may be difficult to relate to the issues and challenges that individuals with SPD face on a daily basis.

How bad can it really be? How can it affect so many areas of functioning? What does paying attention, sleeping, or eating have to do with SPD? Why can't children with SPD just try a little harder to deal with it and manage it? If the parents just did a better job of teaching their kids to cope, couldn't the kids do better? Aren't we just spoiling these kids and feeding into their unwanted and problematic behaviors by accommodating them so much? Won't they just get used to a texture or noise if you let them deal with it?

Those who view this disorder as behaviorally based—as opposed to neurologically or biologically based—often raise questions like this. Therefore, those who view SPD as a behavioral problem tend to propose solutions that are behaviorally based. Better parental discipline and control, less manipulation by the child, a refusal to buy into the reactions of the child, and stronger willpower on the child's part are some of the ways they've suggested parents deal with SPD.

One of the most important points I try to make in this book is that the children's atypical behaviors and responses are the *manifestations* of this disorder, and not the disorder itself. In other words, when a child repeatedly takes off his socks in the middle of winter, it is not because he is being defiant, wants to challenge authority, or is being manipulative to get a parent's attention. Quite simply, he has a sensitivity to touch. His socks provide more stimulus than is comfortable for him, so naturally, he removes them.

Dealing with this issue from a behavioral perspective is as useless and ineffective as dealing with a decrease in a child's blood sugar levels or thyroid level by telling the child to just try harder to stabilize these and other biological entities. This approach assumes that sheer willpower will change one's biology without other means of intervention and treatment.

The danger is that it sends the message to children with SPD that they are failing you, their teachers, friends, and more importantly, themselves, by not trying hard enough and not succeeding. The message is that they are failures, that it is their fault, and that they are internally and at a core level flawed in some way—a disappointment, and a burden. This then becomes a self-fulfilling prophecy. It is difficult, as a child, to fight hard enough not to be or become what everyone thinks you are or will become.

What Causes SPD?

As we have mentioned throughout this book, SPD is a rather newly defined disorder and one that has not yet been fully studied or understood. The answer to the question of what causes SPD is one that, at best, is both tentative and general.

The causes listed below, which may be involved in SPD development, are the same ones that make a child vulnerable to—and may be the source of—many other disorders. Potential causes include hereditary and genetic factors, prenatal issues (such as a mother's use of drugs, alcohol, or medications while pregnant or experiencing major medical complications during pregnancy), trauma during birth (such as a lack of oxygen), and postnatal factors, including substantial neurological and medical conditions and trauma, injury, surgery, and chronic and substantial abuse or neglect. Clearly, there is a considerable void in this area that needs to be addressed through research and investigation, which can then be translated into practical steps and useful information for prevention of this disorder.

How to Step into Your Child's Shoes

My aim in this chapter is to help readers to understand what it would be like to have SPD or to be a parent who cares for a child with SPD. Neither position is easy—both are challenging and at times confusing, frustrating, and bewildering, and, worst of all, can leave one feeling as though everything around them is "out of control" and that nothing makes sense.

Children with SPD may very well feel like their entire day, including all the activities in it, is affected by this disorder. From the moment they open their eyes in the morning to the second they fall asleep to the quality of their sleep, everything is touched by how well they can, on any given day, process incoming sensory information from the environment.

Here are a few exercises that will give you a sense for how it feels to live with this disorder.

For an understanding of tactile overresponsivity, put a piece of sandpaper inside your socks or attach it to the back of your shirt where the tags are, or on the inside of a turtleneck shirt. Then try spending a day going about your normal daily activities, such as work, school, shopping, watching TV, reading, talking to others, and so on, while experiencing the feelings of having sandpaper on your skin.

You will find, no doubt, that not only it is nearly impossible to pay full attention to anything that you are doing, but that as the day progresses, you become more and more irritable, easily frustrated, and distracted, and find it impossible to be fully relaxed, calm, and comfortable. You will experience a general feeling of discomfort that you just can't get rid of. As time passes, you may choose to take comfort in isolating yourself and just shutting down, or, taking the opposite tack, finding yourself overreacting to everything.

Try having every touch on your skin feel like a hard scratch or not feeling any touch at all. Or, walk around with a splinter in your hand all day without noticing it. Or, instead of finding a shower or raindrops on your skin relaxing, imagine feeling the water on your body as if pins and needles were hitting it.

Try overloading your sense of taste by putting too much hot pepper in your food or smelling something that has a noxious odor to you.

Try walking on a balance beam instead of the floor to get to another point.

Turn the volume up on the television or radio all day long. The distress caused by sound that many kids with SPD feel results from their overresponsivity to sound. Therefore, sounds such as that of a vacuum cleaner or fire alarm feel particularly intrusive and uncomfortable.

Try having bright sunlight or bright lights, such as those you'd find at a baseball field, in your eyes while you are trying to read, write, or look at information on a board.

Think back to when you didn't get enough sleep and were tired the next day. Or when you felt tired, it felt as though you had just finished a long run—only it lasted all day long. Or picture a day when you had to go to work with a bad cold. Imagine feeling that way all the time.

Last, but perhaps the easiest example that we can relate to, is that of experiencing each day as if it was your first day at work, with all of the anxiety, novelty, and unfamiliarity of every aspect of the job that leads to an indescribable exhaustion at the end of the day. Keep in mind that it is having a hyperalertness to novelty that takes every ounce of your energy, not necessarily having new things to deal with. So many kids with SPD feel every day that all their experiences are new and unfamiliar, requiring a tremendous amount of energy to get through the day.

It's obvious that these exaggerated conditions would overload your sensory system and make you feel extremely uncomfortable—so much so that some of these methods, such as overstimulating loud noise and bright lights, have been used to break individuals' defenses during times of war or conflict.

Real Stories of Kids with SPD

The following are clinical examples of two children with SPD. The children received either a primary diagnosis of SPD or a secondary diagnosis as part of another disorder. You will learn both the unique and common aspects of their stories, as well as helpful strategies and recommendations in dealing with SPD.

In both cases, I was the first clinician to perform a full evaluation. Please note that the reason for referral in both cases (as with most cases) is not to answer the question, "Does this child have SPD?" or "Can we rule out SPD?" Clinicians can only arrive at such a diagnosis through a thorough assessment process.

In addition, although neuropsychologists and other clinicians may be able to assign the initial diagnosis, only a trained occupational therapist is able to use specific assessment tools to perform special evaluations and create and provide treatment plans appropriate for each child's needs.

In the following examples, the evaluation process, assessment tools, techniques, and report format and style are merely examples of some possible approaches for these particular cases. Other clinicians may perform different assessments that are perfectly appropriate for another child.

Case Study

SAMANTHA, AGE 8—DIFFICULTY WITH SPEECH, MOVEMENT, AND TOUCH

Samantha's parents referred her for a neuropsychological evaluation after becoming concerned over her inability to make friends or form relationships, problems with language development, sensory difficulties, and overall level of functioning.

Samantha had a history of developmental delay, including long-standing difficulties with socialization, movement, fine motor skills, and moodiness.

Amid these concerns, however, Samantha displayed numerous strengths, including a kind nature, an interest in connecting with others, and an enthusiasm for learning. Although she received educational services, Samantha's parents continued to question her diagnosis of learning disorder and the appropriateness of her treatment. The goal of her evaluation was, therefore, to conduct a comprehensive assessment of Samantha's neuropsychological functioning and recommend ways to improve her academic, social, and emotional development.

A Preference for the Familiar

Samantha began talking and was able to walk independently at the expected age, without any problems or delays. However, she found walking, running, going up and down stairs, and holding a pencil challenging. Although Samantha was reportedly a "sweet" baby, she was only comfortable with her mother and cried whenever someone else tried to hold her. She was cautious in new surroundings and had a definite preference for familiarity.

As a toddler, Samantha was easily frustrated and had frequent tantrums. At age 2, her behavior was particularly disconcerting because of a tendency to hit her siblings, not listen to her parents, and behave irritably. As a young child, she would respond only intermittently when her name was called, although a test administered by her pediatrician showed her hearing to be within normal limits.

Samantha, who lives with her parents, older brother, and two younger sisters, had a clinically significant family history in that her paternal uncle had attention-deficit/hyperactivity disorder, inattentive type, and a maternal cousin had mental retardation.

Difficulty with Routines

Samantha continued to have difficulty putting her thoughts into words in the presence of competing and distracting background noise. As a result, her speech was slow, disfluent, and accompanied by word retrieval problems (such as long pauses between words). She also had trouble pronouncing words.

Samantha struggled with fine and gross motor movement and activities. For example, her body appeared awkward and stiff when walking and running, and she had decreased muscle tone in her trunk. Additionally, Samantha's fine motor development was delayed, and she had difficulty with the integration of visual and fine motor skills.

Socially, although Samantha demonstrated an interest in others, she preferred interacting with adults more than peers. She tended to be shy at times, and appeared to lack the skills necessary for entering and exiting a conversation. While Samantha was able to understand some nonliteral speech (such as sarcasm) and interpret facial expression, she had difficulty making and maintaining eye contact. She had less awareness of what her own facial expressions were communicating and often appeared to have a grimace on her face. Due to her seeming disregard of other people's feelings, her mother questioned whether she had difficulty discerning emotion in others.

Samantha's parents indicated that she had particular difficulty with transitions and temporal changes in her routine. She displayed rigid and strict adherence to sequential steps in completing tasks, and could become insistent and easily frustrated when things were not done according to her desire. At home, she continued to hit, pinch, or kick her siblings when she was irritated or tired or when she experienced sensory overload, such as when there was too much noise or too many people around.

Although this behavior had decreased over the past few months, she became increasingly restless in situations involving new people (eg, very quiet, pacing, fidgeting).

School and Learning

A 3rd grader, Samantha particularly enjoyed going to school, where she received speech and language services, occupational therapy, and counseling services. Her classroom teacher described her as a bright, sweet, and affectionate child with a good sense of humor. Although Samantha had a tendency to keep to herself, she was consistently kind to others and did not resist developing friendships with her peers.

Samantha sometimes became overstimulated and distracted by the visual and verbal activity of her peers in the classroom and responded either by withdrawing and ignoring others or by physically rocking in her chair and playing with items on her desk.

She consistently sought out quiet and contained spaces in the classroom and would appear to stay in a physical cocoon if possible. When her attention wandered, her teacher attempted to engage Samantha by making eye contact and repeating a request to complete an instruction. Both Samantha and her teacher were aware that holding a pencil correctly still gave her difficulty, and that although she had been told how to do it correctly, she still needed reminders from time to time. Encouragingly, Samantha was open to help from her teachers and responded well to reminders.

Overresponsivity to Touch, Noise, and Light

Samantha had a history of notable differences in her sensory processing when compared with her typically developing peers. The disparities had been present since her early childhood.

For example, her touch arousal was reportedly highly sensitive, and she had a preference for specific types of clothing (such as shirts without tags, buttons, and collars, and socks without seams). Her other tactile sensitivities included distress during grooming activities, such as brushing and washing her hair, a dislike for splashing water, and rubbing out a spot that was kissed.

Getting dressed every day for school, especially during the winter, was "a nightmare," her mother said. Samantha refused to wear a jacket, did not like the feeling of most sweaters, removed her socks, and could not tolerate boots, hats, earmuffs, gloves, or scarves. When her mother found clothes that Samantha felt comfortable wearing, she bought several of the same item to ensure future cooperation with getting dressed.

"That wasn't always a guarantee either, because she might not feel comfortable today in something that she wore just a week ago," her mother said. At times, she also became tense and stiffened her body when hugged or unexpectedly bumped.

Samantha had an aversion to loud, unpredictable noises, and, until recently, would display an unusual panic reaction to thunderstorms, vacuums, toilet flushes, and fireworks. Competing auditory and visual stimuli were especially distracting, and she had a difficult time selectively attending and sustaining focus to a specific stimulus. This resulted in reduced speed of speech production and often incited frustration with being interrupted. She had trouble completing tasks, for example, when the television or CD player was on.

Her history of unusual visual responses included being bothered by bright and fluorescent lights and fearing public bathrooms, particularly those with black toilet seats.

A Sample Treatment Plan for Samantha

After assessing Samantha's strengths and weaknesses, I made these suggestions: It seems Samantha would benefit from receiving an auditory processing evaluation to more accurately determine the nature of her language difficulties and to rule out an auditory processing disorder. An auditory processing evaluation is performed by a trained audiologist who can see whether Samantha has any problems with, for example, identifying the source of a sound, following a sound, remembering what sound was heard, paying attention to auditory or sound information such as a teacher talking, and distinguishing between background sounds and a primary auditory message without distraction. If a child has any clinically significant problems, then a diagnosis of auditory processing disorder may be warranted.

If Samantha does not demonstrate improvement with increased intervention, she should undergo a thorough evaluation within the next 12–18 months. Her parents may choose to have this reevaluation as a means to measure Samantha's progress and adjust interventions as necessary.

Given Samantha's history of speech, articulation, and expressive language difficulties, she requires intensive services in this area. She should undergo individual speech and language therapy services at least two to three times per week. Additional small group therapy services, if available, would be appropriate, as well.

With regard to academics, Samantha will benefit from the monitoring of her skills across several areas. Tasks requiring copying or tracking should be structured or organized to minimize time demands. Visual supports accompanying verbal descriptions of information will be important. Further, Samantha will need extended time to complete tasks and to organize her thoughts and process verbal information prior to responding.

Samantha would benefit from a small class size with minimal distractions, particularly those of an auditory and visual nature, to help her succeed academically and socially. Samantha's teacher was instructed to present information in different ways—for example, showing it to her, telling her about it, and, when possible, having her actually touch and hold an object. I also suggested, whenever possible, previewing, priming, and reviewing material with Samantha to gain her visual and auditory attention prior to speaking, and providing her with preferential seating.

Changes in routine and transitions are difficult for Samantha, and she would benefit from support to help her prepare and adjust. Providing her with additional time and many verbal cues prior to transitioning between activities may be beneficial. This may be accomplished by clearly identifying a new activity by name, describing the sequence of steps needed to accomplish it, and asking her to summarize the steps.

For example, an activity or task might be for the class to write a one-page description of why they like summer. Here, the activity name would be "One-Page Writing Assignment," describing the sequence of steps would be, "Take out your writing graphic organizer, write the title in the title box, and then write three paragraphs—introduction, body, and conclusion—in the three boxes provided." Then, the teacher might ask Samantha to summarize and show her what she is asking for and to identify the steps to achieve it. This last step assures the teacher that Samantha really comprehended the instructions, gives Samantha an opportunity to run them by her teacher, and allows her an opportunity, before making a mistake, to ask the teacher for any clarifications.

To help Samantha begin to develop organizational skills, schedules and directions should be presented by using visual aids, such as tables, graphs, charts, and checklists. This approach can be useful for both school and home routines, by using laminated cards with pictures. Samantha should also have a checklist of steps so that she can check her work and make appropriate changes on her own.

In light of Samantha's difficulties with graphomotor control, motor speed, and sensory processing sensitivities, she should continue to receive occupational therapy services at least two to three times per week. A trained occupational therapist who specializes in sensory integration therapy should provide these services. At least one to two sessions per week should focus on treating her sensory integration issues, while one session per week should focus on strengthening her fine motor skills, used for such tasks as handwriting, using scissors, and fastening various fasteners (such as zippers and buttons).

Samantha should undergo further evaluation of her sensory integration and processing functioning to accurately identify her sensory processing profile and to develop the most appropriate treatment possible. This can be performed by an occupational therapist who specializes in this area. A sensory diet, which is an individualized list of activities and items to help Samantha reorganize and calm her senses, will be recommended that can be used and implemented at home and at school.

At school, I'd recommend that Samantha receive what I refer to as "sensory integration breaks." These are breaks that students choose to take on an as-needed basis or on a regular basis to reorganize and regroup their senses and subsequently return to the classroom ready to learn. Teachers can determine when younger children should receive these breaks, while older children such as Samantha can identify when they need to take them. During this break, Samantha will have the opportunity to choose an activity that helps her get back to her baseline level, that is, her typical and normal level of functioning. These activities may include taking a walk to the water fountain, to the occupational therapy room, or simply in the hallway. The occupational therapist can predetermine these activities, which should be preapproved by the teacher.

Given Samantha's desire for friendships, I'd recommend continued development of social pragmatic skills. Ideally, social skills training should focus on initiating and maintaining interactions with others, considering others' perspectives, managing emotions and feelings, and developing effective strategies for dealing with transitions and unexpected changes in routine.

Samantha's behavior is an area of concern. Given parent and teacher concerns about her "testing her limits" regarding homework, I'd recommend a functional behavioral assessment and classroom observation to determine why she behaves the way she does when she acts out and what intervention would be most effective. A functional behavioral assessment, or FBA, is a data-gathering and informational tool used widely, especially in public schools, whenever a child has ongoing behavioral problems. The information from an FBA will shed light on the possible function of a behavior, that is, what the child is trying to communicate through the behavior. It is expected that with effective sensory integration therapy and other supports, her behavior will improve.

Samantha's parents are incredibly dedicated, involved, and willing to continue to work closely with all of her care providers and school staff. This home-school collaboration and communication is crucial in ensuring consistency across settings, individuals, activities, and generalization of acquired skills.

HOW A FUNCTIONAL BEHAVIORAL ASSESSMENT CAN HELP

For any child who has behavioral and emotional issues, a thorough FBA is useful in determining the function of the target or difficult behaviors.

Most schools have a counselor or school psychologist who can perform an FBA. A standard form may be used to collect information about the behavior, such as frequency, places, or times when it occurs, and what happened right before the behavior was observed, during the behavior, and right after. This information can help determine what factors may contribute to the behavior. If a factor such as loud noise is the cause of the behavior, for example, recommendations are made on how to reduce the noise level.

As the two case examples in this chapter clearly demonstrate, sensory integration difficulties and SPD can indeed affect many areas of functioning. These areas include social, emotional, attentional, and behavioral abilities that one may not normally associate with sensory processing difficulties.

Case Study

OLIVER, AGE 5—DIFFICULTY WITH SPEECH AND MOVEMENT

Oliver was referred for a neuropsychological evaluation by his parents, who reported unusual sensory responses, such as overresponsivity to sounds, touch, and odors, and social difficulties at school, such as not being able to join in and stay in group activities and isolating himself.

Early Intervention Services

Due to conditions brought on by premature birth, such as poor muscle tone, Oliver's gross motor activity was slow to develop. He was able to roll over at 6 months, sit up at 9 months, crawl at 12 months, and walk at 21 months. Early fine motor abilities were somewhat underdeveloped, and Oliver was in need of therapy services. He was evaluated at age 2 years 9 months, and subsequently received at-home physical therapy services. By age 3, he underwent a reevaluation and showed progress in strength, though he still experienced difficulty in alternating feet on stairs, along with difficulties in postural tone, balance, and jumping.

Though smiling at 4–6 weeks and cooing at 3 months occurred normally for Oliver, there were delays when it came to babbling, jargon ("baby talk"), and his first word, as well as concerns regarding Oliver's ability to speak more than three words at the 12-month mark, and two-word combinations at 22 months. He was given a speech evaluation at age 2 years 2 months, in which delays in expressive language and mild delays in receptive language were reported. Oliver subsequently attended weekly speech and language therapy sessions. An additional evaluation at age 2 years 8 months was reportedly postponed, due to Oliver's inattention and high activity level. At age 2 years 10 months, another evaluation identified Oliver's articulation errors (that is, his omissions of consonants and syllables). In an evaluation at age 3, progress was noted, but some continuing difficulties were cited, including understanding and asking a variety of questions, using four-word utterances, using multisyllabic words, and expanding upon his somewhat limited expressive vocabulary.

By his third birthday, Oliver had shown progress and a growing ability to form three-word combinations. His mother reported that his speech was slow and would include misarticulations, where he would leave out certain letters in words. His inflections were normal, as were the cohesion and logic of his conversation.

At age 3 years 0 months, though able to engage in conversation with adults on topics of mutual interest, Oliver encountered more difficulty conversing with peers. He was, however, able to laugh and smile appropriately in response to peers. Oliver developed early nonverbal communication skills normally. His mother reported that he could interpret others' facial expressions, as well as use his own. He was able to make eye contact and use hand gestures. Slightly abnormal, but still adequate, were Oliver's ability to respond to nonverbal cues while in conversation, awareness of his body in space, and maintenance of his body posture, according to his mother. Oliver's play interests in preschool were reportedly narrow and repetitive in nature, according to his mother, who said that he improved in his second year of preschool. He reportedly engaged in two kinds of play, parallel (beside his peers) and interactive (with his peers), though not cooperative (more complex play, involving negotiation, compromise, and cooperation).

Cold Foods, Low Energy, and Haircut Adversity

Oliver tended to become overexcited and overresponsive to visual, auditory, tactile, and taste stimuli. For example:

Oliver had an occasional tendency to smell his hands after touching objects.

He preferred foods of a cold temperature and soft texture, such as frozen yogurt, pudding, or applesauce.

Oliver occasionally tended to touch people and objects. Also, he might react as if he were "attacked" when unexpectedly bumped, because he experienced difficulty in differentiating accidental and purposeful contact.

His mother also reported occasional signs of Oliver's low energy and fatigue (for example, tiring easily, having weak muscles or a weak grasp).

Oliver often became distressed during grooming and gave his mother "a hard time" during haircuts, nail cutting, and showering.

With regard to auditory sensitivities and sounds, it was reported that Oliver occasionally enjoyed strange noises and/or sought to make noise "for noise's sake."

A psychological evaluation conducted by the preschool sought to clarify Oliver's reported difficulties initiating contact with peers and resolving altercations. The evaluation cited Oliver's mother in reporting that he had temper tantrums and could be irritable and quick to cry.

At present, Oliver's mother reports that he exhibits a full range of affect (immediate expressions of emotion) and changes affect in a smooth manner. However, she also reports that he has trouble calming himself down, particularly at home. She says that he understands a broad range of emotions, nonliteral speech, and joking, and that he can infer others' intent. Further, she reports that he is good with both details and with seeing the big picture. Oliver understands cause and effect and consequential thinking. Though he sometimes has difficulty with problem solving and becomes frustrated quickly, he can typically generate alternative solutions to problems.

Eager to Have, Not Make, Friendships

Just as in preschool, where he needed the teacher's prompts to initiate social interaction with peers, Oliver is still hesitant to initiate play with peers. He tends to follow one friend around, rather than reach out to others.

Oliver's present engagement in play varies between parallel, cooperative, and interactive. He currently relates to toys with more cognitive flexibility and can shift from one activity to another. This past year in particular, Oliver improved his ability to adjust to transitions. In the past, large transitions, such as switching to a new preschool or to kindergarten, caused him some anxiety above the expected level.

Oliver's mother reports his occasional difficulty reading social cues from peers, particularly when they do not want interaction with him. For instance, there was a recent occasion where Oliver followed a peer around and ignored the peer's requests to stop, which led to a minor physical altercation. She believes that with prompting, Oliver would be able to read facial expressions and body language. According to the preschool's evaluation, he is reported to be sensitive toward others, in that he does not like to see anyone sad or hurt.

Oliver reportedly has close friends and takes an interest in friendship. It is noted that he wants desperately to interact, but is not usually eager to greet others. His mother reports that there is some anxiety in situations involving new people, whom he is typically hesitant to meet. Though he has the skills to interact, he has difficulty initiating play with peers. He is willing, albeit hesitant, to enter a group, possibly as a result of his sensory profile. It is reported that Oliver usually engages in a sharing of interests, activities, and emotions, and takes turns willingly. He usually plays well with two or more children; however, his mother reports that he is sometimes better in one-on-one situations. In general, Oliver is reported to function best with low levels of sensory input and stimulation.

Impressions and Sample Recommendations

Oliver is a 5-year-old who was referred for neuropsy-chological testing by his parents because of his reported social difficulties and "unusual" sensory responses. During testing, Oliver was a cooperative, motivated, and engaging youngster.

Overall cognitive functioning places Oliver in a below-average range, compared with his peers, though his unmistakable strength lies in verbal and conceptual reasoning. Here, his scores fall into the average range, demonstrating his good grasp of receptive language and ideas, as well as use of words and sentences to communicate those ideas. He tended to perform better with tasks involving meaningful stimuli, such as stories and concepts. Notably, Oliver had difficulty speaking and pronounced some words incorrectly. Expressive language tasks that called for him to distinguish or analyze phonemes, the sound components of language, yielded results below the expected level for his age.

His visuospatial functioning, assessed by using tasks that helped gauge his level of seeing and arranging visual information, was, overall, below average. Some of the tasks that called for pattern recognition were on the cusp of average and below average. Tasks that employed Oliver's visuomotor integration also tended to fall on the average-to-below-average cusp. Spatial analysis was identified as a shortcoming, particularly in the realm of judging direction and the orientation of lines. A relative strength in this area was Oliver's ability to think categorically and understand the relationships between visually presented items.

In measuring auditory attention, Oliver attended to simple auditory stimuli at his expected age level, whereas complex stimuli proved to be a substantial challenge. In terms of memory and learning, that is, how Oliver encodes and recalls information, his average ability to recall details of meaningful stories substantially outpaces his very compromised ability to remember a series of names. In sensorimotor tasks that measured how well Oliver could control hand movements, he performed in the below-average range. Though his visuomotor precision with a pencil was almost in the average range, he encountered difficulty with imitating hand positions.

In summary, Oliver tends to perform better on clear-cut tasks, as well as on tasks with meaning and language. He tends to struggle more with visuospatial and visuomotor skills, as well as analyzing and sustaining attention to complex neutral stimuli. His abilities in social perception, including how well he recognizes visual cues of affect, fall just below average, which is consistent with reports that he successfully maintains friendships, albeit with occasional episodes of unsuccessful social cue reading.

Behavioral checklists, clinical observation, review of records, and developmental history do not indicate that he has Asperger syndrome. Although Oliver's sensorimotor skills have some elements in common with those typically observed in Asperger syndrome, these symptoms do not warrant this diagnosis.

An SPD Diagnosis

A diagnosis of SPD is likely for Oliver. Sensory processing is the ability to gather information through our senses (touch, movement, smell, taste, vision, and hearing), organize and interpret that information, and generate a meaningful response. This is an automatic process for most people. For instance, when we hear another person talking to us while a car drives by, our brains interpret these sounds as speech and a machine, respectively, and we respond to each piece of information appropriately.

Children who have some form of SPD, however, do not experience this process as smoothly. SPD affects how a child's brain interprets the information, and also how the child acts on that information with emotional, behavioral, social, motor, attention, and other responses.

Children and adults with SPD tend to misinterpret everyday sensory information, such as touch, sound, and movement. They may feel bombarded by information, they may seek out intense sensory experiences, or they may have other symptoms. In Oliver's case, he occasionally makes or enjoys strange noises "for noise's sake," as well as touches people and objects and experiences distress during grooming.

Less frequent is his overexcitability during movement activity, not seeming to notice when his face or hands are messy, and jumping from one activity to another in a way that interferes with play. This sensation-seeking behavior, coupled with his overresponsivity (for example, distress during grooming or reacting to accidental physical contact) and sensorimotor issues (such as difficulties with fine motor skills and coordination), may have ramifications in many aspects of daily functioning. SPD symptoms can affect social and family relationships, regulation of emotions and anxiety, attention, self-esteem, and learning. Additional information in the form of handouts and Web sites was provided to Oliver's parents.

Oliver possesses strengths, as well as intellectual and personal qualities that will be key to his progress. It will be highly useful for regular communication to occur between home and school to monitor his progress, help build skills, and maintain consistent support. In view of the present results, the following recommendations are offered as part of Oliver's treatment plan to address educational and therapeutic needs:

1. Oliver's parents and team of providers should continue to monitor his development, including his social and academic progress, over the next year. They should also pay attention to the type, frequency, and intensity of his inattention and sensorimotor difficulties. He should undergo a reevaluation, including a full neuropsychological battery, in 12–18 months.

2. Oliver should undergo a sensory integration evaluation by an occupational therapist. The therapist would ideally recommend helpful solutions for home and school. Also, there are many helpful online resources to learn more about SPD, such as www .sensory-processing-disorder.com.

3. Should Oliver's reported bouts of temper and frustration persist, he should undergo a functional behavioral assessment to gather precise information about these target behaviors. Once the function of a particular behavior is identified through the use of a functional behavioral assessment, Oliver can be taught a more adaptive and socially appropriate way of communicating his needs.

4. Various social experiences, which Oliver may perceive as unpredictable or unsafe, might prompt him to want to simplify things, reduce unpredictable or novel events, and do things his way (particularly in

light of test results that suggest a decline in cognitive performance in the face of complexity). Helping him to see others' perspectives may reduce any self-centered behavior. Further development of social skills training is also recommended, and should be geared toward developing effective strategies for dealing with unexpected changes in routine. Oliver may need to be encouraged to increase self-monitoring by asking himself, "Did I understand everything this person said?" and by double-checking with the speaker.

5. I've encouraged Oliver's parents to continue expressing their expectations by providing him with clear, brief, and concise directions. This imposed structure will ideally serve to compensate for any lack of inner structure and stability that Oliver may experience.

6. Due to some indications of Oliver's occasional inattention and relative difficulty with visuospatial orientation and complex tasks, his parents and teachers may find it necessary to optimize his productivity by reducing outside distractions, extraneous noise, and unnecessary interruptions. If necessary, his tasks should be short, well within his attention span, varied, and gradually increased in length. Oliver may also benefit from periodic stretch breaks during extended lesson plans. If auditory attention continues to be a problem, it may be helpful if directions are presented one at a time, and he is asked to repeat the direction prior to proceeding with the task.

7. Oliver may benefit from clustering information semantically (that is, giving it meaning and context). Learning to organize information and material in meaningful ways may help him to approach learning tasks more effectively, or to remember where to

locate personal belongings. For example, clothing could be organized into such meaningful categories as school clothes, play clothes, and sleepwear. Also, Oliver is likely to succeed in working in small groups or with one other student. In elementary school, he may benefit from "peer learning" (that is, having someone to share ideas with and to "talk through" tasks).

8. Oliver's teachers should note that he is most likely to grow and flourish in an environment with very clear boundaries, support around social interactions, and predictable social rules. This will ideally foster "internal boundaries" for coping, stress tolerance, and adapting to novel situations. Oliver may find that he needs relationships that evolve at a pace that's comfortable for him to establish trust. An ideal learning environment would include instructions limited to one-to-one or small-group settings.

9. Oliver's teacher and academic team have suggested that Oliver may benefit from repeating kindergarten, due to his difficulty with keeping up with his peers, particularly in completing worksheets. This is not because of Oliver's inability to comprehend or perform the task, but rather his slower rate of performance because of weak fine motor skills. However, given the presenting issue and the cause of the problem, it makes more sense to increase the frequency of Oliver's occupational therapy services, with special attention to handwriting skills so that he can work on keeping up with his classmates' pace.

UNDERSTANDING SPD AS A FORM OF STRESS

Viewing SPD as a type of stress, especially as an ongoing and chronic form of stress, can help parents and other caretakers better understand what a child with SPD experiences on a daily basis, the effect of SPD on the child's body and systems, and the child's physical and emotional reactions in various situations.

Although stress itself is not a disorder or disease, current evidence suggests that it can certainly contribute to a variety of symptoms and may even lead to or worsen various disorders and diseases. Similarly, while SPD is not yet recognized as a disorder by the medical community, we know that it can contribute to—and in more severe cases lead to—behavioral problems, learning issues, and difficulty in social and emotional functioning, attention and concentration, and motor skills development.

Our understanding and view of stress and its effect on individual functioning has changed greatly since the introduction of the idea that stress may lead to disease. In fact, fields such as health psychology, among others, focus on a patient's psychosocial stressors, family issues, job-related stress, financial stress, and such to fully understand and help the patient.

On a broad level, stress as a public health issue has been recognized and legitimized by society in general and the medical community in particular. Along with recognition comes funding for research and treatment programs, and acknowledgement of the suffering stress creates for many individuals and their families. Similarly, inclusion of stress-related disorders in the *Diagnostic and Statistical Manual of Mental Disorders* has paved the way for creating treatment options in the United States that are reimbursable (covered by health insurance). Ultimately, there is a commitment to mitigating the causes of stress and relieving the suffering that stress has caused within our society.

The research and treatment of stress-related disorders can help researchers and clinicians who are in the early stages of understanding and treating SPDs. SPDs are often glossed over or misinterpreted, leading to inappropriate clinical interventions or no intervention—much like the way stress-related disorders were not fully understood 40 years ago. Creating awareness and designating SPD as a public health priority is one of the first steps toward creating diagnostic categories and treatment options.

From a child's perspective, living with SPD is very much like living in a state of constant stress.

The concepts I use below to discuss stress serve as ways to think about SPD. Like stress, SPD causes physiological changes or abnormalities that show themselves and are reported based on how the individual experiences them on a daily basis. For example, in the case of over-responsivity to sound and light in a child with SPD, cognitive and behavioral symptoms emerge, such as having to cover her ears and eyes or leave a room, which compromise the child's ability to learn in school and participate in age-appropriate social activities. From this child's perspective, living with SPD is very much like living in a state of constant stress.

Consider the following example: Arya is a 14-year-old 9th grader with SPD who is hyperalert and hyperaware of (in particular) new sounds, textures, light intensities, and tactile input. In Arya's case, it is not just sensitivities to various sensory input, but also oversensitivity to new sensory input that causes a great deal of stress for him.

On any given day, as he gets ready at home and walks through the hallways of his school and into the classroom, Arya is in a constant state of stress, for the fear that there may be new, unexpected, and unfamiliar sensory input. For example, in the mornings, he worries that he cannot find his favorite hairbrush, in which case he would have to use another brush, one that he is not used to and will feel differently on his scalp. Since grooming activities are already stressful and uncomfortable for him, he is always worried about new and unfamiliar sensations.

Similarly, at school, Arya is hyperalert to having to be in a new classroom, participate in new activities, and adapt to a new environment. From Arya's perspective, "new and exciting" means unfamiliar and stressful. Therefore, while others might view Arya's behaviors as avoidance-based, timid, shy, and isolating, in fact, this is his coping mechanism to lower his stress level and manage his behaviors and reactions.

One Reaction Does Not Fit All

Stress is a phenomenon that most of us have heard about and have experienced, but it's hard to pin down exactly what stress means. Each of us has our own understanding of what it means to be "stressed out" or to experience stress.

While most adults can verbally describe their feelings or thoughts about their own stress, their reactions are not necessarily the same as others. Thus, it remains difficult to apply a one-size-fits-all definition. Defining stress for children can be even more challenging, as children often struggle to connect their feelings with words.

Consider this example: Your heart beats fast, your palms are sweaty, your head hurts, and you can't think straight. You feel like your blood pressure has gone up (and it has), your skin feels clammy, you feel a bit shaky when you walk or stand up, your eyes and ears don't quite work the way you'd like them to, and even though you need a drink of water, you probably don't feel like getting one.

These are some of the typical manifestations of stress that many of us have experienced at some point in our lives. While you may not have experienced all of these symptoms in one stressful episode, you can probably think back to experiences where you remember feeling some combination of those behavioral signs of stress. Each of the symptoms listed triggers a process that "turns on" when we perceive a situation to be stressful. The response that kicks in when we encounter a stressful situation involves many changes, including changes in our body, emotions, thinking, and behaviors.

Children experience basic developmental stages, and their response to and understanding of stress depends heavily on where they are in their developmental journey. For children who, over the years, have developed adequate coping mechanisms and skills and have learned ways of helping themselves through difficult situations, their response to stress may be more adaptive, effective, and socially acceptable. For example, when introduced to a new situation or new group of people, taking a short break by excusing oneself to regroup is a much better strategy than to just run out of the room suddenly and hide in the bathroom.

Consider the following two cases: John, a 14-year-old 9th-grade student, was asked to create a smaller model of a solar-powered car in industrial technology class. The assignment was handed out with all the necessary steps clearly stated. Within the first few minutes, John protested, refusing to work on the project, and stating, "This is stupid, I'm not doing this. I already did this in middle school!" Needless to say, John ended up in the principal's office, who later learned from John's mother that, in fact, due to the fine motor demands of the project, John would have never been able to complete the task without help or modifications. John preferred to be thought of as a kid with behavioral problems than a "dumb" one. His greatest fear was for others, particularly his peers, to view him as a kid who was in need of special education services.

On the other hand, Joe, another high-school student, in the 10th grade, encountered a similar situation in science lab. However, Joe had been prepared by his team of care providers for several years beforehand, and had learned adaptive coping skills in demanding situations. He had learned to inquire about alternative assignments and alternative ways of doing a project, asking to get paired up with peers, and sharing his sensory profile with his academic team at the outset of each academic year. As a result, Joe was able to deal with the situation in a calm and rational manner.

HOW PARENTS AND TEACHERS CAN HELP

As mentioned in other parts of this chapter, more research is needed to fully understand the physiological and psychoneuroimmunological processes driving SPD. Because SPD has not yet been integrated into the mainstream body of medical knowledge, it's important for parents and teachers who want to help children with SPD to keep in mind a few basic ideas about stress and its usefulness as an analogy for SPD.

SPD is not something children can willfully control or change on their own. Much like an individual with chronic stress who experiences physiological, cognitive, and behavioral symptoms, a child with a form of SPD is living with the symptoms of an underlying neuropsychological disorder.

Similar to the outcomes associated with untreated chronic stress, untreated SPD could potentially erode a child's self-esteem, isolate the child from his or her peers, and create vulnerability for depression.

Considering the presence of SPD as an ongoing stressor in a child's life can help family members and teachers understand the toll the disorder can have on a child's daily living. Each behavior that is linked in some way to living with SPD serves some type of function or as a coping mechanism for the child living with the disorder.

Because SPD is an age-old disorder with a new term, it's likely that many individuals in your life and your child's life will not be familiar with it. As the parent of a child with SPD, you may need to take on the role of educating family, friends, and teachers about it. Most individuals have experienced the negative effects of stress, either temporarily or chronically, so they can relate to stress as a familiar concept and understand that it can cause physical and emotional damage. The concept of stress can be a helpful analogy for you to use in explaining the ever-present, depleting effect SPD can have on your child.

Using stress as an analogy for explaining the effect SPD can have on daily living also helps family, friends, teachers, and other important people in your child's life to understand that your child's ability to cope with specific sensory input is compromised, and this causes a ripple effect in other areas of your child's experience. For example, everyone can think of at least one time in their life when they experienced stress of some sort—either minor, time-limited stress, or perhaps more chronic or traumatic stress. It could be helpful to you and your child if you could evoke those references in others by sharing an example of how stress in your own life compromised your daily life. Most people will listen to a story, and some will even gain a better understanding of what it's like to live with a pervasive disorder that affects a child's ability to cope, function, and find joy in his or her life on a daily basis.

How Stress Affects Our Bodies

While we behave outwardly in certain ways in response to stress, our body's complex psychoneuroimmuno-logical, or PNI, system is also involved in the stress response. PNI refers to the interaction between the mind, body, behavior, the immune or defense system, and the endocrine system, which is responsible for our body's hormones.

Our PNI systems involve a complex series of inter-actions between biological systems and psychological functioning. Illness in one biological system in the body affects (either directly or indirectly) the entire body and mind. For example, even a simple cold can affect differ-ent functions of the body. It affects the body's immune system, and as our body starts to fight the cold, the sneezing, sniffling, runny nose, watery eyes, headache, and not being able to get a restful sleep have an effect on our total body functioning and how we feel physically and emotionally. When you think about it, a cold is in essence much like a stressor on the body, a biological source of stress that can affect several of our body's systems—that is, the PNI system. By using this comparison, it's easy to see how the PNI system can be affected in a child with SPD. In other words, if stress equals SPD, and stress leads to changes in our body functioning or PNI system, then SPD can lead to changes in our body functioning and PNI system, as well.

While the different parts of the PNI system are always busy interacting with one another and responding to messages sent to the body, exposure to stressful events turns on a specific portion of the PNI system called the hypothalamus-pituitary-adrenal axis (HPA axis), otherwise known as the stress response.

Consider the following analogy: Imagine if the security alarm was always on in your house (the PNI system), but it only beeped (the stress response) when a specific part of the house, the front door (HPA axis), underwent forced entry. The extent to how the HPA axis responds will vary, from minor annoyances that cause a slight increase in the stress response on one end of the spectrum, to a chronic posttraumatic stress disorder response on the opposite end. In between these two extremes is a wide range of responses to stress.

Such is the case with SPD, in that, depending on how severely and which parts of the sensory system are affected, the responses in a child will vary. Some children may show symptoms of discomfort to several types of sensory input, while others may only exhibit sensitivity to one or two stimuli, such as loud noise and bright lights.

RAISING AWARENESS ABOUT THE EFFECTS OF STRESS

During the early to middle part of the 20th century, a number of scientists began to dedicate their program of research to understanding the physiology of the stress response.

One scientist in particular, Hans Selye (1907–1982), who pioneered studies on the effects of exposure to stressful stimuli on the body, noted that stressful events or experiences caused consistent changes in the body's hormones and immune system. His groundbreaking work helped elevate the scientific study of stress to a notable level. Since then, there has been extensive research on the stress response and its effect on health and everyday living.

Stressed Out and Shut Down

The individuality or phenomenology of stress refers to the way we each experience or make meaning of stressors. Put differently, our subjective experience of stress could be described as the psychology of stress. This is the aspect of stress we refer to when we say things like, "I had a really stressful day at work today." Or "I was stuck in traffic for 2 hours, it was very stressful!"

Interestingly, the subjective experience of stress is elusive because it's difficult to measure and is subject to a multitude of variables. The only clear-cut case of the subjective experience mapping out to the other components of stress is when an individual reports that he or she was in a dissociative state during the stressful event. This means that the stressor was so extreme that he or she "shut down" emotionally, as in the case of combat or some form of abuse.

The subjective experience of dissociation has physiological, behavioral, and cognitive correlates that are all measurable. In more subtle and time-limited exposures to stress, individuals may report that they feel like they've been exposed to something stressful, but physiological measures (such as cortisol levels) don't agree.

When Stress Interferes with Thinking

At one point in your life, you may have been in a stressful situation and noticed that you couldn't think as clearly or remember details as well as you might have under non-stressful circumstances.

Evidence supports the notion that cognition (thinking, learning, and remembering) is negatively affected by immune functioning that has been compromised by stress in some way. This is an important component of stress because if an individual experiences school or work as stressful, then he or she is more likely to underperform. This, in turn, could affect the individual's self-esteem and contribute to depression or a feeling of helplessness. Later on in this chapter, we'll discuss a few research studies that support the concept of stress causing (either directly or indirectly) impaired memory and thinking.

Soldiering On, Fleeing, and Fighting

Behavior is the part of stress that connects everything together—the physical symptoms of stress (physiology), such as increased heart rate and blood pressure, your perception of the stressful event (subjective experience), and the way you solve problems or think while under stress (cognition).

Behavior could mean leaving the stressful event, "soldiering through it," calming yourself down with deep breathing or meditation, or feeling overwhelmed and shutting down. Behavior is key to managing ongoing stress, such as that caused by a challenging school or work environment, and in many situations behavior is critical to maintaining a positive educational experience and supportive social relationships.

As discussed earlier in this chapter, the recently evolved field of psychoneuroimmunology includes behavior as an important variable in understanding the way in which stress affects an individual's physical and psychological health. Many health and wellness facilities understand the value of supporting mind-body balance for individuals who are relatively healthy. Integration of psychoneuroimmunology principles into mainstream medicine and public health policy is still in the early stages of development. On an encouraging note, federal funding for the behavioral piece of disease prevention and management is becoming more common.

Different Types of Stress

Short-term and long-term stress differ in their acuteness and can elicit responses that vary in severity and duration.

Short-term or acute stress in everyday life is time-limited. For example, when you study hard for a big test or finish a complicated project at work, you experience short-term stress. As you'll see later in this chapter, acute everyday stress can boost immune functioning, helping you to reach your goal successfully.

Short-term stress can also be traumatic—losing a loved one or surviving a natural disaster, such as an earthquake or tornado. One of the differences between everyday short-term stress and short-term stress that is traumatic is that when everyday short-term stress is over (the project is done), the individual's physiology, subject experience, cognition, and behavior return to normal. Unfortunately, after a short-term trauma, the individual continues to experience stress, and in some cases, the acute stress can evolve into posttraumatic stress disorder.

Long-term or chronic stress is pervasive and often requires individuals to change the way they live their lives. Examples include an individual who becomes disabled due to an illness or accident, or someone who takes on the long-term care of a chronically ill family member. This type of stress has no real endpoint and requires a massive overhaul of one's life.

Stress connected to a past trauma is neither acute nor chronic because the stressful event or experience occurred sometime in the past; however, the effects of the stress have not faded. In many cases, this type of stressful experience leads to posttraumatic stress disorder.

A CHILD WITH SPD AND THE TRAUMA OF SPORTS

Kevin, a 12-year-old 7th grader, seemed to have weak muscles ever since he was born. He learned to sit up, pull himself up to stand, and walk later than other children.

He tired easily and needed to sit after standing and lie down after sitting. He was not very well coordinated, was slow to respond motorically, and was very fearful of getting hit by a ball during sport activities. Kevin was always "the worst" player in soccer, softball, and basketball, all of which he joined because his parents pushed him to. Kevin got hit by the ball several times, could not keep up with the rest of the kids, was picked last, blamed for the team's losses, couldn't play several different positions, and was left out and ridiculed by the other players. He was always told by his parents, coaches, and the other players to just try harder, be more motivated, and make a real effort.

Yet, Kevin was doing all that. Finally, at the end of 4th grade he absolutely refused to sign up for and participate in group sports. The thought of going through the blame and public humiliation again was too much. On the other hand, not participating in group sports isolated him more and more from other kids, social opportunities, and invitations to birthday parties and other fun social events. To this day, Kevin will not sign up for team sports or camps that require team activities, or even play doubles tennis.

Reliving a Stressful Event Again and Again

On the extreme end of the spectrum are stories about veterans of wars or survivors of extreme abuse who suffer from posttraumatic stress disorder, or PTSD. Their narratives about what they lived through are harrowing, terrifying accounts of extreme suffering and pain. Although we can conceptualize the PTSD experience as an extreme form of stress, it's also helpful to look at some of the unique physiological responses associated with PTSD. In particular, research studies have suggested that there are features of PTSD that differ from chronic or acute stress responses.

Unlike chronic or acute stress, the abnormal psychophysiological response in PTSD is not limited to the actual stressful event. Rather, individuals with PTSD will have a physiological response if they are *reminded* of the traumatic event.

Also, this same individual will have a physiological response to neutral sensory input that is similar to the original trauma. For example, a solider with PTSD hears a book fall on the floor, but his body responds (eg, increased heart rate) as though he is confronted with gun or mortar fire. This type of response indicates that the individual's sensory system no longer discriminates between similar but distinct sensory input.

What Studies Tell Us about
Understanding Stress—and SPD

Numerous studies can help us better understand the experience of stress. We will review a sampling of these studies within the context of considering stress as a model for understanding SPD.

Although the experience of stress usually has physiological changes associated with it, research suggests that in mild, acute situations of stress, individuals may not experience a change in their cognitive functioning or stress hormone levels.

In a 1999 study, for example, researchers in Sweden conducted a study in which 24 men completed a logical reasoning task and a short-term memory task with no environmental stressors. The men completed those same tasks while being exposed to noise or vibrations (or both) similar to the experiences of having a large truck drive by your house. Researchers tested the participants' cortisol levels (stress hormone) in both scenarios, and scored the tasks.

Interestingly, although the men reported that they ascertained the environment to be stressful due to the vibrations and noise, their performance on the tasks didn't suffer, and their cortisol levels were at nonstress levels. This study shows us that the perception of stress doesn't always match up with the physiological or cognitive components of stress. Clearly, the study is limited in that only 24 participants were involved, and there were many variables that were not accounted for or explained. But, this study helps us ask the following question: Are there certain stressors or durations of stress that will "turn on" the HPA axis and impair cognitive functioning?

If you think about stress as being a continuum, then the answer to the question we just raised is yes—extreme stressors such as war, trauma, and fear of imminent death will undoubtedly trigger the physiological and cognitive components of stress. This question becomes more difficult to answer when we look at the less obvious situations in daily life where individuals experience either acute or chronic stress, such as chronic lack of sleep, extensive work hours, or multiple, constant demands. While these types of stressors are common, they are no less stressful!

Three Effects of Stress on the Immune System

In 2004, researchers Suzanne Segerstrom, PhD, and Gregory Miller, PhD, summarized 30 years worth of research on stress and the immune system. Their study, which is referred to as a "meta-analysis" (a study of numerous studies), involved reviewing the results of 293 research studies (from 1961–2001) with 18,941 participants. Their analysis yielded three main outcomes related to immune function.

Short-term (acute) stress gets the immune system working at its optimal level in preparation for injury or infection.

Long-term (chronic) stress damages the immune system (among other bodily systems), and causes illness.

Stress has a greater impact on the immune systems of elderly and sick individuals.

The authors of the meta-analysis study suggested that future research include the role of behavior in the stress-immunity pathway. For example, to what extent can optimism play a role in mitigating the effect of stress on the body? The results cited in this meta-analysis point to the need for more pyschoneuroimmunological studies.

A Predisposition for Stress and SPD

A number of studies have explored the possibility that although posttraumatic stress disorder, or PTSD, is clearly a result of a psychologically traumatic event, such as combat, there may be factors that predispose an individual to being vulnerable to PTSD.

In a study conducted by Roger K. Pitman, MD, and colleagues at Massachusetts General Hospital, Vietnam veterans with PTSD and their twin brothers, who were not Vietnam veterans, were matched with the same number of Vietnam veterans who did NOT have PTSD and had twin brothers who were not Vietnam veterans.

The assumption was that if both the veterans with PTSD and their twin brothers demonstrated a greater number of subtle neurological disturbances (neurologic soft signs) than the veterans without PTSD and their twin brothers, researchers could and, in fact, did conclude that subtle neurological disturbances that showed up in the PTSD group were not in fact caused by the PTSD, but rather, represents a familial (tending to occur in more members of a family than expected by chance alone) vulnerability for developing chronic PTSD when exposed to traumatic events. In other words, those with a familial vulnerability for developing PTSD when exposed to traumatic events are more likely to show changes and subtle dysfunction in their neurological presentation. Pitman and colleagues discussed the many limitations to their study and the need for additional work to be done on this important question of whether there is some type of neurological predisposition in some individuals that makes them more vulnerable to developing PTSD because of psychological trauma.

In another study that used a similar approach, William S. Kremen, PhD, of the Department of Psychiatry and Center for Behavioral Genomics at the University of California, San Diego, and colleagues examined the relationship between cognitive ability and PTSD in Vietnam veterans who received a diagnosis of PTSD and their twin nonveteran brothers. This group was matched with Vietnam veterans who did not receive a diagnosis of PTSD and their twin nonveteran brothers. The results from this study indicated that the Vietnam veterans with PTSD and their twin nonveteran brothers scored lower on various cognitive tests than the veterans without PTSD and their twin brothers. Again, investigators discussed the many limiting factors of the study, including the lack of racial and ethnic diversity, and the lack of female participants. The hypothesis (theory or assumption) of this study was supported; namely, there was a link between an individual's cognitive ability and his vulnerability to developing PTSD because of exposure to a psychological trauma.

Both of these studies provide some evidence for specific predisposing variables, such as subtle neurological disturbances and/or lower cognitive functioning, creating an increased risk of developing PTSD after exposure to a psychological trauma. The idea of predisposing variables or factors is useful for thinking about possible origins of SPD.

HELPING YOUR CHILD EVERY DAY AND AT SPECIAL EVENTS

Children with SPD face daily, sometimes hourly, challenges. Often, these challenges can be overwhelming, exhausting, and isolating.

They may feel like outsiders in their social group, and become frustrated or discouraged with their outsider status. In some cases, children who are socially isolated and anxious are more vulnerable to depression. For example, a child who is overresponsive to auditory sensory input or clumsy due to a postural disorder may find it too overwhelming to participate in a birthday party (especially one with a sports theme). He or she may not have been invited to the party, or if invited, declined the invitation due to embarrassment or feeling bad about him- or herself.

Creating a sensory diet and working with an occupational therapist will help your child learn how to handle his or her SPD. These activities will also help build your child's confidence and self-esteem.

SPD also affects parents—and family members—who can often find it daunting to include their child in everyday activities, especially if those activities involve unpredictable events or environments that are potentially challenging (eg, they include loud music or bright lights).

The following lists of tips can serve as a springboard for helping you plan your outings, events, or activities so that you and your family can feel confident leaving the comforts of your home.

Ultimately, these suggested tips are intended to help you think through ways to increase the probability that your child will enjoy him- or herself, and feel connected to your family events and outings. You and your family will undoubtedly find yourselves in situations outside of the scope of these lists, but in many cases, you can modify a plan to fit your situation and the needs of your child.

SUMMARY EVENTS CHECKLIST

The events listed in this chapter are a sampling of what you and your child might do on a day-to-day basis. In general, when considering any event, it's helpful to try to see the event from the perspective of your child. This will help you prepare him or her for participating in and, hopefully, enjoying the event. Here are some closing thoughts to keep in mind when planning or participating in an event with your child:

Plan as much as you can BEFORE the event. Involve your child's teachers and therapists, and of course, your child.

Listen to your child—read his or her behavior, mood, words, affect. He or she will communicate with you in some way how he or she feels about the event.

Help your child practice as much as possible, and figure out what will work and what to avoid.

Involve as many helpful adults as possible; this creates support for you and your child.

Be creative with alternatives. Yankee Stadium may not work out, but a minor league baseball game in a relaxed environment could work.

Always have an exit strategy that is clear and easy to follow for everyone involved, especially your child.

Accept help from trusted friends and family members!

Strike the balance between helping and overprotecting your child. This is tough, but you can do it!

Be realistic and supportive of your child. Take a moment for a reality check whenever you lose track of how things are going.

There are no failures; each attempt is its own success. Help your child see the value in his or her efforts, and celebrate them together!

Religious and Cultural Holidays

Fortunately, most religious and cultural holidays follow a specific set of rituals, so a number of key environmental components are familiar and, in some cases, soothing and comforting.

In general, it's helpful to find out the social norms associated with the holiday. For example, a 2-hour Christmas Eve mass may or may not work for your child, depending on the type and intensity of his or her sensory disorder. Will there be singing? Will your child need to stand and sit a lot? Will he or she need to sit still and be quiet for long stretches of time? Will the church be packed with people? Will there be bright lights, or dim candlelight? Will there be intense scents or special foods?

Find Out the Five W's of the Event

You'll want to do some homework before the event, and familiarize yourself with the who, what, where, when, why, and how of the event. Try to answer the following questions:

Approximately how many people will be present? Do you know the attendees? If not, will you get to know them before or during the event?

What's expected of everyone—singing, silence, prayer, eating, drinking, sitting, walking, standing, clapping?

Will the event be in a familiar setting? Will you need to travel to get there? How long do you need to travel?

Is the event at a set time, or can you pick an earlier or later time?

How is the event managed? Do you start or stop the event or is it predetermined (eg, a mass or service)?

Why is your family going? Is it part of your religious belief system to attend this function, or is this a secular holiday with a variety of formats and activities?

Tips for Religious and Cultural Holidays

After you've jotted down the who, what, where, when, why, and how of the event, take a few minutes to think through your child's preferences and challenges, and the resources you will have to support his or her participation. Remember, even though the focus of these tips is on your child, you and your family need to make decisions that will minimize your stress and worry, and hopefully enhance your enjoyment also.

Before the Event

Discuss with your child the who, what, where, when, why, and how of the event.

Introduce a sample of new foods, smells, or sounds that might be present at the event—be careful to do this slowly and gently, there's no rush!

If your child needs a particular food to feel comfortable, then bring it along to the event.

Plan your mode of transportation, avoiding extra travel time or potential travel snags by leaving early or taking a less-traveled but well-known route.

If possible, visit the venue before the event so your child (and you) can become acquainted with the environment. Even if you've been to the space before, visit anyhow and discuss how the space might feel different because the event is special or different from what your child might have experienced before in that same space.

Decide with your child which activities make sense for him or her to participate in during the event. Keep the activity age appropriate and time limited so the boundaries are clear to your child.

If possible, expose your child to the content of the event— read prayers, tell stories, and go over the rituals or whatever you think is relevant to the event. This will also help you discover potentially challenging components of the event.

Read a book to your child or give your child a book to read about the event (eg, the story of Hanukah). If reading is difficult, play a CD or DVD, or tell your child a story about the event.

Discuss with your child the props, toys, or special objects that you will bring along to the event. For example, your child may have a squishy ball that he squeezes whenever he feels physically uncomfortable. Your child's therapist or teacher may have some suggestions, so be sure to check with them. Pack these objects in an easy-to-access bag or box.

Discuss with your child familiar coping strategies that have worked at school or home. How can your child use those strategies at this event? How can you help him or her with the strategy?

If appropriate and possible, speak with some of the other attendees—in particular, supportive friends, religious leaders, or family members. Let them know that your child will participate to the best of his or her ability. Let them know if he or she needs special accommodations to participate.

If your child has postural or dyspraxia disorder, discuss and try out the physical requirements of the event. Don't push your child to do everything, and always provide an "out" for making him- or herself comfortable, even if means leaving the event.

During the Event

If you see your child struggling, don't panic! Speak calmly and use language he is used to hearing. Now is not the time to try new techniques.

If the event goes off schedule or becomes unpredictable, explain those changes to your child as best you can. Reassure him that you will help him meet the new challenge.

Praise your child each step of the way, and point out how much he has accomplished by participating in the event.

Encourage your child to use his toys, props, or objects as supports, especially if you think it will help him get through a challenging segment of the event. For example, a child who slouches could make good use of a prop that helps him sit comfortably through the event.

Remember, even if your child does well during "practice," the stress of the real situation could be overwhelming.

Always allow for a way out—such as sitting in the back of the temple or church, sitting at the end of the table, or standing on the outer edges of the congregation.

Remember, the child is not a failure. The only failure may be in accessing the more adaptive and socially acceptable response in the moment. Encourage your child to keep trying and trouble-shooting with you.

After the Event

Gauge how much communication your child is up for after the event. If she is exhausted or craving stimulation, help her address those needs within reason. For example, if it's not possible for your child to go to bed right away because you need to drive home, you can provide a quiet, comforting environment in your car, or go to the playground for a few minutes before driving home. You may have to look for nonverbal cues, such as facial expression, body language, or gestures, to determine how your child is doing.

If your child is able to comfortably engage in conversation, let her know how proud you are of her accomplishments. Be specific and let your child know what specific behavior impressed you. No accomplishment is too small.

Ask your child how she felt at the event. Was it fun? Boring? Too long, confusing, funny? Make a mental note of this feedback, and if possible, write it down. Your child's feedback is part of what makes her sensory diet plan or therapeutic exercises work.

Acknowledge your child's feelings, and offer to help her work on challenges that might have come up during the event.

Communicate with your child's teachers and therapists about the event. The successes and the challenges are all helpful information to have.

Whatever the outcome, don't lose sight of your child's hard work.

Be sure to thank family members and friends who supported you and your child through the event.

Thank your child for trying his or her best.

Give yourself time to rest, reflect, and rejuvenate—whether it's a walk, a trip to the gym, or time alone, make sure you make the time to support yourself.

TALKING WITH YOUR CHILD AFTER THE EVENT

Here is an example of what talking to your child after a social event might sound like. Obviously, the content of the conversation must be adjusted and will be different based on the age of the child: [Parent (P), Child (C)]

P: How are you doing, sweetie? That was a long ceremony. I am so proud of how you were able to sit quietly for such a long time.

C: I was so bored. I wanted to leave so badly.

P: I can see how that might have been boring for you.

C: Do you think people saw me fidgeting?

P: What would you have done if you didn't fidget?

C: I would have run out of there so fast.

P: So you used it to actually help you to get through it?

C: I guess.

P: Next we can think of ways to help you manage the fidgeting so it won't be too obvious.

C: Okay.

P: I am so glad you were a part of this important family event.

TALKING TO YOUR CHILD ABOUT SPD

It's helpful to talk with your child about the biological or physical basis of his or her disorder. Much like any other medical condition, understanding the biological or neurological basis of SPD demystifies it and helps your child understand that there is treatment for the disorder. Talking openly with your child and other family members and friends normalizes your child's day-to-day experience of living with the symptoms of SPD.

One word of caution: Any conversation regarding SPD should be child-directed. As parents, you must follow the child's lead to determine what and how much information your child wants and is ready to hear. More often than not, because of their own anxiety and need for more information, parents spill out much too much unneeded information and complicated explanations and offer unsolicited solutions.

Listen carefully to what your child is asking you, pause to fully understand what it is he or she is REALLY asking you, and determine what the most pertinent information is to the question. You must also, of course, take your child's age and developmental level (level of cognitive and psychosocial maturity) into consideration. If children ask what the disorder is, that means they are not only aware that there is something different about them, but also that they are ready to hear about it.

Take your cues from the question and offer the most concise, simple, direct, and clear answer to that question. Then pause and wait for your child to take the information in and respond to you. If you aren't clear about what it is they are asking, clarify it with them.

Parents should make sure that their children understand that they have SPD, but SPD does not have them. Provide simple examples of common medical conditions that people live with every day, and that they continue to be who they are and do what they do. Some examples may include diabetes, hypothyroidism, or high blood pressure. Acknowledge the challenges that SPD presents for your child. Do not minimize the effect that it has on his or her life. Let them know that there are resources that you, their academic team at school, and their care providers will use to help them. At the same time, remind them that they are their own best resources. Once they know and learn helpful coping strategies, items, and activities—that is, their sensory diet—they can identify what they need at any given moment, access the tools they need, and use them to cope more effectively.

Weddings and Funerals

Weddings and funerals are events that many children would find challenging under the best of circumstances. In some cases, children may not be invited to a wedding, or adult family members may feel that a funeral is "too much" for any child, especially younger ones. If children are not prohibited from these events, it's your call to decide whether your child should attend.

At first glance, it might look like weddings and funerals are very different events. Weddings are usually happy, joyful events, and funerals sad, and perhaps scary events. But, if we look more closely, we can see that both offer profoundly meaningful experiences to their participants. Weddings affirm our faith in love, connection, and family.

Funerals celebrate the life of a loved one and create a space for grieving family members and friends to express their sorrow and, hopefully, find solace.

As a parent, it's important to acknowledge your own feelings about the event, and discuss with loved ones the extent to which you are capable of and available for helping your child participate in an age-appropriate and sensory-appropriate manner.

The Wedding Planner

Unlike religious or cultural holidays, you already have the who, what, where, when, why, and how for a wedding. What you may not know is the magnitude of the event. Will there be 50 or 500 people at the wedding? Will there be a live rock band, a DJ, or a string quartet? Are there provisions for special diets, or is the menu prefixed?

Before you decide to include your child in a wedding, read the following pointers—they will help you decide if your child should attend a wedding, and prepare you and your child for the event.

Before You Accept the Invitation

Review the details of the invitation. Perhaps your child could attend the ceremony but skip the dinner?

Talk with your child's teacher or therapist about the possibility of your child attending. What do they advise?

If it's not clear what the magnitude of the event will be, contact the bride or groom and discuss the details of the event. If you're comfortable, discuss some of your child's challenges and how you will address them so that he or she can attend. Your challenge is to read the bride or groom's response. If you sense discomfort or uneasiness, you can address it in a direct, but kind, manner. For example, "I understand that SPD is not a well-known disorder. We've been working hard to help our son/daughter. We would not put him or her in a situation that could be harmful or detrimental. We also wouldn't want to put undue stress on you on your big day. What do you think?" This type of question gives the bride and groom the chance to voice their support and concerns. In either case, you've opened the door to clear communication.

If you decide that your child can attend some or all of the wedding, discuss with him or her the itinerary and what's involved at each step. If you decided that your child will only attend the ceremony or dinner, then only discuss that aspect of the wedding.

After You've Accepted the Invitation

Similar to religious and cultural holidays, it's helpful to expose your child to examples of weddings—movies, pictures, books, and songs.

Visit the wedding site if possible, and help your child pick out an outfit that he or she will be comfortable wearing. If your child needs practice wearing the new clothes, encourage him or her to wear the outfit around the house or during an occupational therapy appointment.

Request a special meal, or offer to bring your own food for your child.

For the luncheon or dinner, request seating away from the activity hub and close to a quiet lobby or exit. If your request can't be accommodated or seating hasn't been decided yet, consider switching seats at the event.

Together with your child's therapist and teachers, work out a plan of action for handling your child's specific type of SPD at the wedding. Make sure that your child and family members are aware of the plan, and stick to it as long as it makes sense.

If your child is overresponsive to sound and can manage earplugs, discuss with your child's therapist the possibility of wearing earplugs that allow in some, but not all, sound.

Unlike a religious or cultural holiday, a wedding can be unpredictable and outright rowdy at times. Stay attuned to your child's response to the unpredictable or "over-the-top" qualities of the event. If you see him struggling, remove him from the setting (eg, move to a quiet lobby or restroom), and figure out whether it's all right to stay at the wedding.

If you feel yourself getting tense or worried, do a reality check: How is your child doing? Are you needlessly worrying, or is your child struggling to cope with his or her sensory input? If all is well, then enjoy the moment. If your child is not doing well, stay calm and positive, but discuss leaving the room or the event.

Remember: You can leave at any point; don't worry about offending anyone. Your goal is to maintain your child's self-esteem and support his or her development. If that means leaving early, then by all means, leave early.

After the Wedding

Read over the tips previously mentioned for how to help your child after attending religious and cultural holidays.

Thank the bride and groom for including your child, and thank others who might have gone out of their way to accommodate your child (such as catering staff, musicians, and members of the wedding party). Your note or phone call will raise their awareness of the challenges that SPD poses and will make them feel good for helping the event go successfully.

Funerals

The death of a loved one is a complicated, sorrowful, life-altering event. Many adults struggle to attend funerals because the sadness and grief is frightening or overwhelming. For a child with SPD, a funeral could represent one of the most painful and difficult experiences to endure. Alternatively, attending a funeral also provides a way for loved ones, including your child, to celebrate the deceased individual's life, and say good-bye. However, if you think it would be too disturbing for your child to attend a funeral, consider the suggestions below, under "Funeral Alternatives."

As a parent or caregiver of a child with SPD, you could be faced with dealing with your own shock and grief on top of having to comfort and help organize your child's experience. Depending on your faith or the faith of the family of the deceased individual, you may have very little time to decide whether your child can or should attend the funeral. If you think there is a possibility that your child might attend the funeral, consider these tips and suggestions:

Should My Child Attend a Funeral?

- Discuss the death with friends, family, teachers, therapists—anyone who knows your family and your child well. Get a sense for whether you and your family and friends are up to having your child attend the funeral. It's all right to have your child not attend, especially if attending the funeral has the potential to be physically or emotionally overwhelming for you or your child.

- If you belong to a specific faith, seek spiritual guidance. This could help you feel more at ease in your decision to have your child attend or not attend the funeral.

- In a situation where the deceased individual was ill for quite some time, you might have already spoken with your child about the individual's eventual death. If the death was sudden, however, consider the language you will use and amount of detail you will share with your child regarding the death. Depending on the type and severity of your child's SPD, he may have a hard time expressing his emotions and may find it overwhelming to hear too many details about death. Gauge the conversation to your child's needs.

- Consider the unpredictable nature of a funeral—some individuals may express deep pain and sorrow through sobbing and crying. This could be overwhelming for your child to process, especially if this is the first time he or she has witnessed extreme grief being expressed.

- If the funeral includes a wake with an open casket, consider the potential consequences of your child viewing the body of a deceased loved one. This can be difficult for anyone, but for a child with SPD, it could be very traumatic and frightening. Discuss this component of the funeral with trusted family members, friends, and your child's therapist.

- **Important caveat:** If your child is socially isolated, depressed, or struggles with any type of mental health issue, any type of funeral could prove traumatic. Consider some of the suggested alternatives discussed in the "Funeral Alternatives" section.

Attending the Funeral

If you choose to have your child attend a funeral, limit the amount of time she spends at the funeral, and allow time afterwards for her to communicate feelings or "be quiet."

Be sure to bring props, toys, or supports your child may need to feel comfortable in a quiet setting with low lighting. Consider travel time between the funeral and cemetery, and decide whether your child is able to physically manage both settings.

Consider that the transition from the service to the cemetery could mean an extreme shift from a dimly lit, quiet setting, to an outdoor venue involving walking and standing and possibly unpredictable weather conditions.

Like other events, remember that you can leave at any point.

Funeral Alternatives

Invite your child to write or dictate a letter to the deceased individual and have your child keep the letter in a place that is meaningful to him or her (such as a memory box, a simple container or box in which to keep the letter and any other reminders of the deceased person, such as photos or cards).

Help your child create a picture or collage in memory of the deceased individual.

Plan an activity or visit a place that is somehow connected to the deceased individual. For example, if the deceased person enjoyed the beach and your child can manage a trip to the beach, then plan a visit in honor of the deceased person.

Hold a memorial service in an environment that your child is familiar with and is physically able to maneuver. Invite a few close friends and family members. Keep it short, with a focus on celebrating the deceased individual's life. If your child is okay with it, invite him or her to share the letter or collage at the service.

Important consideration: The grief process can be long, and some expressions of grief are hard to respond to over time. If at any time you feel that your child's sorrow or grief is too much for him to handle, or if you are struggling to help your child, seek professional help.

Vacations

Everyone needs and deserves a vacation, including your child! Also, parents and siblings who work hard on a daily basis to help a child with SPD are often running on empty, and could use a break from their daily routines. The following ideas and tips can help you plan your next vacation.

When considering your destination, bear in mind your child's condition. Are there aspects of the destination that will be hard for your child? Are there props or exercises your child can do to help her adapt to the setting?

As you think about your accommodations, try to avoid selecting a setting that is more restrictive than what your child is used to living in on a daily basis. For example, if your child normally has her own room or shares a room with one sibling, it's probably not a good idea to book one hotel room for your entire family. Alternatively, a cottage or suite configuration might be more comfortable for everyone.

If eating and drinking is an issue for your child, be sure to bring food along or prepare food while you travel.

Like religious or cultural holidays, vacations are not the best time to start a new challenge for your child. Pick a destination with activities that you know your child can participate in and tolerate well. For example, if your child is okay with wearing sunglasses and a hat at the beach, but is not okay with large crowds, consider visiting a less populated beach.

It may be the case that your child can participate in some, but not all, of the vacation activities. If that's the case, be clear with everyone in the family how your child will spend his or her time while other family members are involved in another activity. Take turns spending time with your child, and create a situation where everyone is together at least once a day.

Brainstorm a list of activities with your child's teachers and therapists; be creative and fun, but keep the activities simple and the materials portable.

If your child has a goal or desire to do something that she has not been able to do before (such as visit Niagara Falls), discuss with her what it would be like to see and hear the Falls. Is it a goal that will create a sense of accomplishment and build your child's self-esteem? How would your child like to commemorate her goal (with pictures, drawings, or a dictated or written story)?

Try thinking about vacations as events that can be measured in terms of magnitude of difference or change from your everyday life, such as riding in a plane versus car travel, a new language spoken, new landscapes, new foods, time zone changes, different customs, and social expectations. The magnitude of difference you choose will really depend on your child's ability to cope with change. You, your child, your child's teachers and therapists, and other family members can all chime in on the question of magnitude.

Grocery and Department Stores

Trips to grocery or department stores offer a rich opportunity for your child to work on some of his or her daily living skills. While your child need not accompany you on every trip to the store, you can pick and choose which shopping trips will be the most fun and the least problematic for your child. Here are some ideas to get you started:

Planning and Organizing

If developmentally appropriate, put your child in charge of adding to a list of items that are needed from the store on a regular basis. Keep the list in an easy-to-reach location, and help your child keep it up to date. If feasible, let your child search through coupons and mailers for discounts, sales, and other bargains. You could limit the activity to searching for a few items that you need to purchase. As your child becomes more skilled at this task, he or she will notice sale items that you don't need today, but could use in a few weeks (always a nice surprise when your child plans for future needs!).

Have your child help you plan a holiday celebration—the food, decorations, activities, presents, and music. Your child can also help you figure out where to shop for the items you will need for the celebration.

Help your child create a calendar of events. These could be seasonal (such as the Fourth of July), school-based (such as projects and due dates), and social (such as special celebrations). You can include any commitments your child might have with therapists and teachers. This legitimizes and marks the importance of his or her hard work in treatment. Each calendar can include a list of items needed for events, assignments, and celebrations. Make this as fun and creative as possible!

Comparative Shopping

Discuss with your child how you go about selecting a specific store. Does one store offer a better selection? Better pricing? Is the produce fresher or locally grown? Visit two or more stores and compare prices, quality, and availability of products. Invite your child to give his or her opinion, and discuss the pros and cons of shopping for a specific item at a specific store.

If your child has been working on math skills at school or in therapy, ask him to figure out how much a group of items would cost, and then ask him to buy those items. You can, of course, accompany your child and help him work through the process. Another version of this activity involves figuring out how much a few staple items such as milk, bread, and eggs cost, and then have your child total the prices and tell or show you how much money you will need to buy those items.

Ask your child if he is interested in buying a special toy or game. Discuss the qualities of the toy or game that appeal to him. Plan a trip where the two of you purchase that item. To the extent possible, encourage him to help you plan the shopping trip.

Note: All of these suggested shopping activities provide your child with the opportunity to practice writing, planning, computation, communication, and physical movement, as well as support your child's self-esteem and self-worth. Remember: Any of the activities can be modified to meet your child's sensory processing and developmental needs.

Sports Events

Attending a sporting event might seem too daunting or exhausting for you and your child. Under the best of circumstances a sporting event in a 50,000-seat stadium, for example, could be tough for anyone. But before you opt out of attending these types of events, consider some of the following alternatives.

Many individuals find a large stadium or crowded gymnasium to be too loud, too crowded, and too difficult to get to. The distance from your seats to the restroom or parking lot is also a consideration. For a child with any type of SPD, the obstacles are magnified. If, however, you would like your child to experience the thrill and fun of a sports event, consider less restrictive and more flexible environments that you can try out.

Each of the major sports has a local club or league and, in some cases, there are small venues geared toward families. For example, over the past decade or so a number of small, neighborhood-based stadiums were built for minor-league baseball teams. These stadiums are generally easy to get in and out of and have excellent seating (and cost less!). If possible, check out the venues before you attend a sporting event. Discuss with your child what it would be like to attend a sporting event at that venue.

Some local clubs or leagues have dedicated time slots for meeting fans and inviting the public in for tours or special events. These types of events give an extra-special quality to the sporting event.

If your child plays a specific sport, be sure to watch professionals playing the sport on TV. Discuss with your child the aspects of the sport that build on her strengths. Explore with your child how she feels about limitations she may have due to her SPD.

If your child is eager to attend a major sporting event, consider the magnitude of the event and the degree to which the crowd could be a problem in the stadium or gymnasium, as well as in the parking lot (such as, will it take hours to get out of the parking lot?).

Like any other event, talk it over with your child and his or her teacher or therapist, and plan out a strategy. Bear

in mind that it could be hard to leave quickly, especially in a large stadium, so weigh in this factor when
deciding the pros and cons of attending the event.

If other family members will be joining you, be sure to
discuss up front whether they will be expected to
accompany you and your child if you need to leave
unexpectedly. If siblings or other children are involved,
consider involving another adult so that in the event
you need to leave early with your child, the adult can
supervise and transport the other children after the
game is over.

At the Game

You and your child are at the game, the crowd is screaming, and your child is thrilled but struggling. The sensory
overload is too much, but it's hard for him to leave because
his favorite sports figure is in top form. What do you do?

Like any other challenge for a child with SPD, getting
through the excitement of the game can be exhausting and frustrating. Be sure to do a reality test—does
it look like your child has had enough? Is he unable
to participate even minimally? Is your child's level of
participation unmanageable for you (for example, is he
exhibiting sensory-seeking behaviors)? Is your child
putting himself at risk either physically or socially?

As the parent, you may need to tell your child in simple
yet firm language that it's time to leave. As with other
events, mention that your child did succeed in coming
to the event, and that you are proud of his or her effort.

After the Game

If all went well, plan to attend more sports events! If you or
your child felt that there were aspects of the event that

were tough to manage, talk about them and decide how to deal with each problematic aspect. It could be that some of the issues are beyond your control (such as the size of the venue), in which case, acknowledge that it's beyond your control, and come up with an alternative that appeals to both of you.

A Child's Birthday Party

You might think that the process of figuring out whether your child can attend a birthday party would be very similar to the suggestions and tips listed in the "Religious and Cultural Holiday" section. While it is true that many of the considerations listed in the Holiday section are helpful, the birthday party scenario has the added layer of being part of your child's social life. Friends' birthday parties are a window to a child's life outside of your family.

For some children, receiving an invitation to a classmate's party is a huge boost to his or her self-esteem because it means that he or she is accepted beyond the "mandatory acceptance" situation at school. Birthday parties can be tremendously validating and outright fun, but they can also be intimidating and disappointing.

The Invitation Arrives

Your child has been invited to a birthday party outside of your family circle—perhaps it's for a good friend, an acquaintance, or a classmate. In any case, it's a special occasion for any child—in particular, a child who has been living with SPD who has had the added challenge of trying to fit in at school and with other kids in his community. Depending on your child's age and the type of party, there are a number of issues to consider as you discuss the party with your child.

Listen to how your child talks about the invitation—is she happy, excited, apprehensive, distrustful, scared? Ask your child to explain what she is feeling, and let her know that there's no "wrong" feeling.

If your child is eager to go the party, discuss the details of the invitation—the who, what, where, when, and how (you know the why). Listen to determine whether or not she has realistic expectations about the party. If you suspect that your child may not be able to join in all aspects of the party, discuss how your child could participate. For example, if the party involves sports, brainstorm with your child about ideas for getting involved in the sports activity to the best of her ability.

Run your list of alternatives past your child's teacher and/or therapist. He or she could have additional ideas.

If it's not clear from the invitation what the child-to-adult ratio will be, feel free to contact the parents of the birthday child and ask how the activities will be managed. If you think the party could present specific challenges for your child, discuss them in a direct but positive tone with the parents. Volunteer to help—this will make you accessible to your child while supporting her independence. Discuss with the parents whether there is a room or area that your child could go to if she needs a break. Also, let the parents know that it's okay if your child winds up needing to leave the party. This type of conversation reassures the parents of the birthday child that you are being thoughtful about your child's participation in the party.

Discuss with your child a plan for dealing with difficult situations at the party. For example, if your child is overresponsive to auditory input, talk about how she can take a sensory break by leaving the room, or, if needed, by leaving the party. Emphasize that leaving is not a failure, but rather, it's a sign that your child is taking care of herself.

If your child has a sibling or other family member who is also invited to the party, discuss the exit strategy with them. Offer to let the sibling remain at the party, and then confirm with another parent or friend that the sibling can leave with them at the end of the party.

Discuss and plan with your child the items she should take to the party. Keep the items in an easy-to-carry bag. If possible, let your child take responsibility for the bag.

If possible and feasible, offer to drive one or two other children to the party, but have another parent drive the other children home. This gives you and your child the flexibility to leave the party early, but also makes the arrival to the party fun for your child. Consider having another parent drive your child home only if you think that both your child and the parent are comfortable with the arrangement.

Note: It's okay for you to drive alone to and from the party—consider it a sign that your child is doing well!

Your Child Is at the Party

If you have opted to help supervise the party, give your child space and allow him to participate to the best of his ability. If you sense that your child is struggling, do a quick check-in with him. Fight the urge to bail your child out, unless he is truly overwhelmed.

If the party gets out of hand (for example, if there are too many kids and not enough adults), or you are uncomfortable with the way things are going, discuss it privately with your child, and if need be, talk about leaving the party.

If you suspect that your child is having difficulties with his peers, don't rush in to fix it, but do pay attention and intervene if you think anyone is being hurt in any way. Let the hosting parents know about the situation so that they can deal with it, as well. If your child was involved, speak with him as best you can in the setting. Again, leaving is an option if your child is overwhelmed or unable to express himself in an age-appropriate manner.

Whether your child left the party early or stayed until the end, praise him for participating and for doing his best. It's a tremendous step forward for your child!

ASSESSMENT, DIAGNOSIS, AND TREATMENT—WHERE TO BEGIN

You may wonder whether your child or a child you know has SPD. Entangled with that question may be a great deal of anxiety, denial, confusion, sadness, and pain. More important, you may feel overwhelmed about what to do now. "Where do I begin?" "What do I do first?" "Who do I call for an appointment?" "What's involved in the evaluation process?"

This chapter will address the above questions, as well as other questions and concerns regarding the assessment, diagnosis, and treatment process. The recommended steps will help all parents—both those who are in the initial assessment stages and those who have already started the process. This chapter contains examples of how various sensory problems manifest behaviorally, specific steps in getting a thorough evaluation, a sample evaluation report with recommendations, and finally, the role that occupational therapy—particularly sensory integration therapy—plays in the assessment and diagnosis process.

Therefore, whether or not you have already gone through the assessment process, the following information can be useful as a working map to either guide you through the process or help you backtrack to see whether you have taken the most effective route to your goal of getting the best possible evaluation for your child.

The following is a step-by-step guideline for parents who believe their child may have SPD.

Step 1: Make a List of Your Concerns

The first step in this process is to make a list of your concerns. Think back as far as you can remember, and write down any and all your concerns about your child. This step may be a little easier for parents who have other children without SPD. However, the key for all parents is to think intuitively and honestly. If you have wondered about a behavior, had a gut feeling that something wasn't right, or wondered whether your child's reaction was "normal," those are the kind of things you want to include on your list.

You do not need to know the technical term for the concerning behavior—you can just describe it or provide examples to explain what you are concerned about. I suggest you do this before you look at any symptom checklist, so that you create an unsolicited, real, and clear list of your child's symptoms without any confusion or questions.

Try not to feel overwhelmed or stressed by this task. Remember, you are simply trying to create a list of questions, observations, behaviors, examples, and concerns that you have wondered about recently or in the past—as opposed to creating a list of clinical symptoms by using medical or professional language or terminology. It also helps you to organize your thoughts, concerns, and knowledge of your child. Translating your list into a clinical diagnosis is the job of a trained professional.

Some examples of concerns raised by parents might include:

She hates it when I try to comb her hair.

He does not like having socks on.

Certain kinds of lighting seem to bother her.

He only seems to like soft foods.

She is terrified of the vacuum cleaner.

He just doesn't seem to be able to learn how to ride a bike.

She seems tired and has low energy most of the time.

He complains of odors I can't even smell.

She seems to cry harder when I hug her, hold her, or kiss her.

The above are all typical examples of concerns and observations of parents who may not know what, if anything, they will add up to. However, these are all also examples of items that you must include in your list, even if you think they may be silly or sound like making something out of nothing. Your trained professional will review the list with you and help decide what may be part of a bigger issue and what may be an isolated behavior that is not part of a cluster of symptoms.

Keep in mind that one symptom does not make a syndrome. The professional you are working with will consider the symptoms you have noted and gather further information from you to assess to what degree the symptoms interfere with your child's quality of life and day-to-day functioning.

Step 2: Fill Out a Symptom Checklist

Now that you have written down your concerns in your own words, the next step is to fill out a symptom checklist. Again, this checklist does not serve as a diagnostic tool, but rather functions as an educational tool, organizer, and a way to more effectively communicate with your professional care providers.

You can find SPD symptom checklists online on various Web sites or in books on SPD, or you can obtain them from the occupational therapist at your child's school. This chapter will review important components of a good checklist and will offer a basic, but useful, one that you may wish to consider. Please keep in mind that professionals who are trained to assign a diagnosis of SPD have their own diagnostic process, which may include specific assessment tools, tests, questionnaires, and clinical observation of your child.

A good symptom checklist should include items and questions from most of the following 10 areas of functioning:

Auditory—sense of hearing

Olfactory—sense of smell

Visual—sense of vision

Tactile—sense of touch and input from the skin about touch, pressure, temperature, and pain

Vestibular—response to movement

Proprioceptive—input from muscles and joints about body position, weight, pressure, and changes of position in space

Oral—input from the mouth

Auditory processing abilities—processing auditory and language input

Interoceptive—internal regulation

Social-emotional functioning—ability to function successfully within the expected developmental level, in the community, at home, and at school

BEHAVIORS THAT MAY LOOK FAMILIAR

In the next section, I've presented examples of symptoms, behaviors, and responses from all the previously mentioned areas to provide you with a sample of what you may be observing in your child. Keep in mind that not all children will necessarily have every characteristic or show characteristics of a dysfunction in the same way. The child may also be both overresponsive and underresponsive at the same time.

Tactile Sense Difficulties

Children with difficulties in this area of functioning may be overresponsive or have tactile defensiveness to touch, or, conversely, be underresponsive or to touch. Underresponsive children may purposely seek sensation. The following are examples of how these difficulties may manifest.

Reacts emotionally to touch and may become startled, anxious, or aggressive, particularly in response to unexpected touch, such as a pat on the shoulder

Does not like to be held, hugged, or cuddled

Has difficulty standing in close proximity to other people or standing in lines

Complains and becomes distressed during grooming, haircuts, washing of the hair and face, nail clipping, teeth brushing, etc

Is bothered by certain fabrics and textures, will only wear certain clothes, does not like tags on shirts or pants, will not wear new clothes or freshly laundered clothes, will only wear short sleeves even when it is cold, will only wear long pants or long sleeves to avoid being touched on the skin

Does not like splashing water, such as that from the shower, sprinkler, or hose

Avoids touching certain textures, such as slime, foam, or Play-Doh

Does not like to wear socks or shoes, may insist on walking barefoot or wearing only sandals, even when it is cold

Is a picky eater, will only eat soft foods or crunchy foods, does not like two different types of food mixed on the plate

May avoid walking barefoot on grass or sand

May walk on tiptoes

Rubs out a spot on the skin that has been touched by someone

Craves touch, touches things and others excessively

Will only notice and respond to forceful touch

Has a high tolerance for pain

Does not notice or seem to care that hands or face are dirty

Touches lips or mouth, mouths objects, seeks oral input, talks excessively

Is not aware of his or her own strength, squeezes other children or pets while playing or gives them hugs

Appears hyperactive, moves from one activity to another

Seeks and becomes excitable when engaged in movement activities

Has poor fine motor abilities, as manifested by difficulty with fastening fasteners or using scissors, writing tools, or utensils

Does not seem to notice or care if clothes are twisted, may look disheveled

Vestibular Sense Difficulties

The vestibular sense refers to the child's response to movement. The vestibular sense, with receptors located within the inner ear, provides the body with information about movement, the body's position in the air, vibration, and gravity.

Children can be overresponsive or underresponsive to movement, just as they could with their other senses. In other words, they can be hyperalert and supersensitive to where their body is in space, such as in children who feel sick to their stomach when the car goes over a hill. On the other hand, some children might seem capable of walking off a cliff if the parent did not stop them, or they seem to constantly seek movement activities.

The following are examples of over- or underresponsivity to movement and vestibular functioning:

Must have his or her feet on the ground at all times; feels anxious, terrified, and distressed when the feet are off the ground, as is the case with certain play equipment, such as swings

Prefers sedentary and seated activities

Avoids or dislikes elevators, roller coasters, play equipment that spins and turns; is prone to motion sickness

Has a fear of falling

Is afraid of heights

Is fearful of going up or down high stairs, ladders, slides, trees, or rocks

Is afraid of being tipped or having his or her head upside down

Does poorly in sports and activities in which good balance and movement in the air, such as somersaults or rotating movements, are required

May have poor muscle tone (hypotonia)

Has a hard time pulling him- or herself up, as in getting out of the pool by pulling his or her body out

On the other hand, kids who crave motion and are underresponsive to movement activities may exhibit some of the following behaviors:

Behaves like the energizer bunny—moves, climbs, runs, jumps, fidgets, and appears to be in constant motion

Loves and enjoys rotating movements, spinning, being tossed in the air, playing airplane where moved through the air by an adult

Enjoys roller-coaster–like movement, rides, and activities

Enjoys being in upside-down positions

Loves to swing

Rocks body while seated or standing

May need to be rocked to fall asleep or calm down

The following are examples of behaviors observed in children who do not have good muscle tone, balance, and muscle strength:

Has weak muscle tone (hypotonia), "floppy" body, poor muscle strength

Tends to slump or lie down, props self up for support, leans on and against things

Gets tired unusually quickly and easily, seems to have a lower-than-expected level of endurance and energy, may have been thought of as a "lazy" or "unmotivated" child

Has a weak hand grasp and strength and fine motor weakness that translates into difficulty with turning doorknobs, grasping pencils, using eating utensils and tools, holding small objects, and using scissors

Has difficulty manipulating small objects with fingers

Has difficulty fastening fasteners, such as zippers and buttons

Seems clumsy, holds on to the wall, has poor body awareness

Performs below the expected level of gross motor abilities; not good at running, dance, jumping, and sports

Has uncoordinated body movements

Proprioceptive Sense Difficulties

This sense refers to the body's ability to receive information from our muscles and joints and provide awareness about how we move in space. It is critical for the development of body awareness and spatial orientation. This sense allows us to be aware of where our body is in space, and how much force we use to perform any activity. The following are examples of behaviors observed in children who have problems with their proprioceptive sense.

Hugs others (people and animals) too hard and with too much force

Squeezes too hard

Has to touch, mouth, bang, hold, squeeze, and rub objects to get a sense for them

Seems to crave input from the environment, seeks out and enjoys bumping and crashing into things

Enjoys jumping because of the input to the feet, muscles, and joints; loves trampolines

Craves oral-motor input, such as biting, sucking, mouthing, and chewing

Seems to calm down when tightly wrapped in a blanket

Loves heavy or weighted blankets, vests, and coats

Asks others to walk or sit on his or her back

Frequently asks to be massaged or scratched

Cracks knuckles

Craves "roughhousing"

Enjoys pushing or pulling heavy carts and other objects, pushing against the wall

Has difficulty assessing and regulating the pressure of his or her hand when writing, drawing, holding foam or plastic cups, or holding other smaller objects

Auditory Sense Difficulties

Children with difficulties in this area of functioning may have weaknesses in their ability to process sound in their environment. This does not mean that they have a hearing problem. In fact, most children with problems in this area have received normal test results, within normal limits, from their pediatricians.

Here, the child has difficulty processing all the dimensions of sounds and incorporating all of those qualities into effective listening. A child may be overresponsive to sound, or may conversely be underresponsive to sound and therefore underregister auditory input. The following are examples of behaviors observed in children who have problems with their auditory sense.

Notices, is bothered by, or is distracted by sounds, such as the starting and stopping of motors in heating and cooling systems, computers, or refrigerators, or the humming or buzzing of outside or fluorescent lights (sounds typically ignored by others)

Is terrified by the sound of a flushing toilet, to the point of not using the bathroom, especially public bathrooms, those with automatic flushes, and, for unknown reasons, those with black or dark coloring, such as a toilet with a black seat

Is fearful of the sound of everyday appliances, such as the vacuum cleaner, blender, or hairdryer

Is bothered by loud noises, such as a fire truck or fire alarm

Is startled by unexpected sounds, such the ringing of the phone or the doorbell

Appears distracted by and is unable to filter out background sounds

May appear as though he or she has a hearing problem

May have uneven hearing, meaning he or she asks to turn up the TV and radio volume, which may be adequate for others, or asks people to be quiet

Covers ears or hides when there are loud or unexpected sounds

Cries and seems uncomfortable at loud events or places that have an echo, such as parades, concerts, gymnasiums, sports arenas, or skating rinks

Displays inconsistent responses to his or her name being called

May have difficulty orienting to sounds—that is, figuring out where a sound is coming from

May keep asking, "Am I being too loud?"

Oral Functioning and Input Difficulties

This area of functioning has to do with response to oral input. Here, again, a child may be overresponsive to oral input or underresponsive. Oral input includes food, eating habits, taste and texture preferences, and related issues, oral-motor functioning, and comfort and awareness of oral activities. The following are examples of behaviors observed in children who have problems with their oral sense.

May be described as a picky eater

Only eats foods of a certain consistency or texture, such as soft foods or crunchy foods

May not be able to tolerate swallowing textured foods

Has difficulty with sucking or chewing

Only eats foods of a certain temperature

Mouths inedible objects past the expected developmental stage, puts objects in mouth, chews on objects

May exhibit drooling unrelated to teething, due to poor oral motor muscle development and control

Overeats, gains weight, or just needs to eat to have something in the mouth for oral input

Olfactory Function Difficulties

This area addresses the child's response to and processing of various smells in the environment. The child may be overresponsive to smells or underresponsive. This seems to be the least common of the sensory difficulties; however, it can be as uncomfortable as the other sensory processing problems. The following are examples of behaviors observed in children who have problems with their olfactory sense.

Seems to notice and be bothered by smells that may be hardly noticeable to others

Has an unusually keen sense of smell

May not be able to eat certain foods because of their smell

Is unable to tolerate even "pleasant" smells, such as perfumes, colognes, and air fresheners

Is bothered by household cleaning products

May be underresponsive to odors that bother others

Visual Input and Function Difficulties

Difficulties in this area may mean overresponsivity to visual input or underresponsivity, as well as difficulty with tracking, visual discrimination, or perception. It does not, however, mean the child is visually impaired, blind, or has a medical diagnosis indicating a visual problem.

Children may show some of the following behaviors, which indicate an underresponsivity to light:

Exhibits sensitivity to bright lights or fluorescent lights, may cover eyes

Is distracted by visual stimuli in the room, as in an overly decorated classroom

Overfocuses on the irrelevant aspects of visual information, such as the frame as opposed to the picture

Loses place when copying information, such as from a blackboard

Becomes overwhelmed by busy pictures and visual information that has many shapes or colors

Confuses left and right

Has problems identifying shapes

Can't do puzzles

Auditory–Language Processing Dysfunction

This dysfunction indicates problems with the filtering and processing of auditory information. This is different from the ability to hear sounds—rather, it is the processing of sounds and any auditory information. The following are examples of behaviors observed in children who have problems with this function.

Has difficulty orienting to sound—that is, identifying where the sound comes from

Has difficulty identifying others based on their voice, such as over the phone

Has problems with sound discrimination

Has difficulty with auditory discrimination, or filtering out background sounds

Does not learn best when information is only presented orally

Is slow in processing orally presented information and responding—can hear and comprehend the information well, but takes longer to process the data and formulate a response

Social-Emotional Functioning Difficulties

This area refers to the ability to function successfully in the expected developmental level within the community, at home, and in school. Difficulties can include the following examples.

Has difficulty maintaining relationships with peers, is hard to get along with

Insists on having his or her own way, can't negotiate successfully in social play

Prefers to engage in solitary play

Thrives on routine, structure, and predictability of the situation

Gets overwhelmed and frustrated easily, tantrums can go on "forever"

May seem out of control emotionally at times, has frequent tantrums

Seems to overreact to minor problems or to things not going his or her way

Has a difficult time calming down

Functions best individually and in familiar settings

Has rapid and unpredictable shifts in mood, frequent mood swings

Has low frustration tolerance—for example, can't tolerate hunger, thirst, lack of sleep, or change, as is consistent with his or her age and developmental level

Is perceived by others as being a "difficult" and inflexible child

Is easily overwhelmed and bewildered in demanding situations

Does not do well with timed tasks or time limits

Was difficult as an infant

Can't soothe self, and doesn't have or can't access effective coping mechanisms

Has difficulty calming down and falling asleep on his or her own

In addition, for parents, it takes a great deal of energy to provide care for the child and requires a tremendous amount of patience and understanding. Parents or others may misunderstand the child's behavior as "manipulative," mean, rude, or spoiled.

Internal Regulation (the Interoceptive Sense)

This area refers to the regulation of internal body functions, such as attention and arousal, gastrointestinal functions, and hunger and thirst. The following are examples of dysfunction of one's internal regulation and interoceptive sense.

May not feel hot or cold consistent with the weather or how others in the same environment feel

Vascillates and has an unpredictable level of attention and arousal

Has problems with gastrointestinal tract functions, such as producing bowel movements

Is unable to effectively regulate thirst and hunger, has sudden and intense feelings of hunger and thirst that need to be taken care of urgently

Step 3: Get a Referral to an Occupational Therapist

Now that you have taken Steps 1 and 2, and you suspect that your child may have SPD, the next step is to call your pediatrician and ask for a referral to an occupational therapist. Having your pediatrician on board will make matters much easier and more manageable.

By now, most pediatricians are at least familiar with SPD and aware that this is a real diagnosis and that treatment is a medical necessity. This is certainly true, or should be true, of developmental pediatricians. This group of physicians has a subspecialty in child development and developmental disorders. Out of all pediatricians, these are also the folks who are most familiar with autism spectrum disorders, and have familiarity with SPD within that context.

This step should not be an uphill battle. You may be required to see the pediatrician and explain the need for the referral during an office visit. If, after such a visit, you are still unable to get a referral, you may wish to consider changing pediatricians. Although this can be a very difficult step to take, it may be the only way to get your insurance company to pay for the initial and subsequent occupational therapy visits.

For parents of newborns to children 3 years of age, a viable option is your state's early intervention program. This is a free program for all eligible families that covers a variety of services, including occupational therapy.

The initial step typically involves an assessment of your child's development and a parent interview. Once it is determined that your child qualifies for services, a therapist will be assigned to you and will provide in-office or in-home services. Your child's progress will be measured periodically until he or she is too old to participate in the program.

Keep in mind that early intervention services can be supplemented by services paid through your insurance or via a private-payment arrangement. In other words, your child will not be disqualified from early intervention services if you decide to supplement the therapy he or she receives with additional sessions through other means.

Remember that timing is critical, and the frequency and intensity of services make a great difference in outcome.

Unfortunately, most clinics have a waiting list for both the initial evaluation and the therapy sessions. Be persistent and flexible. Ask around and call several places. Get on cancellation lists, and check with the clinic periodically to make sure they have your correct and best contact number. Be clear that you will take the first available appointment. There may also be certain nonprofit organizations in your area that can provide a therapist while you wait to be seen. Explore all the possibilities, and at the very least, get an initial evaluation with a specific treatment plan and recommendations.

Step 4: Educate Yourself about SPD

Although SPD is still a fairly new diagnosis, researchers have managed to compile and produce an impressive amount and array of informative resources on the disorder.

So much of our anxiety about any disorder is tied into our lack of knowledge about it. The experience feels much like being in a completely foreign and unknown country where everything—the language, the culture, the food, the names, the rituals, and the places—seem different and difficult to understand and relate to. If you have ever traveled abroad, you have probably taken some steps ahead of time to prepare for your trip. Perhaps you read some books, watched some DVDs or films, learned a few useful terms, familiarized yourself with the basics of the culture, and so on.

This is a journey you will have to take with your child into the territory of SPD. The more you know, the more prepared you are, and the more educated you become, the easier your journey will be.

Begin by browsing your local bookstore or library. If you cannot find a book on SPD, look for books on autism or Asperger syndrome. You will probably find a chapter or section addressing SPD, with references at the end on the sources of information for the chapter.

Find Internet access and search all the key words you can think of, such as SPD, sensory integration disorder or dysfunction, sensory modulation, and sensory processing. Read everything you can. There are also several DVDs, videos, and audio presentations on this topic. Once you become familiar with the topic, you can scan through educational materials fairly quickly and decide what is most pertinent to your child.

There are also many speakers who regularly give seminars and talks on this topic. If you attend a talk, you will have the opportunity to connect with other families and learn about additional resources.

Keep in mind that the purpose of educating yourself is so that you feel more comfortable with this topic, you're less intimidated when seeing a professional, and you can ask important and relevant questions. In this way, you are an educated and active participant in your child's treatment. The purpose is not to become overwhelmed, paralyzed, and/or further stressed by this task. You are not the clinician—nor should you try to be, as a clinician is a specialist who has attained a specific level of education and expertise. Rather, you are a loving, caring parent who can understand and make educated decisions regarding your child's care and treatment.

Step 5: Find an Occupational Therapist
Trained to Assess and Treat SPD

This may be a more difficult task than one might imagine. Unfortunately, many families report tremendous problems finding an occupational therapist who has additional training in the diagnosis and treatment of SPD. Typically, there are many more resources in larger cities and areas near university programs with a medical school.

Obtaining a correct diagnosis is the first and the most critical step. Treatment planning and services are not of any value if the providers don't accurately know what they are treating. For this reason, the most qualified person to assess the child for an initial evaluation is an occupational therapist with additional training, and preferably, certification in Sensory Integration and Praxis Tests, or SIPTs.

The Sensory Integration and Praxis Tests, by A. Jean Ayres, PhD, is an assessment tool used for children 4 to 8 years 11 months old. The SIPTs, now the standard of reference in the field, show how children in the above age range organize their senses and respond to sensory input. There are 17 brief tests that measure visual, tactile, and kinesthetic performance, as well as motor abilities. Each individual test can take about 10 minutes to administer, but the entire battery of tests can be given in approximately 2 hours.

The SIPTs kit and scoring software is published by Western Psychological Services Publishing, and SIPT-certified occupational therapists are listed on their Web site at *wpspublish.com.* Look under "Occupational Therapy/Sensory Function" and click on the box on the right that says "SI Certified Therapists." Then enter your state to get a list of certified occupational therapists in your area. This company also offers a sensory integration course—a set of four sensory integration workshops—that is the only sensory integration certification program endorsed by the publishers of the SIPTs.

For younger children, a commonly used assessment tool has been the DeGangi-Berk Test of Sensory Integration, or TSI, which is appropriate for children 3–5 years old. This 36-item test measures three relevant developmental areas: postural control, bilateral motor integration, and reflex integration, as well as the child's overall sensory integration. These functions are vestibular based and are critical in the development of motor skills, visuospatial and language abilities, hand dominance, and motor planning. Due to its sensitivity in revealing even subtle developmental deficits, the TSI permits early detection of concerns that, if left untreated, could lead to learning difficulties. The test can be administered and scored in about 30 minutes.

The therapist rates the child's performance by using a numerical scale that ranges from "abnormal" to "normal" development. The TSI yields a total score and provides scores for each of the three subtests measured. The test allows the clinician to compare the child's performance with that of healthy, at-risk, and deficient children.

The above are just two examples of tests that may be used by your child's occupational therapist. Keep in mind that clinicians may not use the same protocol for testing. A good battery of tests is tailored to the needs of the individual child and the reason for referral, as opposed to a cookie-cutter approach for all children. The important point is to have open communication with the evaluator, to feel confident in his or her abilities, and to feel comfortable with that person.

OBTAINING AN EARLY DIAGNOSIS— THE PROS AND CONS

As a parent, it is difficult to decide when to seek professional help when you suspect that what your child is experiencing may be outside the typical and expected realm. As with any other issues, there may be a wait-and-see period, where you hope the behaviors you are seeing will resolve without having to get outside help. No one is well regulated all the time. This means that we all may feel overwhelmed at times by the information and input from our senses, or, on the other hand, we may feel tired, lethargic, and understimulated. Since all of us have some sensory processing problems now and then, the following question comes up repeatedly: When should you consider seeking professional help? A sensible general guideline would be to consider the frequency with which the symptoms occur, the intensity of the symptoms, and the degree to which the symptoms affect your child's day-to-day psychological, social, home, school, and overall functioning. This means that the more impairment, disruption, and difficulties you observe in your child's functioning, the more the likelihood that outside assistance and support may be needed.

When thinking about frequency of a behavior, response, or symptom, think about the following five possibilities: always, frequently, occasionally, seldom, and never. Clearly, "always" and "frequently" would indicate a red flag regarding the frequency of a questionable behavior.

A helpful way to think about intensity is to think about the time period it takes for the behavior to be resolved. An intense reaction, meltdown, or response typically requires a longer period of time to resolve than a minor reaction or response.

The degree to which a response or behavior affects the child's functioning has to do with how much it interferes with the child's day-to-day life. A higher degree of interference may translate into frequently getting to school late because getting dressed appropriately is a daily challenge. This interferes with the child's educational activities on a daily basis.

Consider the following pros and cons of seeking an early diagnosis for your child's behavior.

Pros—An early diagnosis means:

Early intervention, support, and services for the child

Early educational planning, services, and modifications at school

Improved prognosis

Family support

Resolution of diagnostic uncertainty and confusion

Less blaming of the child

Cons—Undergoing an evaluation when the child is very young (early in development) can:

Stigmatize or create unwanted labels for the child

Result in an incorrect diagnosis. As important as it is to get an early diagnosis, there is a risk of incorrectly diagnosing a very young child, age 0 to 5 years, since the diagnostic tools for younger children are more limited. Younger children are typically harder to test and require an evaluator with experience and expertise in this age group. For this reason, and to keep track of your child's progress, follow-up evaluations are important.

Increase stress for the family

Lower expectations for the child at school

Step 6: Connect with Community, Local Organizations, Other Families

Many families feel they are to blame for their child's difficulties with sensory processing issues, despite SPD being a neurological disorder with impairments that are biologically based.

Some mothers report feeling like the "crazy mother" who had nothing better to do but go to the pediatrician's office week after week. Extended family, in-laws, or community members may have criticized parental discipline as ineffective.

Whether you are a parent who is currently going through a difficult time and SPD is a new concept in your family, or you are a knowledgeable parent who has dealt with this disorder for some time, this step of finding support is an important one in your journey. If your family is new to this disorder, you need all the information and support you can get. Being connected to those who can truly understand your feelings, experiences, and frustrations without judgment is a gift that is invaluable to you at this phase of your journey.

In addition, you will benefit tremendously from others' wealth of knowledge, information, and experiences. As a parent who has dealt with this issue for a while, by reaching out to other families, you will have the opportunity to spare others a very difficult time and inspire them to give back when the time is right.

To attract the much-needed support, understanding, and attention from the community at large to this disorder, the SPD community must first come together and form a strong network.

A fast and effective way to connect with others is through the Internet and online resources via parent forums and support groups, such as sensory integration dysfunction/dysfunction of sensory integration, or SID/DSI, AllAboutKids, or *spdparentshare.com*. There are also resources at the end of this book that you may wish to consider using.

The Assessment Process:
What You Need to Know

The occupational therapy and sensory processing evaluation is a long and involved process, much like the neuropsychological evaluation process, which may require a couple of appointments, depending on the child's attention span, level of energy, and cooperation at any given time.

The following components should be included in the evaluation-based report, as much as possible: complete background information, early developmental history, child and parent questionnaires, observation of the child during free play and during structured and standardized assessment activities, individualized recommendations, and an individualized sensory diet that can be implemented at home and at school, as well as during therapy sessions.

The observation of the child during structured and unstructured activities is an important part of the evaluation. It provides firsthand information about the child that goes far beyond what the therapist can learn from the parent interview, the questionnaires, or previous reports. While all that information is invaluable, watching children do what they normally do—interacting in their everyday life, reacting and relating as they normally would, and performing and struggling as they would outside the office—can open a window into their true day-to-day functioning.

Of course, the standardized portion of the evaluation is crucial to obtain a true and scientific measure of where the child's abilities are at the time of evaluation and prior to intervention. This allows for using follow-up evaluations as a measure of the child's progress and response to treatment over time. Several questionnaires may be used, and your child's evaluator will choose the one most appropriate to address the specific referral questions and concerns. While questionnaires are typically completed by parents and/or teachers, older children who are willing to do so may fill them out themselves. It can be insightful to learn directly from the children how they see each challenging situation and what they identify as their strengths.

What a Sample Evaluation Looks Like

The following is a sample occupational therapy evaluation, which may be helpful to look at as a point of reference. Please note that reports may vary in their length, format, content, and writing style. Due to space constraints, we have abbreviated certain sections of all the evaluations presented in this book.

The child presented in this example, Ariel, was referred for an occupational therapy evaluation after undergoing a neuropsychological assessment. This is perhaps the most common way of accessing an occupational therapist— through a referral by a psychologist, teacher, nurse, or pediatrician.

So that you can fully comprehend the process and experience the journey with Ariel's family, who graciously shared the occupational therapy report, I've first presented the neuropsychological report, followed by the occupational therapy evaluation. In looking at the evaluations of the same child, from the perspectives of members of two distinct disciplines, the role and function of each specialty may become clearer.

Sample Neuropsychological Evaluation

Confidential

Client Name: Ariel

Age at Testing: 3 years 5 months

Identifying Information and Reason for Referral

Ariel is 3 years 5 months old and was referred for a neuropsychological evaluation by her parents, due to a series of concerns regarding her overall functioning, including her speech and language skills, social development, and daily living skills. Ariel has a history of developmental delay and has previously received a diagnosis of autism spectrum disorder.

The goal of this evaluation is to provide a comprehensive assessment of Ariel's neuropsychological functioning and treatment recommendations to improve her academic performance and planning, social-emotional abilities, and adaptive functioning, or activities of daily living.

Relevant History

By the time she reached age 1, Ariel's parents became concerned about her delayed language development. Her first words were spoken around 26 months of age.

Ariel's mother reported that Ariel received occupational therapy, speech and language services, and applied behavioral analysis (a form of behavior therapy) through an early intervention program. In light of her difficulties with verbal and nonverbal communication, mild stereotypic behaviors, and impaired social development, Ariel received a diagnosis of autism spectrum disorder at the age of 2 years 10 months.

At present, Ariel's mother indicates that Ariel's non-verbal communication skills are better developed than her verbal abilities. Ariel can interpret some facial expressions, is beginning to point, and tends to use hand gesturing to communicate. Although she does imitate sounds and word approximations, Ariel is functionally nonverbal. When she has trouble communicating her needs and desires, she will physically prompt her mother by taking her hand and leading her.

Socially, Ariel has difficulty making eye contact, engaging others, and making friends. While she enjoys being around people, her play with toys is restricted to mouthing and banging toys. Ariel's mother indicates that her social interactions with peers are limited, due to her lack of functional and pretend play. According to Ariel's mother, although Ariel is not toilet trained, she will use the toilet if placed on it. Ariel's mother also reports that if she asks Ariel if she is wet or soiled, Ariel will inconsistently nod in response.

When Ariel was 2 years old, she participated in an 8-hour day program, consisting of applied behavioral analysis, or ABA, and speech and language therapy, for about 3 months. At the end of the summer, Ariel was able to say approximately 50 words.

Ariel currently attends her preschool ABA program. This 6-hour-a-day program uses the Progressive Academic Learning System, or PALS, and consists of ABA, speech services, and occupational therapy. In addition to school-based services, Ariel receives supplementary speech therapy through an independent provider in the community.

Ariel's classroom teacher identified difficulties associated with her ability to sit still, remain focused, and follow multistep directions. Stereotypic behaviors, including high-pitched vocalizations and motor movements (such as clapping), were also noted in the classroom. Ariel reportedly responds well to frequent and consistent reinforcement with praise and tangible rewards.

Behavioral Observations

Ariel was an alert and playful girl, who was accompanied by her father when she arrived for her evaluation with me. Ariel made intermittent eye contact. She inconsistently responded to her name being called. In terms of attention, Ariel had substantial difficulty focusing for extended periods of time and required frequent breaks.

She was very curious about the testing activities, although she occasionally became frustrated with challenging tasks. She was able to orient to sounds in the environment and occasionally used gestures to indicate objects she wanted during the evaluation. She pulled on either my hand or her father's hand to communicate her needs. Although Ariel required frequent and continuous redirection, she was able to focus her attention and cooperate with most tasks.

Although she didn't use any words, Ariel was able to imitate sounds and word approximations. She also frequently made vocalizations of a high-pitched sound and occasionally some sound blends. She had significant difficulty understanding verbal instructions, so we had to modify several tasks for her. For example, nonverbal means of communication accompanied verbal instructions, and/or fewer response options were offered. Here, the purpose was to determine if Ariel could perform the same task in a more limited way or with some prompts and cues. (As a parent, please note if items are modified—the examiner will only report on the performance, since the results, while valuable, are no longer based on standardized administration). She tended to perform better when test items were more concrete and when there were fewer stimuli to choose from.

Ariel struggled with fine motor skills. For example, she was able to grasp a pencil, but did not demonstrate a hand preference. She mouthed various items continuously and required a great deal of redirection regarding this behavior.

Because of Ariel's adequate level of attention, arousal, and cooperation, this assessment was felt to provide an accurate measure of her current abilities. However, given her young age and difficulty attending, this evaluation should not be considered predicative of Ariel's full potential in the future.

As part of the evaluation process, all of Ariel's past and current medical, testing, and academic records were reviewed, her parents and teachers were interviewed and asked to fill out various questionnaires, and she was observed at home and in the classroom during free play and structured activities. Also, standardized assessment tools were utilized to measure her current level of functioning. Feedback regarding diagnosis and treatment recommendations was provided to her parents at the end of the evaluation process.

Recommendations

Ariel's neurodevelopmental profile, clinical presentation, and history are consistent with a diagnosis of autism spectrum disorder, characterized by language impairment, reduced social functioning, and repetitive patterns of behavior. These areas of vulnerability contribute substantially to her difficulties with following directions, resulting in difficulty processing social and interpersonal information and poor inhibition of behavior. Ariel also has marked areas of weakness in her adaptive functioning, including self-care skills, social skills, and motor functioning.

Without support and comprehensive programming, these delays will likely place Ariel at risk for continued difficulties at school, at home, and in the community.

When developing academic programming and modifications, it is important to maximize Ariel's strengths and acknowledge her abilities. It will also be essential for there to be regular home-school communication and collaboration to maintain consistency in the approaches used at home and at school, to monitor her progress to ensure she is in fact benefiting from the interventions provided, and to generalize skills to natural environments. This last piece is important, because a child might be able to perform a task in therapy but not at home or school. Some examples may include using utensils, using the word "please," and zipping up his or her jacket.

In view of the present results, the following recommendations are offered as part of Ariel's treatment plan to address her social-emotional, educational, and behavioral needs.

Because of Ariel's history of marked speech and language delay, she requires intensive services in this area. Individual speech and language therapy services are recommended at least five times per week. Additional small-group therapy services, if available, may be appropriate, as well.

Ariel requires an educational program that will focus on improving her play, nonverbal communication skills, and independent living skills (such as using the toilet). A parent training component should also be included to assist her parents in working with her in environments outside of school.

To increase Ariel's chance of succeeding academically and socially, she would benefit from a small class size, with as much one-on-one attention as possible. It will be important for her to have a quiet room, with minimal distractions and a low noise level.

To help Ariel begin to develop organizational and self-help skills, schedules and directions for home and school use should be developed by using visual aids, such as tables, graphs, charts, checklists, and laminated cards with pictures.

Given Ariel's weaknesses in fine motor skills, continued occupational therapy services, provided by therapists trained in working with autistic children, is recommended at least three times per week. This service should also include a sensory integration component to address Ariel's repetitive mouthing of objects, seeking of tactile input, poor muscle tone, and other sensory processing deficits and difficulties.

Ariel should undergo a full occupational therapy evaluation that assesses her sensory processing abilities and creates an appropriate sensory diet plan.

Ariel needs numerous opportunities for healthy social interactions and exposure to her peers. Therefore, she would benefit from remaining in the classroom whenever possible to give her the opportunity to have positive interactions with her classmates.

Ariel needs help in developing independent, functional skills. Particular areas include daily living skills (eg, feeding, toileting, and dressing) and socialization skills. A very structured, behavioral approach to teaching such skills will be most beneficial. This is a marked area of deficit for Ariel that needs continued attention and active interventions.

Ariel's development should be carefully monitored over the next year and reevaluated in 12–18 months.

Ariel's parents are incredibly dedicated and involved parents who have learned a great deal about their daughter. They are very willing to form an active partnership with all of her outside care providers and school staff. This home-school collaboration and communication is crucial to ensuring consistency across settings and generalization of acquired skills. I've encouraged

Ariel's parents to share this report with her school-based team, who will consider whether her current service profile is sufficient to meet her academic, social, emotional, and behavioral needs.

Sample Occupational Therapy Sensory Evaluation

Ariel's responses during this evaluation were typical of her general performance and a valid appraisal of her present abilities. Her mother was present during the evaluation and reports that the day of the evaluation was typical of each day in the household.

The evaluation lasted approximately 4 hours and included observation of the child, interview with the parent, completion of parent questionnaires, and formal testing of the child by using standardized assessment tools. Feedback was provided to her parent after the evaluation.

Ariel showed difficulty in the area of auditory processing, which encompasses the ability to process sounds in the environment. She appeared not to be aware of external, salient sounds. She did not respond when her name was called, but her hearing was normal. She appeared not to hear what you were saying, as if she was tuning you out. She responded after her name was called at least three times, but this was not always consistent.

Overall, Ariel exhibited visual processing abilities that fell within the normal range. Her mother indicated that Ariel has difficulty doing puzzles and has a hard time with finding objects in competing backgrounds. Occasionally she will become frustrated when searching for objects.

Vestibular Processing

This section of the evaluation measures a child's response to movement. There are receptors located in the inner ear that are responsible for telling the body about its movement as it relates to gravity. Ariel exhibited a Probable Difference in this area.

Ariel exhibited a low level of affect. When using suspended equipment, such as the platform swing, Ariel's affect immediately changed. Her eye contact increased, and speech production increased. There was no safety awareness, and she often appeared clumsy during any movement. Her mother indicated that Ariel will seek out all kinds of movement activities and will twirl and move throughout a room during the day.

The first sensory system to fully develop by 12 weeks of gestation is the vestibular system, which controls the sense of movement and balance and the inhibition of emotion. This system is the sensory system considered to have the most important influence on the other sensory systems and on the ability to function in everyday life. Directly or indirectly, the vestibular system influences nearly everything we do. It is the unifying system in our brain that modifies and coordinates information received from other systems. The vestibular system functions like a traffic cop, telling each sensation where and when it should go or stop.

The sense organs for the vestibular system are located within the inner ear and consist of three semicircular canals, the utricle and saccule. Projections from the vestibular system to other parts of the brain and sensory organs serve as communication channels. Sensory receptors in the inner ear provide a person with crucial information about movement, gravity, and vibration. The vestibular system is considered to have the most important influence on the other sensory systems.

When the vestibular system is affected, it also affects the following structures in the central nervous system: the cerebellum, thalamus, ocular and auditory nuclei, and cerebral cortex. The cerebellum is responsible for selective attention and inhibition of motion, rhythm, and timing, all coordinated movements, and proprioception. The thalamus is responsible for sequencing and organization of movement. The ocular nuclei are responsible for teaming and smooth movement of the eyes. The auditory nuclei are responsible for auditory processing and spatial relations. The cerebral cortex is responsible for higher-level sequencing and organization of movement, such as motor planning.

The vestibular system relies on the cerebellum to act on perception. If there is a problem with vestibular perception, but not on the action itself (proprioception), then hypotonia (poor muscle tone) exists. Ariel exhibited poor muscle tone in both upper and lower extremities. Muscle tone is described as the muscle's passive resistance to movement. Hypotonia is then defined as decreased resistance to passive movement, soft muscle bellies, and hypermobility of the joints (that is, locking joints for stability). It can delay the development of gross, fine, and perceptual motor skills and can limit endurance in functional activities and postural stability. Ariel maintains a "W" sitting position when sitting on the floor or in a chair. The "W" sitting position supports the hips for increased trunk stability. It prevents fluent movement from her left side to the right side of her body.

Ariel's weak muscle tone, or hypotonia, directly affects her generalized muscle strength, which appears weak for surface and core muscles.

Muscle weakness can delay the development of gross, fine, and perceptual motor skills and can limit endurance in functional activities and postural stability. For Ariel, transitioning from the supine position (lying down) to sitting on the floor required the use of bilateral arms for support and the use of abdominal obliques (she would turn to the side). The use of the abdominal obliques when transitioning indicated that the rectus abdominus and transverse abdominus were weak. This lack of muscle activity indicated weak core muscles. The core muscles are those muscles that are closest to the bone. They are the muscles that ultimately allow respiration and coordinated movements to occur. The core is the part of your body where all movement originates—all of the muscles around the spine, the abdominals, and the muscles that lie beneath the "six pack." When transitioning from a supine position to sitting on a 75-cm ball with support, Ariel required the use of both hands and her abdominal obliques (she would turn to the side). Ariel appropriately crossed midline, demonstrating the integration of both sides of her brain during gross motor activities.

The cerebellum is like a "mailroom," as it organizes where all information goes. It controls emotional outbursts and impulsivity. Ariel appeared passive during occupational therapy; however, a tantrum and/or resistance was observed when waking from a nap. Overall, Ariel did not appear to be affected by activity in the treatment room, nor did she respond negatively to transition from one activity to another.

The ocular nuclei are directly affected by dysfunction in the vestibular system. Ariel exhibits zero eye contact. She requires physical prompts to her nose to elicit a midline for her eyes. She is unable to follow any pursuits (her eyes cannot follow an object moving in the environment), and she does not exhibit saccades (her eyes do not move from one stationary object to another object) or convergence (her eye movements do not become esophoric [move inward] as an object is brought toward her nose). It is the job of the vestibular system to control movement of the eyes separate from head movement.

As the vestibular system is activated (as in spinning), it sends information to the muscles of the eyes to move in response to the movement sensation it receives (postrotary nystagmus reflex). The more a person is spun, the faster the information is sent from the vestibular system to the ears and eyes. Nystagmus is the involuntary, rhythmic oscillations of one or both eyes. It is the job of the vestibular system to move the eyes separate from head movement. This is why a person presents with a postrotary nystagmus reflex. The postrotary nystagmus subtest of the Sensory Integration and Praxis Tests was attempted. Ariel did not exhibit the reflex, as she was spun three separate times with zero response.

The cerebral cortex is responsible for higher levels of motor learning, such as motor planning. Motor planning is the ability to conceptualize, plan, and execute a non-habitual motor act. Ariel has much difficulty in this area, as demonstrated in difficulties with eye-hand coordination and eye-foot coordination. This is evident in Ariel's increased difficulties with object manipulation skills (in this case, skills with a ball). Ariel demonstrated the ability to fling a ball. She was unable to throw a ball over-hand or underhand. She was unable to catch a ball. Ariel was unable to lift her foot to make contact with the ball independently.

Children who have weakness in the vestibular system may have problems with balance, core muscle strength, midline crossing, and bilateral integration (using both left and right sides of the body together). Ariel exhibits asymmetrical tonic neck reflex, or ATNR, which measures the degree of inhibition of the ATNR in the quadruped position, when looking at the ability to maintain postural stability. ATNR is a reflex response that diminishes by 6 months of age. When it lasts longer, however, central nervous system immaturity is indicated. Persistence of the ATNR interferes with bilateral coordination and is affected by poor muscle tone.

The vestibular sense provides information related to movement and head position. It is important for development of balance, coordination, eye control, attention, security with one's movement, emotional security, and some aspects of language development. Disorganized processing of vestibular input may be seen when someone has difficulty with attention, coordination, following directions, or eye-hand coordination.

Touch Sense (Somatosensory Sense)

Items in this section indicate a child's ability to process information related to touch. Ariel indicated Typical Performance in the area. Her mother indicated that Ariel avoids wearing shoes and loves to be barefoot. She will occasionally touch people and objects.

The somatosensory sense is the largest sense in the body. It determines our ability to navigate in the environment. The skin is the key component in the somatosensory sense, as the receptors on the skin increase our ability to discriminate. Our skin is our largest sensory organ, followed closely by our muscles and skeleton, connected by our nervous system and governed by our brain. The touch section measures a child's responses to stimuli that touch the skin.

Multisensory Processing
(Arising from Stimuli within the Body Itself)

Ariel exhibited a Probable Difference in this area.

With regard to proprioceptive processing, or the unconscious perception of movement and spatial orientation, her mother indicated that Ariel always has a difficult time paying attention. She will look away from tasks to notice all actions in the room. Ariel appears oblivious within an active environment and is observed climbing on furniture and/or hanging on people. Ariel exhibited differences in the following factors that contribute to problems with regulating the proprioceptive system: 1 (sensory-seeking behavior), 3 (poor endurance and muscle tone), 5 (inattention/distractibility), and 8 (sedentary tendencies).

Proprioception involves the use of unconscious information from our muscles and joints to give us body awareness about how we are moving. This is very important for the development of body awareness. The nucleus of the proprioceptive system is housed in the cerebellum and works in tandem with the vestibular system and tactile system, where special receptors in muscles and joints travel quickly from the cerebellum to enhance tone and joint stability. It is the ability to sense the position, location, orientation, and movement of the body and its parts. A person performs proprioception during push-pull activities. It is a calming, safe input to use with a child who appears disorganized. Problems with the proprioceptive system can be the main contributor to difficulties with motor planning tasks, which is the ability to figure out how to use one's body and body scheme, especially under time constraints. It is also closely associated with an inability to focus on the task—the need to know everything that is going on in the surrounding environment. For this system to work properly, it must rely on the receipt of accurate information from the sensory systems so it can then organize and interpret this information efficiently and effectively. Some common signs of proprioceptive dysfunction are a lack of awareness of body position in space, the need to be hugged and held tightly or snugly (or just the opposite—maneuvering away from hugs or cuddling and avoiding all types of touch), bilateral coordination difficulties, and clumsiness. Children with disorganized proprioceptive systems will demonstrate dynamic balance difficulties secondary to decreased awareness of their bodies in space and in relation to gravity. Falling results in increased pressure along the muscles and joints, which increases awareness and organizes the system. This is why children with SPD will crave activities such as wrestling, which target the muscle bellies, giving them the necessary information for the brain to process.

In general, dysfunction within the proprioceptive, vestibular, and tactile systems manifests itself in many ways. A child may be over- or underresponsive to sensory input; activity level may be either unusually high or unusually low; a child may be in constant motion or fatigue easily. In addition, some children may fluctuate between these extremes. Behaviorally, the child may become impulsive, easily distractible, and show a general lack of planning. Some children may also have difficulty adjusting to new situations and may react with frustration, aggression, or withdrawal. This will definitely increase anxiety levels, as the child does not have the spatial or body awareness to navigate through the "sensory environment."

Children will use the mouth as a means of increasing sensory input (increasing focus or attention to a task). This is because each tooth in the mouth is a joint. A child is capable of increasing joint attention in the mouth, as there are 32 teeth (joints) in this area alone. The tongue also has a large amount of sensory receptors, which increase a child's sensory input.

Introducing weights into a child's routine will increase her body awareness, allowing her body the ability to understand where she "is" in relation to gravity and the ground or the floor. The increased weight on her lap is directly related to increasing attention, as weight affects the proprioceptive system. Heavy-work input releases serotonin, which sets the firing levels of all neurotransmitters. Many children experience body awareness for the first time when they start to use weights.

Modulation Section

Sensory modulation occurs at the lower brainstem and acts like the brain's "security guard." It is a term that refers to an individual's ability to process and organize relevant sensory information that is detected both internally and in the environment. The central nervous system determines the relevant amount of information and prepares the individual to respond appropriately. Adequate modulation of input is essential for appropriate arousal level, organized behavior, safety awareness, and attention. If a child overresponds, underresponds, or fluctuates in her response to sensory information, sensory modulation difficulties may be present. Modulation can only be expressed behaviorally, and the psychosocial patterns are consistent with the child's behavior. Ariel demonstrates modulation difficulties related to endurance and muscle tone, body position, and activity level.

Sensory Processing Related to Endurance and Tone

Evaluation in this section measures a child's ability to sustain performance. Ariel presented with a Definite Difference in this area. She performed with differences in Factors 1 (sensory-seeking behavior), 3 (poor endurance and muscle tone), and 8 (sedentary tendencies). Ariel demonstrated weak core muscles and locked joints. She exhibited a weak grasp and poor endurance, and she tired easily when activities were graded for quality. Ariel appeared to have low endurance and appeared lethargic.

Postural instability was noted in Ariel's gross motor coordination. In strength-type activities, much difficulty was noted in this area secondary to muscle weakness, phasic muscle bursts, holding of the breath, and low levels of endurance (as demonstrated in poor performance in gross motor locomotion and object manipulation skills, in this case skills with a ball). Ariel would lock her joints to increase her stability, as in when she performed quadruped activities. The decrease in core muscle strength makes postural support difficult to attain. The core is the part of your body where all movement originates—all of the muscles around the spine, the abdominals, and the muscles that lie beneath the "six pack." This was all clinically significant when observing the manner in which Ariel participated in gross tasks. Balancing skills were difficult, and she appeared very clumsy. Ariel also performed most gross skills at an increased speed, which is indicative of a child with muscular weakness, as when grading the activity halts muscle movement and relies on muscle memory. Muscle memory is very poor in children with hypotonia.

Modulation related to body position and movement. Evaluation in this section measures a child's ability to move effectively. Ariel demonstrated a Definite Difference in this area. Her mother reports that Ariel has a high tolerance for pain. She appears very clumsy, and can just be walking and trip over her feet. She often climbs on furniture and lacks safety awareness. Her mother indicates that Ariel appears to be accident prone, as if she enjoys falling. This feeling is directly related to the sensory system seeking proprioceptive input. She requires physical "information" to be sent via her muscles and joints.

Modulation of sensory input affecting emotional responses. Items in this section measure the child's ability to use body senses to generate emotional responses. Ariel needs more protection from life than other children. She tends to be overly affectionate with others and is not able to interpret body language.

Modulation of visual input affecting emotional responses and activity level. Items in this section measure the child's ability to use visual cues to establish contact with others. Ariel always avoids eye contact. She does not appear to notice when people come into a room. Once they are there, though, Ariel watches what everyone is doing in the room.

Behavioral and Emotional Responses

Sometimes behavioral problems are the first indicators that the child may have SPD. Sometimes children are extremely rigid in their behaviors and are described as "perfectionists." This extreme rigidity is necessary for the child to maintain external control of her body, especially when she is unable to control her body internally. On the basis of information provided in Ariel's sensory profile, her mother's concerns, school reports, and clinical observations, Ariel demonstrates behaviors typical of a child with difficulties regulating the sensory system.

Summary and Recommendations

Some of the recommendations based on the sensory integration evaluation are similar to those from the other areas of the overall neuropsychological evaluation, such as working with an occupational therapist three times a week. In addition, I would recommend the following:

1. Occupational Therapy—It is recommended that Ariel receive direct, 45-minute-long occupational therapy sessions no less than three times a week, involving the use of a sensory integration and developmental frame of reference.

2. Physical Therapy Evaluation—It is recommended that Ariel undergo an evaluation for physical therapy secondary to her decreased endurance and hypotonia (poor muscle tone), which affect her ability to perform in her environment.

3. Sound Therapy—It is recommended that Ariel complete a therapeutic listening program. Therapeutic listening is a sensory integrative technique that utilizes altered music to strengthen the muscles in the inner ear and stimulate and exercise the vestibular and cochlear system and the attending and organizing mechanisms of the middle ear.

4. Core Strengthening Activities—A swimming program is recommended for Ariel, as a means of increasing her generalized muscle strength. The water provides isometric resistance to each of the muscles of the body.

5. Sensory Tools—A weighted lap animal or blanket is recommended, which can rest on her lap during tabletop activities at school or at home. The increased weight on her lap is directly related to increasing attention, as weight affects the proprioceptive system. Weighted lap animals can be ordered through Theratoys of America, Inc [call (646) 529-8939].

6. Implementation of Sensory Diet Activities—Sensory diet activities can be performed at home and school and during therapy sessions. These activities are designed by an occupational therapist and are developed to meet the needs of a child's nervous system. For Ariel, some of these activities may include play activities with a variety of textures, such as Play-Doh, slime, Floam, silly putty, cornstarch and water, sand, feathers, beans, sandpaper, tin foil, salt, shaving cream, and finger paint. There are a number of rubber-based "squishy" toys on the market that are great fidget toys. Use of oral input activities, such as resistive blowing and sucking activities, provide organizing "heavy-work" input. Also, the use of chewing gum during homework time sometimes increases focus. During fine motor activities, encourage your child to maintain active compression (touch pressure) around the object before she manipulates it. For example, have her squeeze a pencil or crayon prior to asking her to draw.

What Is a Sensory Diet?

A sensory diet is an individualized treatment plan that, after a thorough evaluation, outlines a set of specific activities that will effectively treat a child's sensory problems. The plan will also include specific items and objects that may be used to perform the specific recommended activities.

There are a few key components to an effective sensory diet. Perhaps the most important component is first performing a full and careful evaluation of the child's sensory functioning. Next, an individualized plan is developed on the basis of the evaluation findings. As much as possible, the plan should be practical, fun, accessible, and usable everywhere the child goes (whether at home, at school, or in the community).

An important goal of a good sensory diet is to take the behaviors or activities the child thrives on, which may be maladaptive, socially unacceptable, isolating, disruptive, or odd, and replace them with more adaptive behaviors. For example, if a child craves oral-motor sensory input and mouths, chews, and bites inedible objects, the sensory diet may direct you to give your child sugarless gum. If he or she likes jumping on the sofa or other furniture, provide a safe and comfortable alternative, such as a trampoline, instead.

As you can see, the target behaviors are not stopped by telling the child repeatedly not to do them; rather, the child is given other viable and adaptive alternatives to use. This is particularly important as the child gets older. Odd and peculiar behaviors can set a child apart from his peers, and even make him an easy target for bullies at school. Younger, less socially sophisticated children may not even notice most of these "maladaptive" behaviors. However, as the child gets older it becomes more and more important for them not to stand out because of such behaviors.

It is important to emphasize that the home-based component of a sensory diet is absolutely crucial and necessary for the success of the proposed interventions. The skills that your child learns in therapy must be mastered and generalized to places outside of the occupational therapist's office.

Suggested Sensory Diet Activities

"Heavy work" is organizing for the senses. Propriocep-tive input (sensations from joints, muscles, and con-nective tissues that lead to body awareness) can be obtained by engaging in the following activities: lift-ing, pushing, and pulling heavy objects; engaging in activities that compress (push together) or distract (pull apart) the joints, such as playing tug-of-war or jumping on a trampoline or a hard surface to send information directly from the nerve endings in the foot and improve motor planning skills; climbing on top of balls, barrels, a makeshift "mountain" (a mat placed over ball), stairs, and ladders; wearing a backpack filled with objects; using a weighted lap animal or a weighted blanket; pulling a wagon full of toys or books to help normalize the somatosensory system and increase body aware-ness; giving bear hugs; performing animal positional movements; using massagers, especially along the oral cavity; jumping; climbing over a blanket that covers a variety of ball sizes; rough and tumble play; sitting on squishy cushions and pillows, also of different sizes; shoveling snow; raking leaves; pushing heavy objects like firewood in a wheelbarrow; doing push-ups against the wall, wearing a heavy backpack or pulling one on a luggage cart; mowing the lawn with a push mower; and wearing a weighted vest, available at a sporting goods store that sells equipment for martial arts or weightlifting.

Tactile activities stimulate the sense of touch, involv-ing texture, temperature, pressure, and more. Don't forget that the tactile system includes not only the skin covering your body but also inner skin linings, such as inside the mouth. For example, the taste and texture of foods can affect tactile arousal levels. Some activities to increase oral input include resistive blowing and sucking (to provide organizational "heavy work" input) blowing whistles and bubbles, eating frozen foods (popsicles and frozen fruit and vegetables), drinking (slushies, smoothies, and milkshakes) through thin and crazy straws, drinking plain seltzer water or carbonated mineral water to experience the bubbles in the mouth (they can even be flavored with lemon, lime, etc), eating lollipops or other foods that require resistive sucking (such as spaghetti), introducing chewing gum to activate the 32 joints in the mouth, and using sour candy to arouse the oral cavity. You can organize tactile processing by providing play activities with a variety of textures (cooked spaghetti with oil mixed in, sand, feathers, cornstarch, Nickelodeon Splat [found at WalMart or Target], shaving cream or whipped cream, finger paint, water, salt, and Mylar foil). You can fill textured bins with rice, beans, or sand, and hide small objects (like money or alphabet letters) for her to find.

Auditory activities draw attention to what we hear, but they can also affect the vestibular sense, as the vestibular and auditory systems are connected neuroanatomically. In addition to listening to various types of music, both recorded and live, here are some ways to provide calming and organizational auditory input. Get out into nature, and listen. Go to the beach, or sit still and listen to a thunderstorm or windstorm. If you hear birds singing, try to identify what direction a given bird is calling from. Listen to natural sound recordings, such as a rainstorm, waves crashing against the beach, or birds in the forest—sometimes, these recordings also feature light instrumentation (with flutes, keyboards, etc). Play a listening game: Sit quietly with your child and try to identify the sounds you hear (traffic, the hum of the refrigerator, a door closing, etc). Encourage your child to play a musical instrument. For a child with auditory sensitivity, controlling the sounds she hears can be especially helpful. If your child is fearful of loud noises, let her control the volume on the stereo, and explore soft versus loud music.

Vestibular input (the sense of movement, which is centered in the inner ear) can be obtained by spinning and swinging, and, to a lesser extent, by performing any type of movement. Some suggested activities include: Swing on a hammock, on playground swings, or a merry-go-round (you're never too old!); do cartwheels and dance (also provides proprioceptive input); hang upside down from the monkey bars at the playground; roll down a grassy or snowy hill (good proprioceptive input as well); ride a roller coaster; and when using swings, try various types of swings and movements, such as front and back and side to side. Spin on a Sit 'n Spin, a Dizzy Disc Jr, or an office chair. Run in circles, ride a carousel, jump down from a step or from playground equipment, slide down a slide on your belly, walk on a balance beam, and hold your child's arms and legs and spin her around like an airplane.

During seatwork, the feet should be flat on the floor (or other surface, such as a box). Use a removable chair cushion or weighted lap animal, if needed.

In the classroom, try using easels for drawing and coloring and removable chair cushions. Vary positions for play and work (such as lying prone on the belly, lying down on one side, kneeling, or sitting cross-legged). Never sit in a "W" position (a "reverse tailor" position, where the knees come together and the feet point outward in opposite directions; this position is not possible unless there is an underlying issue of poor muscle tone).

Provide a variety of snacks with different tastes and textures, especially sour, crunchy, and chewy. Suggestions include pretzels, mini-bagels, granola bars, pieces of lemon, and raw vegetables. Sour candy can be used to arouse the oral cavity. Encourage your child to drink water from a bottle with a sports top, or through a straw.

Use creative arts, such as drawing or painting, to encourage your child to express herself. Such activities can also increase her self-confidence.

Adding rhythm to an activity makes it more organizing for the senses. Encourage dancing and moving to different types of music, drawing and coloring to music, beating drums or other rhythm instruments, and clapping in time to music.

Taking movement breaks during the day can be important too. During a movement break, have your child march in place, jump on a trampoline, stomp around the room, run up the stairs, or carry heavy books to another classroom.

What You Can Expect from Treatment

As has been mentioned in other chapters of this book, the most effective treatment for children with SPD is sensory integration therapy combined with traditional occupational therapy (to strengthen fine motor skills and hand and finger abilities), provided by a trained occupational therapist.

The treatment is delivered after a careful assessment of the child has been performed and an individualized sensory diet has been determined. The sensory diet is a customized program of activities that are designed to help the child with self-regulation, sensory integration, and sensory management. Since occupational therapy has been mentioned as the treatment of choice for SPD, let us consider what this entails and what specific problems occupational therapists treat.

Here is how the American Occupational Therapy Association (originated in 1976) defines occupational therapy:

> *The therapeutic use of work, self-care, and play activities to increase development and prevent disability. It may include adaptation of task or environment to achieve maximum independence and to enhance the quality of life.*

As is clear from the above definition, occupational therapy is so much more than what the general public typically thinks of. It can be used to help individuals strengthen their fine motor skills, to better handle such tasks as writing, typing, manipulating utensils, and fastening fasteners (eg, zippers and buttons).

The three areas mentioned in the above definition include work, which can broadly be defined as performing any task; self-care, which entails such activities as bathing, combing or brushing one's hair, clipping the nails, brushing the teeth, using the toilet, eating, meal preparation, and cleaning; and, finally, play or leisure activities. These include activities undertaken during one's free time, such as reading, watching television, playing games, exercising, socializing, dancing, and traveling. Occupational therapists are also an integral part of many multidisciplinary teams, such as those who provide services at schools, hospitals, and rehabilitation centers.

When considering these areas of functioning and the sample activities mentioned, it is hard to imagine occupational therapy not being able to improve our functioning in every facet of our lives. By the same token, should an incident affect our normal level of functioning, it would be hard to think of a function that would not benefit from occupational therapy. The activities addressed by occupational therapists are those that we may think of as functional activities in our daily lives.

Whether you are learning a task for the first time, mastering a task you can only partially perform, or relearning a task or skill, occupational therapy can be instrumental in achieving that goal. Occupational therapy services can offer so much more than teaching individuals to type or developing better handwriting. So many skills involved in the day-to-day activities of children with SPD can benefit from utilizing occupational therapy services. These skills and abilities will in turn improve their social lives, confidence levels, peer relationships, and ability to participate in activities such as sports; increase their independence; and add to their overall quality of life.

Just briefly and for the sake of clarity, let us say a word or two about physical therapy and how it is similar to or different from occupational therapy. Although there is some overlap between the two disciplines, in general, physical therapists focus on strengthening one's gross motor skills. These are skills that involve the body's larger muscles and are involved in one's ease of mobility. Occupational therapists tend to focus on the development of fine motor skills, which involve more subtle body movements and muscle groups and allow a person to perform "routine" tasks that are necessary in day-to-day life.

Sensory Integration Therapy

Sensory integration therapy is based in occupational therapy, with some specific differences. While traditional occupational therapy focuses on improving fine motor skills and the skills needed for activities of daily living (as described previously), sensory integration therapy focuses on using very sensory-rich activities in a room specifically designed for the activities to take place in safely and is performed by a qualified therapist who has specific training in providing this form of therapy. This distinction is important when parents are looking for an occupational therapist to evaluate and provide therapy for SPD. Again, it is worth repeating that not all occupational therapists are trained in and qualified to provide sensory integration therapy. Therefore, parents are encouraged to specifically inquire about the qualifications of the therapist who will be providing sensory integration therapy for their child.

In sensory integration therapy, the goal is to provide opportunities for the child to have as many sensory experiences as possible, involving as many senses as possible in a safe environment. Ideally, every activity will provide an opportunity for two or more of the senses to be engaged.

These specific activities are chosen by the therapist to be fun, enjoyable, and encouraging to the child and to meet the specific sensory and motor/praxis needs of the child. As with any therapeutic relationship, it is crucial to have a trusting and mutually respectful relationship between the child and the therapist. While the activities are child directed, they are structured by the therapist to provide the most favorable arousal level and increase the likelihood of success for the child.

Below is a list of just some of the activities with which an occupational therapist can help. By strengthening a child's fine motor skills, many other necessary skills will be learned. These skills are considered "functional" skills, since they are necessary for a child's everyday activities.

Occupational therapists can be of assistance in tying shoes; styling, brushing, braiding, and putting hair into a ponytail; using fasteners, such as zippers, snaps, buttons, and buckles; manipulating small objects, such as small pieces of food like cereal or puzzle pieces, beads, and arts and crafts objects; manipulating lids and scissors; writing and drawing; opening door knobs; using keys; using utensils; and any and all activities that require the use of the hands and fingers.

There are a number of factors that can make therapy a successful experience. One is that, as always, when working with children, the work must feel as much like play as possible. If therapy can be play based and fun, the child will be motivated and invested in participating in the activity. First and foremost, any successful form of treatment requires patient compliance. Put simply, the patient must do what needs to be done to get better and improve his or her condition. This is perhaps even more true when treating a child. Therefore, make sure you work with a therapist that understands this principle and employs it every time.

A second factor is the generalization of the acquired skills. This means that you practice at home what your child has learned in therapy. One hour of therapy a week is a good start and a very useful foundation, but for the learned skills to become second nature for the child, he or she must practice and keep practicing. This is no different from learning any other new skill, such as playing the piano or tennis. If a child only plays piano 1 hour a week during a music lesson and does not practice between lessons, he or she will probably never learn to play the piano fluently. The same is true for skills such as tying your shoelaces or zipping up your jacket. If, instead of practicing with your child patiently, you rush to do it for him, progress will be very slow. Be patient, and teach your child to also be patient with himself. Once he masters a skill, the joy and pride he feels will be enormous.

A third helpful hint is to work with the therapist to purchase and bring home some key therapeutic items for practice and use. These may include a small trampoline, a weighted blanket or vest, a therapy ball, and Theraputty. These items are fairly inexpensive and available through various occupational therapy Web sites.

In providing sensory integration therapy, it is of great importance that parents familiarize themselves with fun and easy activities that help their child explore opportunities for a variety of sensory experiences. *The Out-of-Sync Child Has Fun,* by Carol Kranowitz, is full of wonderful, enjoyable, and simple exercises that parents can do with their children.

Lastly, be creative, have fun, follow your child's lead, and encourage your child.

Hopefully, this chapter has shed some light on the process of assessment, diagnosis, and treatment of SPD and has taken some of the mystery and anxiety out of this process for you.

6

HOW TO HELP CREATE A SENSORY-FRIENDLY CLASSROOM

The life of a child essentially takes place in two environments: home and school. Children typically spend 6 to 7 hours a day, and about 190 days a year, at school. These numbers may be higher if the school day runs longer or if you count after-school hours and summer camp.

When children with SPD are not at home and they're away from their primary caretaker, it's during these times that parents are most anxious and worried about how their child will feel and respond. At school, the safety and protection of the familiar setting at home is missing. Furthermore, the adults at school not only do not know the child as well as his or her parents, they are also responsible for many other children in their care and are restricted by the parameters within the school setting.

The school environment is typically much more demanding for the child than that at home, as it brings heightened responsibilities and pressure to perform, frequent and abrupt transitions, more socially complicated situations, more noise, more bodies in motion all around the child, a faster pace, unspoken rules, greater demand for organization, a pull for flexibility and the ability to conform, the expectation to function independently, and a requirement to think fast and on your feet. School is the kind of environment that assails all the weaknesses of children with SPD.

The Effect of SPD on Learning and Functioning at School

During my years of working with children with SPD, parents have often asked me why their children act differently at home than at school. "How come my child does so well at home, but not at school? We never see any of these problems (especially behavioral issues) at home," and vice versa.

This is a very common and valid question on the part of the families. It is not that parents don't want to acknowledge that their kids have problems at home; they just don't see what teachers see at school. Many families are surprised and shocked to hear that their child pushed another child or staff member, ran out of the classroom, refused to take part in a project, had a meltdown when a scheduled event changed, or seemed to completely shut down. Although these families are well aware of their child's SPD, they have never observed such behaviors at home, or at least not to the degree reported by the school.

School is the kind of environment that naturally assails all the weaknesses of children with SPD.

At times, it may be hard for school personnel to believe the parents when they say they have never seen a certain behavior at home. Teachers and administrators may feel parents are blaming them for "bringing out" these behaviors in the child, or worse; no one at school is know-ingly or purposefully "setting off" the child. School personnel may feel that parents are not being sincere about their child's functioning at home.

In the opposite scenario, the child functions beautifully at school, but completely falls apart at home. Parents hear from their child and teachers that he or she "had a good day," and there were no issues to report. However, shortly after the child gets picked up or goes home, he or she falls apart over what seems like the smallest thing. The meltdown takes on different forms depending on the age of the child. Preschoolers may literally fall on the floor rolling, crying, or hitting their heads. Middle school children may have verbal tantrums, slam doors, and lock themselves in their rooms.

To better understand the above scenarios, let us consider for a moment how we, as adults, deal with any situation that pulls at our weaknesses and exposes them not only to us, but also to others around us. To begin with, none of us likes to be put in that kind of situation, much less have to face that kind of demand several hours a day.

It is human nature to flee from any threatening condition—this is a basic survival strategy. If overwhelmed and unable to physically flee, we tend to mentally shut down and block out any incoming stimuli. Imagine the stress if you were put in that kind of state every day, year after year.

When the nervous system can't process sensory input properly, it feels like an assault to the body, with tremendous psychological consequences. It is absolutely exhausting. The child experiencing these feelings has limited internal resources for dealing with stressful events and has to fall apart at some point. That point could be at school, when facing demanding situations, or at home, after having held it together for hours that day.

Most children, if they can help it, tend to let go and melt down at home, where they feel safe in the presence of loving parents who will help contain and hold them. These children use every ounce of their energy to get through the day and do it so that they do not stand out in the classroom. Unfortunately, not all children are able to cope while at school and will exhibit behaviors that make them look like a child with behavioral issues.

Creating Sensory-Friendly Classrooms

Throughout the book, I've offered suggestions to make the life of a child with SPD easier, less eventful, and less stressful at home. In this chapter, you will find strategies to share with your child's teachers that will make the school day more pleasant and manageable both for your child and for the teacher. In fact, these strategies can be helpful for every student and make learning easier and more fun for all kids.

Let us begin by defining what the most important lessons are to teach a child. How many of you can recall what ocean the Strait of Malacca is connected to? Or how to find the volume of a cone? These are pieces of information learned in 6th grade social studies and 7th grade mathematics classes, respectively. While schools are mandated to teach specific curricula and prepare students for various state assessment tests, learning meaningful, functional, and adaptive skills is what gets us through life's everyday challenges.

It is important for educators not to lose sight of the big picture—the importance of the process of learning—and not to get swept up in a meaningless race to get through the most amount of information possible—especially if the fast pace means leaving behind many students who do not fall in the average range for one reason or another.

Convincing Schools to Help Your Child

How can you get your child's teacher on board with making changes at school? The following are some tips for convincing your child's teacher to implement some of the classroom changes proposed in this chapter.

Educate your child's teacher. SPD is a fairly new diagnosis and is most typically associated with autism spectrum disorders. Many people, including teachers, are not familiar with SPD as its own diagnosis, representing a real clinical issue outside the realm of autism. Therefore, sometimes, it is difficult to get an already busy and overwhelmed teacher to believe that an otherwise perfectly typical child may need special accommodations in the classroom.

> Here, the responsibility to attend to the child is a shared one. Parents must take the responsibility to meet with their child's teacher at the onset of the school year and to give simple, practical information to the teacher about SPD and how it affects their child. Teachers truly appreciate having critical information about a child early on, instead of following a difficult incident at school.

> One key person who is often overlooked at school is the principal, who, in fact, can make a substantial difference in the child's school experience. Parents must remember to include the school principal in informative discussions regarding their children. Suggestions about having a speaker talk to teachers or administrators about SPD should be presented to the principal. Also, when your child is involved in an incident at school, having met with the principal ahead of time makes dealing with the issue a lot simpler.

Educate the students. There are many times during each school year when parents are asked to speak to students on a variety of topics, such as their career, ethnic background, and foods from around the world. This is a great opportunity to talk to students about SPD. Parents are always pleasantly surprised to find that once kids know about differences, they are much more respectful, compassionate, and tolerant.

Help teachers to understand SPD as a medical issue. SPD is a neurological issue and must be treated as such. When talking about SPD, cite other medical examples that others can easily relate to, such as accommodating a child with diabetes by allowing the child to have frequent snacks, or wearing orthotics or reading glasses.

Help teachers relate to and connect with you. When sharing information about your child and SPD, help teachers to think about questions such as, "If it was your child, what would you want teachers to do for her?" This goes back to treating others the way you want to be treated, and deciding how you want your loved ones to be treated and cared for. If done gently and respectfully, this approach goes a long way.

Volunteer, help out, and appreciate. Public school teachers, in particular, have their hands full every year. There are typically 20 to 30 students in each class, each of whom teachers must get to know, teach, and manage. Any help that a parent can provide in the classroom goes a long way and is appreciated by teachers. Helping out and volunteering is, more than anything else, a simple way of showing your gratitude for all that your child's teacher does and an acknowledgement of all of his or her efforts. As an involved parent, when you are talking to the teacher about your child, you are not the parent who has no idea about what the teacher has to deal with on a daily basis, but rather one who can talk with firsthand classroom experience. For example, if you suggest that tennis balls should be placed on all the chair legs in the classroom to reduce sudden noises, offer to donate the balls and/or place the balls on the chair legs yourself.

Explain the cost and consequence of not making the necessary accommodations. Finally, help teachers understand the real cost of not accommodating children with SPD. These can include losing a child's attention, reducing his motivation for learning and self-esteem, and not being able to prevent or address disruptive or problematic behaviors in the classroom.

TEN STEPS TO BETTER ORGANIZATION

Both teachers and parents can use the following strategies to help students with SPD improve their organizational skills and assist with day-to-day school and home functioning.

Keep in mind that because your child has a deficiency in internal organizational skills, you must provide external and assistive organizational tools to remedy the problem. Identifying various helpful tools and practicing use of them also prepares your child for future years, when school and life require more and more complex organizational skills.

Set the alarm for "early." Have your child up and ready for school with plenty of time to spare in the morning. Children with SPD do not do well with a rushed morning routine. The period between waking up and getting to school often sets the tone for the rest of the day. Give your child's body and senses time to awaken slowly, in an unhurried manner. Most kids with SPD require warm-up time to begin their day.

Have everything ready to go. Do not leave anything to be done "first thing in the morning." As difficult as it is to get something done the night before, it will be ten times more difficult to get it done in the morning, right before school. This could include tasks such as printing an assignment, getting a form signed, and packing a lunch.

Of special importance is choosing and setting aside clothes for the next day. This is especially true for children with heightened tactile sensitivities and those living in cold climates. Finding just the right fabric is a great challenge in and of itself. Other things, such as tags, socks, jackets, hats, and gloves, make getting dressed an eventful time in many households. Figuring out what to wear, and even wearing the selected items the night before, may take one stressor out of the day.

Arrive ahead of time. A simple, yet critical, strategy is to get the student to school before the first bell rings. If possible, try to have your child at school about 20 minutes before the first class starts. This gives children plenty of time to get to their locker, take out what they need, and get settled for first period.

Many teachers will have the day's assignment and events listed on the board. The student can use this planner to face the day in a more predictable fashion. Additionally, many teachers will make themselves available before the start of the day to answer questions and help students catch up on unclear assignments.

Create a checklist. Writing a checklist of things to do before entering the classroom is a good strategy to remind children what they need to do. At the elementary school level, many teachers are willing to provide this list, which can be placed either outside the door or in every student's locker. The list remains the same all year, and needs to be created at the beginning of the academic year, since the basic schedule typically remains the same for kindergarten through 5th grade. Middle-school and high-school students may create their own list and place it in their locker. Tasks such as "place lunch money in brown envelope, put signed forms in purple bin, and choose a book for quiet reading" are some examples of checklist items.

Separate each subject. It would be helpful and worth the extra expense in the long run to provide a specific zip-up folder for each subject, with a different-colored cover for each subject. This simple strategy alone will prevent many of the difficulties that children with SPD face on a daily basis at school. They can get the folder they need quickly and without drawing too much attention to themselves, and make sure they do not lose any papers by the time they come home. Parents can help children organize and go through their folders periodically to discard old papers and notices.

Plan to get a planner. A daily planner can help children with SPD keep track of all assignments that are due and cross out those that have been completed. If you prefer to keep a large, wall-sized planner, make sure to include your child in using it. This is a useful, lifelong strategy that is never too early to learn. With younger children, use pictures or stickers to mark upcoming events or tasks. Daily planners are great visual, organizational, and time management tools that help reduce the occurrence of surprise due dates and anxiety and prevent the child from feeling overwhelmed by having to do last-minute projects.

Separate, organize, and store. Clear plastic bins are probably the most efficient and cost-effective way to get organized. Get as many as you need to organize your child's home and school life, and label them. This will also allow your child to be more independent and self-sufficient, and therefore, more confident. Aside from storing items that he or she needs on a daily basis, such as various kinds of paper (lined, clear, and graph paper), coloring pencils, and pens, you can use these bins to organize your child's paperwork. As every parent knows, every day children come home with an impressive amount of paperwork. These papers can be separated and organized with such labels as "old homework/projects, upcoming projects, need parent signature, tests/quizzes, need filing in binder," and other headings as it pertains to each student.

Plan ahead. Provide written and verbal schedules and use priming or preteaching (exposing the child ahead of time to what may arise later) to prepare kids for what is coming up. This strategy helps with organization and reduces anxiety. In addition, identifying, planning for, and rehearsing the steps involved when facing a novel situation will allow children to access effective coping skills and adaptive ways of managing the anxiety associated with a specific task.

Manage your minutes. Teach time management skills at home and at school. At school, a simple way to do this is by using a digital timer with a pleasant, 1-minute alarm signal. Many inexpensive models are available and come with a magnetic strip, base, and clip so you can place them anywhere. Timers may be placed by the classroom computers and various work stations. These timers allow children of all ages to participate in time keeping and eventually take charge of their own time management. With practice, even children who have difficulty reading clocks or keeping track of time will "get a feel for" how long 10 minutes is, for example. More importantly, such strategies will teach, promote, and foster self-management skills, which are critical for any individual who seeks a productive and independent lifestyle.

Practice beforehand. Rehearse any strategies suggested here or by others ahead of time to make sure they are viable options that your child can use at school. This will give you and your child a sense for his or her comfort level with various tools, and help you identify any glitches in the plan. For example, if your child is allowed to use a laptop but does not sit near an outlet in the classroom, a change in seating may be necessary. Informing your child's teacher and including him or her in these decisions is important, since he or she has the final say in making any changes. Remember, the partnership of home and school and the communication between them is the key to successfully implementing any of the proposed strategies.

Consider technology as an aid. Provide and allow the use of assistive technology tools whenever possible. These can offer your child a simple, discrete, socially acceptable, and quick way to get organized, help him or her to make and follow a plan, and make each day as predictable and manageable as possible.

These tools range from a laptop computer and electronic organizer to more sophisticated tools, such as a BlackBerry, which features a memo pad for quick notes on the go, calendars to provide reminders on upcoming assignments and due dates, and writing programs. Having access to such devices may be critical, especially for students with graphomotor weaknesses. (Graphomotor abilities generally refer to fine motor skills and the use of the hands and fingers.) From a vocational perspective, all the skills used in conjunction with the use of assistive technology can be helpful and marketable, as well.

Finally, talk to other parents of children with SPD, as well as to your child, about what has worked in the past for them. Use their input to add to this list.

Behavior as a Form of Communication

Teachers must think like detectives when encountering a problematic child, a difficult child, or a child who has trouble paying attention, learning, or following directions.

Instead of focusing on the behavior and what your child is doing or not doing, try to figure out what your child is trying to communicate to you through his or her behavior. In other words, what is the behavior telling you? What is the message being communicated to you via the behavior?

All behaviors are a form of communication. For example, a child who is sensitive to touch may refuse to attend a family gathering. If the child's parents just focus on the "refusal" part of the behavior, they may view the child as defiant, hard-headed, stubborn, rude, uncooperative, isolated, or antisocial. However, if they keep the child's sensory profile in mind and think not about the behavior (in this case, refusing to go) but rather the reason for the behavior, they will see that the behavior makes sense.

A child who is sensitive to touch is particularly sensitive to unpredictable touching. The child may remember past family gatherings, where greetings, goodbyes, and other interactions during the event involved being "touched" by a family member. These touches could include hugging, kissing, shaking hands, bumping into others, brushing against someone, getting a pat on the head or a tap on the shoulder, and so on.

Looking at the situation from the child's point of view, you can see that such a child is far from stubborn, defiant, and uncooperative; rather, he or she has learned to avoid situations that are uncomfortable and uneasy for him or her. The function of this child's behavior is avoidance (of an unpleasant event), which, in this case, is an adaptive and appropriate response in the context of his or her SPD.

This is called the function of the behavior in a functional behavioral assessment, an innovative method of observing and addressing children's unwanted behaviors. This method of behavioral intervention is effective and helpful not only in children with SPD, but in children of all ages and in a wide array of behavioral challenges and levels of functioning, including typically developing individuals.

Officially, a functional behavioral assessment involves observing the child at various times during the course of the day and recording on a form specific information about certain targeted or unwanted behaviors. This information is then used to develop a specific behavioral intervention plan. This assessment and intervention tool has proven to be so successful that staff at all public schools in the United States are now required to complete this assessment when facing a child that demonstrates a pattern of challenging behaviors (Individuals with Disabilities Education Act, 2004).

This method asks that parents, teachers, and care providers look for and identify the factors contributing to the occurrence and reoccurrence of the problem behavior. It requires care providers to take a step back, and instead of focusing on the behavior, focus on what the child is trying to communicate with the behavior. What purpose does the behavior serve for the child? Why does the child engage in this behavior knowing that he or she may lose privileges, such as use of a phone, TV time, or time with friends?

The answer to this question is imbedded in (a) what occurred just before the undesirable behavior that may have triggered the behavior, (b) what the child is trying to tell you with his or her behavior, and (c) what the child is gaining from the behavior.

As noted previously, all behaviors are a form of communication. The parent or teacher's challenge is to try and figure out what the child is trying to communicate through a specific behavior.

Some examples of what a child may be trying to communicate are as follows: getting attention, getting a specific person's attention, being the only child who gets attention, getting physical attention, continuing the use of an object, continuing engagement in an activity, avoiding a socially demanding situation, escaping having to perform a task, escaping a potentially embarrassing situation, escaping a group activity or other form of involvement, or escaping a highly demanding situation.

Think of children's behavior as their sign language and their way of telling you what they are feeling. How does the mother of an infant know what each cry of a baby means? If the mother keeps telling her baby to stop crying without figuring out what the baby is trying to communicate or addressing the reason is behind the tears, the communication is useless and superficial. Similar situations will come up again and again that will be exhausting for both the mother and her child.

You can use this analogy to understand a child's behavior at school. In the moment a child is not able to function according to expectation, a teacher must shift the focus from the behavior and ask him- or herself, "What is this child trying to communicate to me through this behavior?" The following real-life examples will demonstrate just how effective this method can be in addressing "problem behaviors" in children with SPD at school.

Case Study

RAY—AVOIDING EMBARRASSMENT BY ACTING OUT

Ray is a 16-year-old who has SPD and Asperger disorder. As part of his SPD, he has a low activity level in general. He has poor muscle tone, poor balance, and fine and gross motor weaknesses. He's overresponsive to sounds, particularly echoing sounds, and overresponsive to touch and light. He has a very poor awareness of where his body is in space.

For Ray, this means that he does not have a good sense of his body in relation to space and to others, his own strength and force, his lack of coordination, where his body ends and others' begin, his proximity to surrounding people or objects (for example, he's likely to stand too close to others or bump into things), and the ability to modulate his volume and tone of voice. In addition, he has poor regulation of body temperature, or sense of hot and cold, and impaired perception of pain (for example, he might experience a light touch as uncomfortable but not feel pain from a cut).

Ray also lacks organizational skills and displays challenging behaviors, such as aggression, when he's overwhelmed, anxious, or "not in a good place." He demonstrates delays in gross motor skills and clinically significant weaknesses in fine motor abilities.

Since Ray is 16 years old and has dealt with these difficulties all his life, he knows, even before attempting a task, what he can and cannot do. He also knows how he can get out of having to do things that are beyond his abilities. His ways of avoiding them are not all adaptive, socially acceptable, or appropriate methods; nevertheless, over the years, he has found that they work in getting him out of a potentially embarrassing situation in front of his peers. Ray, like most children with SPD, would rather have a reputation as a "behavioral" child than a "stupid" child or one that is unable to manage a simple task like the rest of his classmates.

One day, in his social studies class, the students were told to make a globe. They were given materials and were asked to mark various points of interest on their globes. They were instructed to draw the shape on paper by using exact measurements and to cut out the pieces accordingly, color them, and paste the pieces together to complete the project. All the steps were written on the board, and the materials were placed on each student's desk.

Ray walked into the classroom, sat at his desk, and glanced at the board and the assignment. "All of a sudden, he went from zero to a hundred," reported Ray's teacher. Ray grabbed the papers on his desk, crushed them in his fists, and threw them on the floor. He left the classroom, repeating all the while that "this is stupid."

On the surface, Ray's outward behavior makes him seem like a defiant, rude, and terrible student, who deserves strong consequences for his behavior. On the other hand, if we consider what Ray was communicating with his behavior, a whole new picture emerges. Every step of this assignment assailed Ray's core weaknesses, skills that he knew very well he did not have. He knew it was only a matter of time before he felt humiliated in front of the class. How humiliating must it be at 16 to be unable to use scissors to cut around a shape or to use glue to paste small pieces of paper together?

Ray would much rather leave the classroom and not participate in this "stupid" assignment than to have to raise his hand and announce to the entire class that he could not do what a 5-year-old could do easily. The assignment wasn't "stupid"—Ray felt "stupid" for not being able to do it. When he said, "this is stupid," he really meant "I am stupid" for not being capable of doing what seemed like a very simple task.

In the above example, if the teacher had only focused on Ray's behavior, he would have been mis-labeled, punished, and made to feel even worse about himself. He would have felt even more disconnected from school, his peers, and his teacher. More importantly, missing all the important information about Ray's SPD would have led to similar situations for the rest of the academic year. Encouragingly, the teacher in this case was able to see the problems with the assignment for all the students with SPD in her classroom, and was very willing to adapt future projects to accommodate students with SPD.

Case Study

ALI'S STORY—FEAR OF FAILURE

Another example is that of Ali, a 6th grade student who was taking a culinary arts class. Ali's SPD profile included overresponsivity to sounds, sights, touch, and textures. In addition, he had difficulty with coordination, delay in auditory processing, and weaknesses in fine and gross motor skills, in addition to an apparent lack of organizational skills.

The inefficiency of Ali's tactile system made him especially sensitive to and defensive against certain textures that touched his body. These included soft, sticky, and squishy liquids. Many of the recipes in culinary arts include eggs as an ingredient and require the students to break an egg. During the first class, in which students were required to break and add eggs, Ali bravely attempted the directions. Due to his difficulties with fine motor skills, he could not "feel" how hard he hit the egg on the side of the bowl, and he shattered the eggshell. Raw egg, with its unique soft texture, ran down Ali's hand. He could not contain himself. Crying, he tried desperately to wipe his hands off. Needless to say, Ali was not able to finish the project that day.

In Ali's case, it took a patient and talented teacher to look beyond the student's disruptive overreaction to a minor mishap. At a later time, when Ali was able to talk about this experience with his teacher, she understood how Ali's sensory overresponsivity played a role in his reaction. For the remainder of the classes that year, Ali was able to fully participate in the class and enjoy himself. As his teacher said, "He just doesn't crack eggs, but he still has fun."

As we have seen, SPD can affect every aspect of a child's functioning at home and at school. A good day at school makes a world of difference. Since the school environment is so different from that at home, and parents can't be with their children in the classroom, how can we make sure that the child has a chance at success at school?

SPECIAL EDUCATION AND THE LAW

Parents need to know that under the federal Individuals with Disabilities Education Act, 20 USC section 1401(8), "free and appropriate public education" means that special education and related services are available to all children, free of charge and in conformity with the child's individualized education program.

This interpretation means that with sufficient support services, the student has access to and benefits from the educational instructions in the least-restrictive environment. The least-restrictive environment means that the school districts must, to the extent appropriate, educate students in a regular classroom with "supplementary aids and services," which refers to supports and aids to help students attend classes along with their nondisabled or healthy peers.

In addition, students with disabilities tend to receive the most meaningful education when it is tailored to meet their specific and unique needs, through the development of an individualized educational plan. Depending on the needs of each student, accommodations may vary. Examples include:

Receiving preferential seating

Being accompanied by a teaching aid

Being able to drink during class

Receiving prearranged breaks from class

Being able to use a tape recorder or a note-taker (either a person or an electronic device)

Receiving photocopies of notes in advance

Allowing for changes in test format, such as receiving extended time; having exams read orally, scribed (having someone take notes during an oral exam or having it noted down in some written form), or typed; taking segmented exams that allow the test to be completed over several sessions; allowing the use of computer software during an exam

Receiving substitute assignments or extensions on due dates

Providing students with alternative ways of demonstrating their mastery of materials

For older students, schools may provide administrative accommodations that include assisting with registration or financial aid, modifying degree requirements, providing access to a quiet lounge, or giving an incomplete grade rather than a failure if the student is unable to finish all of the course requirements on time.

Communicating with Your Child's School

Disability laws may vary from state to state, so parents need to check their state's laws and regulations.

Having said that, the first step for parents is to decide whether to share information about their child's SPD with their child's teacher and school. When considering this question, think back to when you didn't know what was going on with your child, why your child could not stand being even lightly touched, or when all the kids at a birthday party were running around, screaming, singing, and clapping while your child was hiding under a table covering his or her ears. Think about how frustrating it was not to be able to go to the mall for just a little bit, because your child would have a fit as soon as you were in the store. When you didn't know about your child's SPD, his or her behaviors and reactions didn't make sense, and nothing seemed to help.

For these reasons, I encourage parents to share information about their child's SPD with teachers. How much you share is up to you, depending on your comfort level and that of your child. Just like you, if teachers don't know anything about your child's condition, they can't help your child. Most teachers mean well, and do their best to teach their students effectively. However, if they don't know what helps your child, despite their best intentions, they may miss the real issues.

At the beginning of each school year, make an appointment to meet with your child's teacher or teachers. Try to make a special appointment, at a time when the teacher is not being pulled in ten different directions by kids or parents during parent night. The best time may be before school starts in the morning or after classes end. If you wait until something terrible happens that requires a meeting, it may be too late.

The main goal of informing the teacher is not only to make your child feel more comfortable at school, but also to protect his or her dignity, self-esteem, and pride. Therefore, it is important that teachers are aware of your child's condition so that they can make the often simple but crucial changes that make a big difference in your child's comfort level and safety. In simple, nontechnical terms, try to convey who your child is, noting her strengths as well as her weaknesses. Work with your child's teacher to arrive at the most effective and practical solution to meeting your child's needs.

For example, if your child is easily distracted, look around the classroom with the teacher and determine whether moving your child's seat is feasible. You will find that there are some teachers who are very open and willing to work with you and your child in addressing your child's needs, and there are some who may be more resistant to making changes. If possible, have your child assigned to a teacher who is willing to listen with an open mind and has a willingness to try different strategies to accommodate your child.

At the beginning of each school year, make an appointment to meet with your child's teacher or teachers. If you wait until something terrible happens that requires a meeting, it may be too late.

Talk to other parents about their experience with various teachers. They can offer helpful information, such if teachers are strict or prone to yelling; if they have favorite students or they care too much about homework; if they're sweet, fun, or flexible; if they call parents back right away; or if they sometimes conduct class outside.

Once your child has been placed in a classroom, communicate regularly with his or her teachers. Let them know that you are available to brainstorm strategies for various problems that may arise in the classroom. Many strategies that benefit children with SPD can also benefit all the other students.

Tips for Parents and Teachers on Making the Classroom More SPD Friendly

Be flexible, because the child cannot be. This is perhaps the most important recommendation for teachers. SPD is a neurological disorder in which the nervous system is unable to effectively process sensory information that it receives from the environment. This means that children cannot modulate and modify their responses to various stimuli.

A useful analogy here may be an individual with diabetes who does not have any control over having diabetes and does not have much flexibility with foods that he or she can have. You can't just decide to stop being a diabetic because it is inconvenient for others, or for yourself. However, with certain changes, such as choosing a proper diet, getting exercise, and taking the right medications, you can make a difference in how the condition affects your day-to-day life and functioning.

Similarly, children with SPD cannot be flexible about their sensitivities. If, for example, they need oral-motor input (or stimulation of the oral cavity and the muscles of the mouth) while in the classroom, allow them to chew gum. If unexpected noise bothers them, consider carpeting the classroom or placing tennis balls on all the chair legs.

Start with the premise and the mindset that kids with SPD are doing their best every day. Children with SPD are not necessarily uncooperative, difficult, willful, rude, malicious, or spoiled, only looking for secondary gain or manipulation or pretending to have sensitivities to get special attention. No child wants his or her parents to have "a special meeting" with the teacher to talk about how they are different from others. No child wants to stand out in a crowd of their peers. Even if they don't show it, every child wants to do better. It is not worth the physical and emotional agony to have a major meltdown just so you can get out of wearing a jacket in the morning. If you change the way you think about these kids' behaviors, you'll see and understand their behaviors differently.

Children with SPD have many strengths—identify and build on them. This is especially important when it comes to nonpreferred subject matter and nonpreferred activities. All children, including those with SPD, have special interests and areas of expertise, whether it be dinosaurs, trains, computers, or leaves.

Allow children to choose projects, and give them an opportunity to include their area of interest. Let them show off and build their confidence by teaching their peers about what they know so much about. This does a great deal for a child's social life at school, as well as his or her academic standing.

Just because they did it once doesn't mean they can do it all the time. Teachers can find inconsistent performance in their students challenging. For instance, it is hard to understand why a child who was able to sit through a whole class period yesterday cannot pay attention today, or why a child could tolerate certain stimuli two days ago but cannot do it every day.

Children, especially those with overresponsivity, feel various sensory stimuli to be too much or too harsh. Depending on what events may be going on in the moment, what went on earlier, and what they are anticipating and anxious about taking place soon, kids with SPD may be able to deal with environmental factors better at certain times than others. They often use all their internal resources, strength, and coping skills to deal with the demands placed on their nervous system. Their lack of success at times does not mean they are being lazy or pretending or not putting enough effort into the task.

Identify your child's "sensory diet," and share the information. A sensory diet is essentially a list of specific activities that have been deemed helpful to children with SPD in regulating their senses. An occupational therapist with a special interest and expertise in sensory integration will conduct a thorough assessment of your child and determine an appropriate sensory diet. The diet includes activities to help your child organize, focus, and feel alert and calm. The therapist or other evaluator may also be available for consultation with your child's educational team or outside service providers.

The therapist ensures that identified strategies are an integral part of all daily activities, with consistency across settings, staff, and occasions. For example, if the therapist has determined that the student benefits from having a vibrating pen, which provides input to the muscles of the hand or the mouth, the teacher is informed so that one can be used in the classroom. Allowing the student to take frequent breaks is another example of a strategy identified by the occupational therapist, to be shared and utilized by all teachers. It is important to use these strategies throughout the day and as needed by your child, primarily as a preventive measure—and not just an attempt to manage a difficult behavioral situation.

Any items and activities that help your child manage his or her responses to the environment must be made available to them readily and as covertly as possible—so that the child does not feel singled out and different from his or her peers. For example, if doodling allows your child to be more attentive in class, extra paper and pens should be placed in your child's desk or nearby for his or her use, as needed. When beginning the implementation of a sensory diet, teachers and staff may act as an external organizer to remind your child of the activity that might be helpful at a given time.

For example, a teacher may say to a child who is having difficulty remaining seated on a chair, "Johnny, the ball is available to sit on for the remainder of the class." Clearly, such interventions will feel more natural and less obvious and isolating in younger children's classrooms, especially if these options are open to all the students in the classroom.

As children get older, the strategies used must be adjusted to ensure the older child's need to blend in with the rest of his or her classmates. For this reason, it is important that with time, teachers, staff, and parents allow and encourage their child to remember, identify, and access the activities and items on their diet on their own.

Identify a designated person who can serve as a source of in-school support to your child. Children with SPD face many situations at school that lead to feeling overwhelmed, frustrated, and anxious. Having an informed, sensitive, and nonacademic counselor available to a child can be an extraordinarily important resource for your child. The student knows that in difficult situations, he or she can connect with the counselor, address emotional issues, and explore adaptive coping mechanisms. This counselor can serve as a resource not only to the child, but also to the family, facilitating communication between the school and home, consulting with school staff, monitoring progress, and participating in and sharing information at important educational planning meetings.

Teach organizational skills. Parents, teachers, and clinicians working with children with SPD will tell you that a major stumbling block for these kids is their deficient organizational skills. I have dedicated special attention to a section about this at the end of the chapter, since this area, by far, is one that parents and teachers are most concerned about.

Organizational skills are part of what neuropsychologists refer to as executive function tasks. These tasks include, among others, problem solving; planning, assessing, and foreseeing consequences of behavior; inhibiting response; controlling impulses; thinking with flexibility; participating in organizational activities; learning from experience; integrating and extracting information from experiences, feelings, and behaviors; finding the most efficient way to do a task; and practicing time management.

For school purposes, perhaps the most effective strategies can be simple, reasonably priced, and accessible. Please see the section "Ten Steps to Better Organization" at the end of this chapter for specific suggestions on this topic.

Simplify and modify the classroom. Here, I encourage you think the opposite of what you normally would when you imagine a typical classroom. Reduce the amount of "stuff" on display as much as possible. This "stuff" could be maps, artwork, pictures, written directions, written rules, items hanging from the ceiling, art supplies, projects on the bulletin board, and so on. This type of a classroom is a nightmare for a child with SPD, and may even be distracting to other children. All the textures, colors, and shapes are nothing but a means of visual sensory overload for children with SPD.

Simplifying the classroom environment requires a shift in thinking by the teacher. Having all the work displayed on the walls at once does not prove that a lot of teaching or learning took place. In fact, cluttering the walls may detract a child's attention from his current project. Limiting the display time for each project may be a sensible compromise for everyone.

Avoid sensory overload by first putting yourself in your child's place. Think about when you need to relax and regroup. Think about the kind of environment you seek when that happens. You might seek a simple, quiet place with the least amount of clutter, noise, and light possible. As an exaggerated example, think about the atmosphere at a spa or meditation room. Now think about how that kind of environment allows you to not only relax, calm down, and regroup, but also reenergize, think more clearly, and focus your attention. This kind of a classroom will not only keep children awake but will also allow for better and more efficient learning.

Other suggestions include reducing the noise level as much as possible or creating white noise, by using a pleasant sound machine or playing classical music in the background. Covering the classroom floor carpeting and the walls with corkboard reduces and absorbs classroom noise substantially. Also, increase the physical space between a child with SPD and his or her classmates by allowing the child to choose a seat in the front or back of the classroom. Fluorescent lights are often distracting and difficult for some children with SPD to handle. If possible, use incandescent lights with an adjustable light switch. Consider this option at the very least for the occupational therapy room and/or office where children with SPD receive their sensory integration therapy.

Make sure the child's seat is stable, comfortable, and cushioned if needed. Since body awareness and the relationship of the body to space is an area of weakness in SPD, this stability prevents falling off one's chair. If possible, particularly for younger children, allow the child to sit on a therapy ball appropriate for his or her size.

Sensory integration breaks are key components of a successful program. Sensory integration breaks are brief timeouts that a child takes as needed and/or on a scheduled basis to regroup, modulate, reorganize the senses, and regain the ability to return to the activity at hand. These breaks can occur through reminders from an adult or by the child's own initiative as a way to prevent problems such as shutting down, meltdowns, overactivity, inattention, fidgeting, and other unproductive responses to sensory problems.

Identify specific areas that children can have access to, should they need to leave the classroom. These areas should be quiet places with minimum sensory stimuli, where they can regroup and return to the classroom.

Reconsider timed work. Could the child do the work if there was no pressure about time? Provide the option for the child to finish the work in segments, or allow extra time. From a teaching perspective, the real question is: Has the child learned the material and can he show it, not can he show it in 30 minutes or less. As mentioned previously, many children with SPD struggle with anxiety and disorganization. The idea of performing in a limited amount of time only magnifies the underlying and ever-present anxiety and adds to the disorganization.

Let the child choose tasks and how to do them. Whenever possible, use multiple modes of teaching, and allow students to demonstrate what they have learned in different ways. As all teachers know, one of the best ways to get students excited about a project is to incorporate his or her special interest and/or expertise into the assignment. This approach not only motivates the student, but also makes up for any areas that may not be a strength for the child.

This is particularly helpful with group projects, where the student with SPD may not be very skilled at making a poster or diorama, but can do research. Again, be flexible, because the child cannot be.

Here are some real-life examples of creative teaching: A student who did not want to write an article for the class newsletter was given the option of drawing a cartoon. He does not like to write because of fine motor weaknesses, and has an electronic scribe device for tests. However, he enjoys drawing cartoon characters.

Similarly, another student with fine motor weakness who "refused" to write out full answers was given the option of writing the first letter of each answer next to the question (for example, "R" for "Rome"). His refusal could have been misinterpreted as a behavioral problem; however, the teacher thought about the function and reason for the behavior. This allowed the student to complete the work successfully, and made the day an uneventful one. Another student "refused" to read a social studies packet. The teacher recognized that the student felt overwhelmed by the packet, and allowed the child to use an appropriate Web site to access the same information.

The thought of creating a diorama of life under the sea (an actual 3rd-grade science assignment) may be dreadful for a 9-year-old with SPD. However, having other options to show his or her understanding of the material can save the child and the child's family a great deal of heartache and tears the night before.

A good strategy is to try to make the accommodations universal and available to all students, so that the child with SPD does not feel isolated and less capable than the other students. At the outset of each project, assignment, or piece of homework, think about at least two different ways of teaching the material and allowing the students to demonstrate their knowledge.

Allow movement. When and if possible, allow students with SPD to move, stretch, and use their bodies. Movement "wakes up" the body and the senses. It is organizing for the senses, energizing, and improves attention and arousal. This is true of and beneficial for all students, not just those with SPD. Movement does not necessarily mean disruptive activities within the classroom, rather having natural opportunities built into the day to allow students to get out of their chairs and not remain sedentary for long periods of time. The idea that "good" students sit at their desks quietly and pay attention all day is preposterous, and needs revisiting.

Begin with taking a close look at your classroom setup. If possible, provide enough space for all students to be able to stretch their arms and legs about their desk without impinging on another student's space. Similarly, a student should be able to stretch his shoulders and tilt his head without ending up in another student's face.

Set up common classroom supplies, such as an electric sharpener, a box of tissues, a calendar, and so on to provide opportunities for students to get up to access these items. If possible, provide a space, such as a book corner, for the students to sit on the floor for certain activities.

With permission from his or her parents, ask the student with SPD to help push, pull, or move light furniture and objects in the classroom. This provides proprioceptive input to their muscles and joints. The proprioceptive system, again, refers to components of muscles and joints that give us an awareness of body position and allows us to monitor and adjust our bodies in relation to objects. For example, this system provides the body with signals to allow us to take smooth steps on the street, manipulate bumps as needed, step off a curb effortlessly, and sit in a chair properly. In addition, helping the teacher move objects boosts a child's self-esteem by being useful to the teacher and demonstrating physical strength.

Monitor yourself when directing kids to sit up and keep still. Again, despite our old-fashioned ideas about attention, sitting quietly in the same position does not necessarily facilitate learning. In fact, many individuals, both children and adults, learn and work better and are more productive with some background noise or while moving around.

Do not take away recess or break time because a child misbehaves in your classroom. This is a mistake that leads to further problems in the classroom, and in fact, feeds into the very issue you're trying to address. As we know, for a consequence to be most effective, it would have to be directly related to the unwanted behavior. For example, if students leave the reading area messy, it is more effective to take away their classroom library privileges for a day or two than to take away recess. Here, students understand the natural consequence of their behavior, the true cause and effect, in a way that makes sense.

The previous suggestions are examples of ways to provide natural opportunities for movement within the classroom. However, clearly, not all of them can be implemented in every classroom, given each school's limitations and boundaries. Teachers, as always, need to be creative and think about unconventional ways to accommodate their students.

Use humor, allow healthy humor, and have fun. It is no mystery that when used appropriately, laughter and humor can almost immediately lighten up the mood, relax a tense moment, and reduce stress, anxiety, and frustration. This is an amazingly helpful tool that can diffuse a potentially embarrassing, stressful, or explosive situation rather quickly.

In this case, humor works best when it is generalized or when you joke about yourself to make a point. For example, when you observe a child struggling to manipulate a pair of scissors, make a lighthearted comment about how it can be frustrating for anyone or how sometimes the same thing happens to you. Be genuine, and treat the child in an age-appropriate manner. Older students are especially sensitive to comments and treatment they consider "babyish," so be especially mindful of your tone of voice and the words you use with them.

Be cognizant of the classroom noise level, your own volume, lighting, environmental odors, and others' proximity to a child with SPD. The importance of this recommendation may be best understood by individuals who have severe migraine headaches that last for days. As they will tell you, during those days, people with migraine headaches are overresponsive to any stimuli to which others are oblivious. It feels as though all their senses are heightened, and their nervous systems are on high alert.

You may know of people who turn off all the lights in their room or turn down the ringer on their phone, or who cannot tolerate being around perfumes or certain foods. This is how many children with SPD feel on a daily basis.

For children with SPD, most incoming sensory messages are amplified and feel harsh, intrusive, and overwhelming. Despite this, these children have to get through the day at school, at home, and in the community. What is remarkable is that small and seemingly minor changes can make a huge difference in the daily lives of these children. Consider these ten recommendations to address sensory input in the classroom:

Be cognizant of your volume. Keep in mind that the teacher's volume can set the tone for the classroom, and that students would have to quiet down to hear a quieter voice.

Be aware of everyday objects that can make noise in the classroom, and adjust them. For example, if possible, fix a squeaky window, replace an older classroom pencil sharpener with a newer, quieter model, and lower the ringer volume on the classroom phone. You can install sound-reducing boards, usually made of dense cork or foam, on walls to reduce excessive noise. This is especially helpful if you share a wall with another classroom.

Install dimmers on light switches to control the amount of lighting in the classroom. Most kids with SPD prefer incandescent lights to fluorescent, due to a buzzing sound they hear from fluorescent lights.

Install shades or drapes on classroom windows.

Use white dry erase marker boards instead of traditional chalkboards.

For quiet activities, consider playing some form of relaxing, neutral music in the background.

Provide earplugs for students with SPD and any student with reduced attention capabilities.

Create one or two individual workstations that face the wall as additional options for those who need a little more separation.

If your classroom is near the school cafeteria or kitchen, keep in mind that certain odors can be noxious to some children with SPD. Think of any other space away from the kitchen that may be a viable option for the child.

Making all the above changes is likely not possible for most classrooms. Many factors, such as the classroom budget, available space, and physical setup of the classroom play a decisive role in this matter. The point to take away from this discussion, however, is to be aware of these issues and to address any that may be possible, given your specific set of circumstances.

On a final note, be aware of your bodily proximity to a child with SPD, and that of others. Respect his or her bodily space and be aware that for some, even a seemingly gentle touch may feel harsh. In addition, practice not getting the child's attention by tapping him or her from behind. Many children with SPD are hypervigilant and experience unexpected physical contact as a threat to their bodies. Along the same lines, consider the setup of your classroom and decide whether there is comfortable space between the students' chairs and desks, which prevents most accidental body contact and the possibility of bumping into furniture.

Give simple, precise directions, and break tasks down into smaller steps. Do you recall what a 6th-grade-math word problem sounds like? Have those of you who do not teach math ever read one and said to yourself, "Huh?" If you have experienced this difficulty, you are not alone.

Do not make your directions into math word problems. Use simple, multistep directions that break the task down into smaller, more manageable components. Speak the directions and write them on the chalkboard or on paper as a reference for all students. Remember, the simple way is the best way.

If there are many steps, ease any anticipated confusion of the students by saying something to the effect that, "I know this is a lot," or "this can be confusing," and offer students an opportunity to ask questions. One caveat—due to their levels of anxiety, most students with SPD may need a separate time of the day or class to clarify any confusion they may have.

Recommendations for
Physical Education Class

It is perhaps obvious, but certainly worth a reminder, that children and adolescents with SPD often find most physical activities, including physical education classes, challenging. In fact, for many students with SPD, this class poses more difficulty than any of their academic classes.

One can guess about the reasons why the above statements may be true, but let us consider all the elements, skills, and innate qualities that go into successful participation in gym class.

Remember what a typical school gymnasium looks, feels, sounds, and smells like? Many school gyms are big, colorful, loud, smelly, and have unpadded floors and walls that echo any sound. Based on what we have discussed so far, it is basically a nightmare for children with SPD to have to spend 3 hours a week in the gym. This is sensory overload at its worst.

Here are some suggestions for successfully including children with SPD in physical education classes:

Shorten the classes or build in break times that allow a student with SPD to leave the gym for 5-minute periods.

Place students into smaller groups, and limit the number of participants in each group.

Establish clear physical boundaries. Visual guidelines are always helpful. It can be useful to indicate, for example, what the perimeters of the play space are, or where each player should stand.

Concentrate on one skill at a time.

If possible, assign staff to fill highly coveted positions. If, by chance, a student with SPD who has poor muscle tone or fine motor skills is assigned to a critical position on the team, this may create a great deal of anxiety and pressure for that student. It may also lead to pressure and blame by other students who just want to win.

Explain the rules clearly, repeat them, and ask students to repeat the rules. Make sure they understand why each rule is important.

Do not call attention to every rule infraction, especially overtly. Take special care not to embarrass students with less-developed skills by pointing out their weakness or mistakes in front of all students. Be aware of more athletic students making unkind comments, as well.

Modify the game as necessary; remember that not all participants are at the same level.

Make plans, but be flexible. A "lesson plan" or game plan is only successful if it works.

Remember the group activity is for *all* the students, and the students only (not the teacher).

Lastly, the students look to you to gauge how the game is going. Have fun—it's only a game.

7

THE DIFFERENCE BETWEEN SPD AND LOOK-ALIKE DISORDERS

Several disorders share similar features and symptoms with those in SPD. The overlap of these symptoms makes deriving the correct diagnosis a challenging task that requires a certain level of expertise and attention.

There are children who appear to only have SPD. On the other hand, there are children who have SPD as well as a psychiatric and/or developmental disorder, such as attention-deficit/hyperactivity disorder, learning disorder, a pervasive developmental disorder such as autism or Asperger syndrome, nonverbal learning disorder, and obsessive compulsive disorder. In these children, SPD can amplify and exacerbate their primary condition.

Keep in mind that SPD occurs in varying degrees, from very mild symptoms in some otherwise typically developing children to severe symptoms in children with autism, for instance. In the following section, I discuss a number of psychiatric and developmental disorders in greater detail to provide you with a better understanding of how two disorders, SPD and another disorder, can simultaneously affect a child and his or her behavior. I'll also go over some overlapping symptoms.

The following descriptions and essential diagnostic features of the disorders mentioned previously are based on the guidelines provided by the *Diagnostic and Statistical Manual of Mental Disorders*, fourth edition. Individuals with these disorders have symptoms that mimic SPD more than other psychiatric disorders.

As you read through the descriptions, note that a symptom does not necessarily constitute a syndrome. Symptoms are basically the signs of an illness that are observed by patients, the people around them, and a physician. They are also the complaints of the patient that are usually noted in the "chief complaint" section of the patient's history. A syndrome, on the other hand, is a collection and group of signs and symptoms that together form an entity. For example, autism is a syndrome, while a failure to develop age-appropriate peer relationships is a symptom of autism. An accurate diagnosis can only be assigned by a trained specialist, who also gathers input from a child's parents and from all service and care providers involved.

Pervasive Developmental Disorders

There are five categories under the heading of pervasive developmental disorders in the *Diagnostic and Statistical Manual of Mental Disorders.* These are:

Autism

Rett syndrome

Childhood disintegrative disorder

Asperger syndrome

Pervasive developmental disorder not otherwise specified

Those with a pervasive developmental disorder are markedly impaired in the areas of reciprocal social

interaction and verbal and/or nonverbal communication. They exhibit stereotyped (repetitive) behavior and
have stereotyped interests and activities. These may
include an intense interest in specific topics, such as
trains, dinosaurs, maps, or computer games. In addition,
all the disorders in this category usually appear in the
first years of life and are typically associated with mental
retardation.

It is important to say a word or two about pervasive
developmental disorder that is not otherwise specified,
since it is a diagnosis and a term that is used more and
more in the field. Here, the impairments mentioned previously are observed; however, the diagnostic criteria for
autism, in which the symptoms may have begun at a later
age, may occur in milder forms or atypically, or both.

The first clinical example in chapter 3 of this book, that
of Samantha, is an example of a child with difficulties in
various areas of development who received a diagnosis
of pervasive developmental disorder of a not-otherwise-
specified type.

Autism

Those with autism find social interaction difficult, including forming and sustaining appropriate peer relationships. Their language development is often delayed, or,
with young children, they are unable to engage in make-
believe play and activities. Finally, they often display
stereotyped patterns of behavior, such as odd motor mannerisms or very narrow and specific interests.

Autism is a biological and neurological disorder
involving the brain and its various functions and prop-
erties. Often there are clinically significant associated
medical and/or genetic disorders that are present in
individuals with autism, including mental retardation,
epilepsy, chromosomal abnormalities, and structural

brain abnormalities. In addition, there may be conditions that occur along with autism, such as aggressive behaviors, temper tantrums, self-injurious behaviors, and psychiatric problems, such as mood instability or seizure disorder.

An important feature and component of autism is an individual's difficulty with sensory processing. Although there is a limited body of research on this topic at present, anecdotal data and small studies show that more than half of children with autism have clinically significant symptoms of SPD. However, the reverse does not seem to hold true. SPD and autism can overlap as co-occurring conditions, SPD can exist without autism, and autism can occur without SPD.

Often, individuals with autism struggle with various sensory functions, as well as emotional regulation. These individuals also seem to demonstrate clinically significant impairment in the areas of social interaction, affiliation, and functioning; spoken and nonverbal language; and restricted patterns of interest.

Although these sensory processing difficulties are not included in the *Diagnostic and Statistical Manual of Mental Disorders* diagnostic criteria for autism, they are recognized as an area of impairment. They are listed under "Associated Features and Disorders" as "odd responses to sensory stimuli" (page 72). This recognition exists even more strongly among parents, teachers, and clinicians who witness the child's struggles with processing sensations and the way in which it affects his or her day-to-day functioning. Thus, the question is not whether sensory processing issues affect children with autism, but rather, what interventions and services can we provide to assist children in dealing with these difficulties.

Many screening tools used to assess autism include questions about sensory processing difficulties. One such tool is the Modified Checklist for Autism in Toddlers, or

M-CHAT, a parent-report questionnaire used with children aged 18–24 months that contains 23 yes-or-no questions. This tool includes questions about the child's motor abilities and responses to sound and noise.

Asperger Syndrome

Asperger syndrome was first described by Hans Asperger in 1944 on the basis of a small sample of four girls, aged 6–11, all of whom had good language and cognitive skills but had motor weaknesses, circumscribed interests, and a paternal history of similar problems.

Today, to meet the *Diagnostic and Statistical Manual of Mental Disorders* criteria for Asperger syndrome, individuals must have impaired social skills, such as difficulty establishing and maintaining peer relationships, difficulty with emotional reciprocity or emotional give-and-take, an unawareness of others' feelings, and problems with social pragmatics. (Social pragmatics is basically the social use of verbal and nonverbal language skills to communicate with others in various social settings.) Restricted and stereotyped patterns of interest, inflexibility in thinking and routines, and odd motor mannerisms are also observed. Individuals with Asperger syndrome have substantial difficulties in social, academic, community-oriented, and occupational functioning. On the other hand, they have no difficulty with daily living skills, self-care, and cognitive skills, and display normal curiosity about their environment.

The most highly affected area of difficulty for individuals with Asperger syndrome is that of appropriate social skills, peer relations, and social functioning. However, the ineffective processing of sensory information not only contributes to and amplifies these social issues, but it may also lead to behavioral problems. Children with Asperger syndrome may have behavioral problems because of their vulnerability to anxiety, poor coordination (particularly in sports), and problems handling sensory information. Some conditions that may trigger behavioral issues include stress (perceived or real), anxiety (general or specific), sensory overstimulation, excitement, fatigue, interruption of a desired activity, fear of failure, and fine motor weakness (which may lead to frustration). A behavioral problem may also result from requiring a child to multitask or not providing ample time to process incoming information.

For children with Asperger syndrome, sensory integration therapy—including an individualized sensory diet—is crucial to improving their functioning and attention, reducing anxiety levels, boosting motor skills, and improving the likelihood of social success.

Compared with their autistic peers, children and adolescents with Asperger syndrome generally function better socially and have higher cognitive and language skills. Therefore, they can take charge of the sensory breaks throughout the school day that can make a substantial difference in their academic and social success. They can either set preplanned and specific times for these short breaks or take them on an as-needed basis. This is an adaptive way of dealing with sensory overload or sensory understimulation in advance and in a socially acceptable way. Sensory integration intervention not only gives control to children who have the verbal and cognitive abilities to know and determine when they need a break, but is also discreet. It is less socially odd and noticeable than asking a teacher repeatedly to take a break or, even worse, to run out, act out, or lose control in front of peers.

Creating an individualized sensory diet that includes regular sensory breaks will allow children and adolescents with Asperger syndrome to reorganize, regulate, and effectively modulate their senses so that they can be more productive, attentive, and successful at school, at home, and in the community.

Nonverbal Learning Disorder

Nonverbal learning disorder, or NLD, is a neurological syndrome thought to relate to white matter dysfunction in the right hemisphere of the brain. It refers to a pattern of strengths and weaknesses in a person's cognitive functioning.

Simply put, NLD involves dysfunction in how a person's brain is wired. This atypical wiring can cause a person to be very good at certain tasks, such as verbal expression abilities, attention to details, and rote memory, but have great difficulty with reading comprehension, math, motor functioning, and abstract tasks.

Functionally, the individual with NLD has great difficulty integrating incoming information and experiences, making sense of them, and making accurate and helpful inferences. For example, a child might just pick up bits and pieces of information and miss the big picture. Social functioning and peer relations are perhaps the most adversely affected areas of functioning in NLD. Children with NLD typically play with either much older or much younger kids. They may be very naïve and gullible, may appear odd, seem anxious and isolated, and have difficulty with control and modulation of affect.

Children with NLD have a particularly difficult time understanding, interpreting, and responding to nonverbal cues. Therefore, because they cannot draw on past experiences and have the benefit of that bank of information, many experiences feel new to them. This is perhaps the reason for the high level of anxiety observed and reported in kids with NLD.

For example, a child with SPD may experience an equal or even higher level of anxiety than a child with NLD before going to a birthday party. Each might worry about unknown and unpredictable aspects of the party. For example, what do I do when I first get there, what do

I do with my gift, who do I say hello to, what if the person who opens the door is not from my class, and such. This child has substantial difficulty drawing on past experiences of a similar nature and applying those learned skills and social knowledge to a situation that is not exactly the same.

Imagine the combination of going to work every day and feeling like you are going through your first day of work. Imagine your level of anxiety and stress. Think what it would be like not to be able to draw on your past experiences to help you get through the day. In addition, picture not being able to read and benefit from nonverbal cues in communication to interpret social interactions. This combination of difficulties would probably drain every ounce of your energy to get through the day.

Other areas of difficulty in NLD include weaknesses in social perception, psychomotor coordination and motor learning, balance, visuospatial perception and organization, visual discrimination, reduced attention, spatial orientation, difficulty with dealing with novelty, and an overreliance on literal language. However, the area of dysfunction that is most relevant to this book is that of sensory processing difficulties. SPD underlies many of the weaknesses of a child with NLD and is a real, substantial, and debilitating deficit.

For children with NLD an individualized sensory integration therapy program can be helpful and beneficial. When recommendations are made for occupational therapy services, it is indicated that the child will receive not only traditional therapy services to strengthen fine motor skills, as in handwriting and fastening fasteners, but specific sensory integration therapy, too.

Children with NLD have a number of strengths that must be identified, noted to them, and built on. Some of these strengths include good cognitive skills, simple motor skills, rote verbal memory and storage, verbal output, and auditory perception, attention, and memory. Knowing these strengths, particularly in an academic setting, can facilitate learning and boost the child's confidence in his or her own ability to learn various academic skills.

One last point about NLD that is worth mentioning is that it is currently not included in the *Diagnostic and Statistical Manual of Mental Disorders*. Clinicians have commonly categorized NLD under the learning disorders umbrella for the purposes of treatment delivery. In most cases, a diagnosis of NLD in and of itself does not necessarily render a student eligible for special education services, unless it co-occurs with an eligible condition.

The Learning Disorders

Children can receive a diagnosis of a learning disorder or a learning disability when their academic performance falls significantly below the expected level, given their age, grade, and level of cognitive skills and intelligence. On the basis of the *Diagnostic and Statistical Manual of Mental Disorders*, learning disorders include:

Reading disorder

Mathematics disorder

Disorder of written expression

Learning disorder not otherwise specified

Simply put, a learning disorder interferes with a child's ability to perform and learn arithmetic, reading, and writing, and may even cause problems in all of these three areas. In addition, as one might expect, learning disorders also interfere with any of the activities of daily living that require reading, writing, and arithmetic.

In the event of a reading disorder, on standardized reading tests the student's reading accuracy or comprehension is significantly below the expected level and interferes with his or her expected level of academic achievement. (In general, all diagnoses are assigned by using standardized measures.) Dyslexia is a common form of difficulty in reading, writing, and spelling. A child's struggles in these areas exist despite his or her good efforts, motivation to learn, and cognitive abilities.

In mathematics disorder, the child's mathematical ability is substantially below the expected level in calculation/numerical operations or math reasoning (using graphs, charts, tables, and such to draw out and reach conclusions and information). Here too, the difficulties must be pronounced enough to interfere with the child's expected academic achievement. Also, these problems interfere with activities of daily living that require math abilities, such as calculating prices, distance, percentages, and discounts.

With regard to a disorder of written expression, the focus of concern is the child's writing skills and performance on functional assessments of writing abilities. Poor handwriting or copying ability is often observed in children with this disorder as soon as they begin elementary school, and the disorder itself is often apparent by the 2nd grade. Similar to the diagnostic criteria for reading and arithmetic disorders, writing performance on standardized tests is important, as is the assessment process. Significant interference with academic achievement and performing activities of daily living that involve writing must also be considered.

In all of these cases, if a child has a sensory deficit and weakness, then the problems with reading, writing, and math learning must occur independently of those usually associated with sensory deficit. In other words, the learning problems must stand on their own.

Similar to pervasive developmental disorder not otherwise specified, learning disorder not otherwise specified is a diagnosis assigned when problems with reading, writing, and mathematics do not meet the diagnostic criteria for any one specific subtype, but difficulties in all three areas together are pronounced enough to interfere with the child's academic performance.

Given the fact that low self-esteem, school dropout, sadness, feelings of isolation and defeat, demoralization, and heightened social problems go hand in hand with learning disorders, the presence of sensory processing difficulties can only exacerbate all the other issues. We know that SPD may affect visual, auditory, motor, attention, alertness, and processing abilities of a child, making it difficult to access and benefit from an individualized education program. If students with a learning disability also have SPD, their education team must ensure appropriate sensory integration therapy as an integral part of treatment delivery. In such cases, math tutoring or working with a reading specialist alone would not treat the whole child.

Many of our senses, such as visual, auditory, and motor senses, are involved in learning and academic achievement. All of the above disorders of learning require multisensory processing and functioning. As such, any proposed intervention and/or treatment plan must focus on strengthening, integrating, treating, and addressing all of the senses to be effective.

Attention-Deficit/Hyperactivity Disorder and Disruptive Behavior Disorders

Approximately 3% to 7% of school-aged children have attention-deficit/hyperactivity disorder, or ADHD, according to the *Diagnostic and Statistical Manual of Mental Disorders*. In most cases, parents of toddlers initially observe excessive motor activity, though not all children go on to develop ADHD.

There are three subtypes of ADHD:

ADHD, combined type (the most common type), where symptoms of inattention, hyperactivity, and impulsivity occur

ADHD, predominantly inattentive type, if more symptoms of inattention than hyperactivity and impulsivity occur

ADHD, predominantly hyperactive-impulsive type, when there are fewer symptoms of inattention; impairments from the symptoms of inattention, hyperactivity, and impulsivity must be present in two or more settings, such as at home and at school

The main feature of ADHD is the child's marked difficulty focusing on the task at hand, hyperactivity, and/or impulsiveness. Some of the symptoms may have been reported prior to age 7, although most cases of the predominantly inattentive type of ADHD are often diagnosed later.

Forming the correct diagnosis is critical in creating an effective treatment plan for ADHD, as the treatment is different from that of SPD. To better clarify and distinguish between the two, consider the symptoms of ADHD as described in the *Diagnostic and Statistical Manual of Mental Disorders.* With regard to the symptoms of inattention, some of the following may be present:

The child frequently has difficulty focusing on a given task, such as sustaining attention to required details.

The child tends to make careless errors when doing tasks and projects such as homework and tests.

The child may seem as though he is not paying attention or following the speaker when spoken to.

The child may have a hard time filtering out extraneous stimuli and is distracted by them.

The child may lose things or seem unorganized.

The child may have a difficult time following instructions, which may lead to an inability to complete a given assignment or project.

With regard to the symptoms of hyperactivity-impulsivity, some of the following symptoms may be observed:

The child struggles with having to sit for a given period of time. She fidgets, moves, and changes position frequently and may look like she is falling out of her chair. In her struggle to remain seated, she may give up and leave her seat for various reasons, even though there is a clear expectation for her to remain seated.

In younger children especially, there may be a "maladaptive" and excessive amount of climbing, moving about, and running—these children may look like the "Energizer bunny" and be able to keep going without needing to stop, as though they are "driven by a motor." The child seems as though she cannot stop talking.

The symptom of impulsivity encompasses behavioral symptoms often associated with impulsive individuals; he or she has an overall difficulty with controlling responses and output, either verbal or physical, or both. A child may have a hard time waiting for his turn in play, conversation, and other interactions; he does not give the speaker ample time to finish a question before blurting out an answer; and he has problems with interrupting others' social interactions, such as conversations, games, and activities.

Individual Treatment for Similar Symptoms

The behavioral manifestations of SPD can be similar to those observed in ADHD. Behaviorally, the two disorders do indeed look alike. However, the reasons for the behaviors differ, and so should the treatment.

Some children may have just SPD or just ADHD, but some children may have both. A single symptom does not make a syndrome, and does not necessarily lead to a diagnosis. SPD can be present alone, can co-occur with another disorder, or can be a component of another problem.

As we have seen throughout this book, the hallmark of SPD is a markedly atypical, abnormal, or impaired ability to adjust to incoming stimuli from the senses and perform sensory discrimination, sensory regulation, and sensory-based motor activities. As with any disorder, the frequency of occurrence, duration, and intensity are important factors to consider. These factors determine the effect of the disorder on the child's level of functioning, as well as the level of impairment.

As far as the distinction between SPD and other disorders is concerned, consider the child's reactions and responses to sensory input. In particular, pay close attention to the child's responses to touch and movement. In general, a child with SPD will have unusual and unexpected responses to sensations of touch, sound, smell, odor, and movement. While a child with ADHD may be distracted by noises outside the classroom, a child with SPD seems pained, uncomfortable, and truly uneasy when a loud sound occurs nearby. Children with ADHD will also eventually get used to various sensations and sensory input. On the other hand, without proper intervention and treatment, most children with SPD will not habituate, get used to, or react normally to sensory input. Clearly, the severity of SPD will make a difference in the severity of a child's responses.

The area of motor functioning may be helpful in making the distinction between SPD and ADHD, as well. Most children with SPD have clinically significant weaknesses in motor coordination, balance, and movement. The opposite is true for most children with ADHD. As was mentioned in the diagnostic criteria in ADHD, children with this disorder are on the move and love to climb, run, jump, and engage in physical activities.

Once the correct diagnosis is established, appropriate intervention must be put in place. It is a well-established fact in the field of psychopharmacology that most children with ADHD benefit from a class of drugs called psychostimulants. An example of such medicine is methylphenidate, or Ritalin. In addition to pharmacotherapy, behavioral interventions have proven an effective treatment modality for children with ADHD. A child with SPD alone will not respond to such interventions. For children with SPD, a regular and tailored sensory integration therapy program continues to be the best course of treatment and produces the most favorable outcome.

WHEN YOUR CHILD IS EVALUATED—TIPS FOR PARENTS

The following are tips and suggestions that may be helpful as children go through a neuropsychological evaluation to arrive at a diagnosis, to clarify a diagnosis in light of their symptoms, or to get a sense for what they can and can't do on their own and what they may require help and support with.

Also, after an SPD evaluation is done, a family may wish to add a neuropsychological assessment to make sure the child is performing at the expected level in all other areas of functioning and to address additional concerns or problems.

As a starting point, it may be easier to get a referral and reimbursement for a neuropsychological evaluation than an occupational therapy evaluation. Please be sure to let the psychologist know all of your sensory-related concerns so that he or she can, at the very least, do a screening for SPD.

Since SPD can affect most aspects of a child's life, including learning and social-emotional functioning, it is helpful to have a neuropsychological assessment in conjunction with a sensory processing evaluation. This is particularly true if there is diagnostic uncertainty and can be tremendously useful in developing a well-rounded treatment or service delivery plan.

Parents need to know that, at this point in time, most insurance companies consider a neuropsychological evaluation a medical necessity and, therefore, will provide some coverage of the cost of the evaluation. Check with your insurance carrier to determine what your specific coverage is for this service. Also, please note that with certain plans, a referral may be required from your child's pediatrician.

If you must choose a clinician from your panel of providers, make sure you get the names of a few, so you can interview them to determine if they're a good fit for you and your child. Once the initial, expected rapport-building period is over, your child should feel fairly comfortable with his or her evaluator.

Talk to other families you know who have had such evaluations done. A referral from another family speaks volumes to the work of the clinician.

Talk to your school staff, especially the school counselor and/or school psychologist. They receive and review several reports from the school every year and talk to families who provide information and feedback about their experiences.

Although most neuropsychologists would want to meet with you first, please make sure that this step is not skipped in the interest of "getting your child in quickly." Talking without your child in the room, particularly prior to the first appointment with your child, will provide the opportunity for you to speak with the evaluator openly regarding your concerns. It is also usually during this meeting that the clinician takes a thorough history and explains the evaluation process.

Be honest with the evaluator. It is important that you are forthcoming about such questions as family history of medical and psychiatric issues, ongoing couple and/or marital conflicts, any significant and recent changes, and any previous testing and records. Revelations that may be painful or embarrassing (such as those about the child's behavior or other family members' quirkiness, etc) will be totally confidential. Aunt Sally's nymphomania and Cousin Billy's picky eating and the child's frequent foamy bowel movements are all pieces of the puzzle. Talk about stuff like this, because it matters!

In the case of divorced, blended, or multiple–care-provider families, it is important that all the caregivers form a united front in this process, especially when filling out forms, providing history, and talking to the child.

A neuropsychological evaluation contains information on family history, as well as your child's developmental history. In preparation for this, consult your child's baby book, first photo album, early videos, and other family members.

Learn about what the testing process will be like, and explain it in simple language to your child ahead of time. Try to answer any questions as best as you can. Do not put pressure on your child to "do well," since the last thing you want is for your child to develop test anxiety.

At the time of testing, do not be surprised if you are asked to wait outside while your child is being tested. Except in very special cases and with very young children, children will work one-on-one with the evaluator.

Be sure to bring in drinks, a snack, and food for your child, since the evaluation can take a day or two and require long stretches of time. This is particularly important for children with various food allergies.

Bring in items from your child's sensory diet list, if you have one, or just a couple of small, calming, favorite items to be used during break times. Bring books, puzzles, and toys, too.

Once the results are ready, you will meet with the evaluator to review the findings. Take paper and a pencil with you and write down any information you need—don't trust your memory! This meeting can feel overwhelming, so don't hesitate to jot down information and ask questions.

At some point during the process, the evaluator will provide feedback to your child about his or her performance and the findings of the assessment, as appropriate to the child's age and developmental level. However, be prepared to talk to your child about the findings of the evaluation, and ask for suggestions on how to phrase things from the clinician.

Share the results with those involved in your child's care, including teachers, school counselors, other specialists (such as occupational or speech therapists), and your child's pediatrician.

Children with Bipolar Disorder

Mood disorders typically encompass feelings of depression, mood swings, and mania (elation and giddiness), and cause pronounced mood shifts and changes. The main feature of a mood disorder is a mood disturbance. The two most widely known categories of mood disorders are depressive disorder and bipolar disorder. We'll focus specifically on bipolar disorder and any overlapping or similar symptoms to that of ADHD and SPD.

The essential feature of bipolar disorder is one or more manic episodes, during which the individual may experience distractibility, increased motor activity, hyperactivity, and psychomotor agitation, impulsivity, racing thoughts, inattention, a pressure to talk excessively, a decreased need for sleep, and an inflated self-esteem. The depressive symptoms, on the other hand, include sadness; a decreased interest in most activities; insomnia; a feeling of worthlessness; reduced motor activity or restlessness; an inability to think clearly, pay attention, and concentrate; and finally, feelings of suicide.

There is an overlap of some symptoms of SPD, ADHD, and mood disorders. Some of these include poor attention, "zoning out" or not being able to listen; poor organization; inability to keep up with various tasks; atypical motor activity and ability; distractibility; sensitivity to sensory stimuli; problems with sleep and eating; difficulties with social functioning, social skills, and peer relationships; and poor self-esteem.

However, treatment differs on the basis of an individual's primary condition and symptoms. In ADHD, the treatment goal is to help the child slow down, reduce impulsive behaviors, and concentrate. In bipolar disorder, treatment focuses on helping children mange their moods, so that the shifts from normal to elated and giddy, to sadness, depression, and suicidal thoughts, are reduced. In

SPD, on the other hand, the treatment goal is to help the child to modulate, regulate, and integrate all sensory input through sensory integration therapy.

How Behavioral Challenges Play a Role

Many children with SPD have behavioral challenges and difficulties. If that is indeed what is going on with the child—that is, if SPD is the cause of the behavioral problems—it is of crucial importance to determine and recognize this matter. As has been mentioned in other parts of this book, to mislabel a child with SPD as a "behavioral" child is a great disservice that can have terrible future implications. It may be worth stating the obvious, that most children with behavioral issues do not have SPD. As we have seen with other disorders discussed in this chapter, arriving at the correct diagnosis is imperative in determining the most effective course of treatment.

Again, the most effective treatment for SPD continues to be sensory integration therapy and using an individualized sensory diet, assigned by a trained occupational therapist. On the other hand, treatments for behavior problems vary, from such simple methods as giving the child a "time out" to limit setting, anger management, coping skills training, and, in some cases, medication.

It is only through a thorough functional behavioral assessment that unwanted and challenging behaviors can be addressed. Once this has been accomplished, an effective behavior plan may be developed. This method can be relevant and useful for typically developing children, those with developmental disorders or psychiatric disorders, and children with SPD.

Many clinicians prefer using functional behavioral assessments, since they can be used with any age group, from toddlers to adults. The one point that is certainly worth repeating in this chapter is that due to overwhelming supportive research on functional behavioral assessments, public schools in the United States are legally obligated and mandated to conduct this type of assessment of a child's behavior when creating a treatment plan and addressing behavioral problems (Individuals with Disabilities Education Act, 2004).

Parents of children with any of the previously described disorders should communicate and collaborate with their child's service providers, clinicians, and school staff to determine whether conducting a functional behavioral assessment would benefit the child's treatment plan.

The following is a sample neuropsychological evaluation of a 6-year-old child who was referred for symptoms of difficulty with mood regulation, sensory processing difficulties, behavioral challenges, and ADHD-like behaviors. The task here was to tease out exactly what was causing this child's behavioral problems—in other words, what syndrome(s) was producing the reported symptoms in the child.

This particular case example shows that the referral symptoms can be a part of any number of disorders. Note that neuropsychological evaluations and reports come in various styles and may have different formats, involve the use of different assessment tools and methods, have different lengths in terms of number of pages, and have different headings, depending on the clinician's style.

Case Study

EMILY, AGE 6—MOOD INSTABILITY

Emily was referred by her parents for neuropsychological evaluation. They described her as an active, inquisitive, and friendly girl, but were concerned by behavioral and psychological difficulties. The most prominent of her recent and current difficulties was the instability of her mood, which ranged from flat to elated to sad to unusually excited.

"Her moods are so intense, it's hard to deal with them," her parents said.

In addition to her increasingly defiant behavior, Emily had been having greater difficulty controlling and managing her mood and emotional reactions, which sometimes escalated into temper tantrums. Emily was not always "tuned into others," or did not listen to them. During these times, she exhibited poor attention and concentration and appeared distracted. Further impeding her social functioning was her impulsivity and tendency to interrupt others and speak so rapidly that her ideas could not be fully expressed. Her thoughts seemed to be racing, and her parents reported that "she couldn't stop talking." She also lacked organizational skills.

Emily had trouble going to sleep and remaining asleep, and told her parents that sometimes a voice spoke to her, telling her what to do and frightening her. She awakened frequently with nightmares and asked to sleep in her parents' room. She was sensitive to some sensory stimuli, such as bright lights and unexpected touch. At times she said she felt sad, had trouble eating, and had poor relationships with children her age.

A Paternal History of Mental Illness

An only child, Emily lived with both her parents. In terms of family history, there was no clinically significant psychiatric or developmental health issue on her mother's side, except for Emily's aunt, who had dyslexia.

However, there was a history of psychiatric problems in two of Emily's paternal aunts, who had depression and bipolar disorder, respectively. Her great paternal aunt was also reported to have had major depressive disorder. In addition, her great paternal uncle had schizophrenia. (Note: Obtaining an accurate and detailed family history is important, since many psychiatric disorders, such as depression and schizophrenia, are now thought to have a genetic component and run in the family.)

Adaptive Behaviors

Emily completed kindergarten, and her parents reported that she was active, inquisitive, and social. She initiated conversations easily with peers and adults. Outside of her home, she was friendly and understood the necessity of social manners. Full of affection, she enjoyed giving hugs and kisses and snuggling on the sofa. This was especially true when she initiated physical contact.

When speaking and socializing, Emily tended to express much emotion. She enjoyed talking with her parents, dancing, climbing, singing, role-playing, cooking, reading, drawing, listening to music, watching movies, and playing with a variety of toys, including video games. Emily participated in weekly gymnastics and swimming lessons and had expressed interest in learning to play the drums.

Her day care and kindergarten teachers said that she generally behaved well at school. However, at times, she had difficulty with tasks that required sustained attention and organization. Her teachers reportedly spoke of her desire to read and her motivation in completing assignments. On occasion, Emily would report being bored in school and attempt to stay home by claiming she was ill or needed more sleep. Once at school, she would cooperate with both work and play. Teachers' verbal and written reports indicated her occasional refusal to do required tasks and activities.

Disconcerting Behaviors—Defiance, Temper Tantrums, and Anxiety

Emily's parents reported her resistance to complying with requests, as well as arguing with family members and sometimes teachers. She yelled, made excuses for not complying, or ignored or overtly refused requests by proclaiming, "No," or "I am not listening."

Emily had also begun refusing to take responsibility for her mistakes and started shifting blame toward others. She would say, "See what you made me do?" or "It is your fault," or "See, you got me in trouble." Emily talked excessively and provided detailed reasons for why she was not responsible for something that she had done, or why a given mistake was not solely her doing. Nevertheless, Emily's parents also noted that she sometimes apologized of her own accord for various mistakes (such as spilling or dropping something, forgetting to flush the toilet, or not putting away her belongings).

Lately, Emily had thrown more frequent temper tantrums and overreacted in various situations. Her happy and content moods could very quickly shift to anger and upset, prompted by seemingly small details and otherwise normal routines. She reportedly became anxious about various scheduled activities and plans, such as the arrival of her parents or other family members. Requesting that events be marked on the calendar so that she knew when it is happening, Emily had been observed checking and rechecking when the given event (or person) would happen (or arrive). She inquired about details regarding what was going to take place, who was coming, and why, and seemed to take comfort in having this information. Within minutes of initially asking about plans, she tended to ask the same question repeatedly. She would ask questions even if they were already answered, and await a response.

"I Am a Devil"

Emily often had between two and five tantrums in a given day, each lasting between 5 and 15 minutes. During a tantrum, she would cry, clench her fists, growl, yell, make high-pitched screams, bang her head against a pillow or furniture, hit objects, and, at times, hit her parents.

After an episode, Emily typically became calm and sometimes apologized. She then either complied with what had been requested of her or returned to playing as if nothing had happened. In many instances, such as when Emily was not allowed to watch television, she yelled at her parents in an angry tone, which her parents described as a "voice from beyond." She had more recently begun referring to herself as a devil, saying, "I am a devil," or "I am evil." She said this in passing, as well as in moments of anger.

Emily's parents provided the following as an example of an incident that led to a long temper tantrum. In a recent incident, Emily "ordered" her long-time babysitter, who was watching her one afternoon, to take her to a fast-food restaurant. Disregarding the babysitter's explanation of how they were to follow her mother's plans for the day, Emily tried to lock herself in the car. Once at home, Emily told her babysitter not to read the note of instructions left by her mother, and to listen to Emily's instructions instead. Emily grabbed the note out of her babysitter's hand and threw it out. She then proceeded to have a meltdown that involved crying, yelling, and screaming at her babysitter, and throwing her toys and other small objects around.

Frequent Nightmares

Emily began having chronic nightmares shortly before her evaluation, which contributed to her awakening one to three times a night. After a nightmare, Emily typically left her bedroom and slept on a couch or in her parents' bed. She had been disturbed by these nightmares to the extent that her body shook, and to feel safe, she needed her parents to sleep with her. She had difficulty settling down to sleep, which could take 5 to 45 minutes, as well as trouble waking up in the morning.

Further, Emily disliked being in the dark, even when there was enough light to see her surroundings. She wouldn't enter a dark room unaccompanied. If she did, she attempted to turn on the light immediately, but should this fail, she tensed, exhibited a frightened tone, and whined or yelled. She reacted similarly to heights. Emily's parents also reported that when she was out of their sight (or out of the sight of other family members), she called out to them for help, and once they responded, she simply replied, "I love you."

Hearing a Voice

Shortly before her evaluation, Emily began reporting that she heard a voice, both at night when she sleeps and during the day. She had described the voice as having a low tone, at times sounding more like a man.

Nevertheless, Emily had said that the voice was that of a girl, of whom she had drawn a picture for her parents, and who told her frightening things, such as, "Be scared, be afraid, there is a spooky ghost that is going to come get you." The voice had also told Emily to push her friends and "mess up their block towers." Emily claimed she ignored the voice in these instances, recognizing that its orders were morally wrong. Furthermore, Emily claimed to see ghosts of animals, including a horse and a cat.

Rapid Speech and Constant Movement

Emily's rapid cadence of speech could cause her to stutter or lose track of her words and repeat what she had just said. According to her parents, she seemed as though she had too many ideas to convey at a given instance. In her haste to communicate she could become extremely agitated, particularly if she felt unsuccessful at it.

She often needed reminders to slow down and take a minute to consider what she was trying to say. In these verbose moments, Emily could lose her temper if she erroneously perceived others as not giving her their full attention.

Emily's parents described her as "constantly in motion." She exhibited motor movements with her hands and feet that distracted from and disrupted her performance in various activities (such as reading, playing, talking, sitting, eating, and preparing for sleep). Although easily distracted by external stimuli (such as sounds and the activity of others), encouragingly, Emily was still capable of promptly returning to the task in which she was engaged prior to the distraction.

Hard-to-Control Impulses

Emily was often prone to interrupting or intruding on others' conversations. Even after being redirected or asked to wait a moment, she insisted on interrupting and knowing what was being said. Her parents reported that she purposefully stood between others when they were talking and tapped them, even when redirected to wait a moment. Emily was also apt to interrupt those who directly engaged her in conversation.

Emily's impulsivity sometimes manifested in inappropriate ways with family members, such as tapping their breasts or buttocks or making attempts to pull down their pants or the front of their shirts. Emily was also fond of playing jokes on others, such as hiding important objects (like keys or the phone). In one instance, she poured milk on her aunt's head. At times this was done in good fun, but as her parents reported, she could take it to an extreme and could not inhibit or withdraw from her behavior.

SPD Similarities

Some of the problems reported by Emily's parents, particularly those related to her social and emotional functioning, arousal, activity level, attention, sleep problems, and inability to self-regulate and self-soothe, are similar to those seen in children with SPD. Therefore, Emily may benefit from a sensory integration evaluation and respond favorably to a planned and individualized program (a sensory diet) to help her become more regulated, focused, and more attentive (see recommendation 4 at the end of this report).

An Initial Diagnosis

What seemed to have the greatest effect on Emily's learning style and capacity to adapt to life's demands was her apparent difficulty handling her feelings, mood, and emotional responses.

Her unique set of symptoms, history, and problems appear consistent with childhood bipolar disorder. A somewhat classic definition of bipolar disorder in adults would include extreme moods, cycling between a hyperenergized, grandiose, elevated mood and deep depression.

In children, early onset bipolar disorder may cause sudden rage, continual irritability, and talking nonstop very suddenly and without provocation. They may engage in oppositional and dangerous or risky behaviors, such as running into the street.

The depressive stage is usually preceded by a worsening of aggressive and irritable mood, as well as rage. The so-called "aggressive depression" usually happens suddenly and takes parents by surprise. Though there are minimal reports of Emily's strictly depressive behaviors, there are aspects of her reported anxiety that could reflect a depressive tendency. Therefore, Emily's mood in the coming months should be monitored closely, in case of further outbursts or a possible "decline" into depression.

The majority of cases diagnosed with childhood bipolar disorder are also diagnosed with ADHD. However, Emily does not fully meet the criteria for this diagnosis, given her age and idiosyncratic set of symptoms. Emily's current symptoms are most consistent with a mood disorder—formally, mood disorder not otherwise specified. This is a more generalized category and therefore a cautious diagnosis. Mood disorder not otherwise specified emphasizes the need for further evaluation over time to arrive at a more precise diagnosis and avoid potentially false labels.

It will be highly useful for regular communication to occur between home and school to monitor Emily's progress, help build skills, and maintain consistent support. Such communication might be carried out more effectively by arranging for a "service or case manager" to serve as a point person at school.

Immediate Recommendations

In the interest of prompt intervention and services, the following outlined recommendations were presented to Emily's family immediately after the evaluation.

A referral was made for a consultation with a child psychiatrist who specializes in treating young children with mood disorders. (This clinician is also currently providing opportunities for families to participate in various research studies, with close monitoring and evaluation of participants, should the family choose to do so now or at a later time). This is not necessarily a referral to start treatment with psychiatric medication; rather, it is a way to connect the family with a specialist who can become familiar with the family and available to them should the need arise in the future. It is not a good idea to start looking for a specialist in an emergency, since it reduces parents' choices of service providers.

An immediate referral was also made to a child psychologist who specializes in the treatment of young children with mood disorders, ADHD, and behavioral concerns. In this capacity, the clinician can address and work on such concerns as Emily's nightmares, voices that she reports hearing, impulsivity, mood management, temper tantrum reduction, and social skills improvement.

Emily's parents must observe and monitor her behavior closely for any changes, regressions, or new symptoms, and share this information with all service providers.

Emily's parents were encouraged to share the findings of this evaluation with her pediatrician, since that person will coordinate her care through referrals to various specialists and can also consider any relevant medical issues.

Her parents were encouraged to share these results with Emily's clinical and academic team at school, since, at this age, some of the services can be provided through their local school district. Also, she may qualify for special education services under the social/emotional category and thus receive some much-needed special accommodations, including counseling, participation in social pragmatics groups, and occupational therapy.

In view of the present results, the following recommendations were offered as part of Emily's treatment plan to address her educational and therapeutic needs:

Emily's development, symptoms, and progress should continue to be monitored carefully over the next year. A reevaluation, involving a full neuropsychological battery, is recommended in 12–18 months.

Though Emily is quite young to be treated with medication, a consultation with a child psychiatrist, preferably one with a subspecialty in mood disorders, is recommended. Making this connection now ensures the availability of a specialized service provider who is familiar with Emily's history and symptoms, in the event that the need presents itself in the future.

A functional behavioral assessment conducted at school may shed light on some of Emily's problem behaviors in the classroom. The findings of this assessment can be used to create an effective and targeted behavioral intervention plan. In addition, the initial assessment can be used as a baseline tool against which future assessments and progress can be considered and measured.

Given the fact that some of Emily's symptoms are similar to those observed in children with SPD, an evaluation by an occupational therapist who specializes in SPD is recommended. While Emily's primary diagnosis is one of a mood disorder, she can benefit from a setting and approach that can teach her how to calm herself, better control her emotional responses, lower her anxiety, manage sensory input, find ways to regroup when things do not go her way, and learn the skills and develop the tools necessary to help herself in difficult social and emotional times. As such, a preliminary sensory diet, with objects and activities to help with sensory integration, was developed for use while the family awaits an appointment for an evaluation by an occupational therapist.

Emily would benefit from regular weekly meetings and therapy with a child psychologist skilled in play therapy and experienced in working with a young child. This would provide a safe forum for Emily to express herself and her feelings verbally. Emily should also be connected with her school counselor, who can provide a safe haven at school.

Behavioral management at home and at school is recommended to help with impulse control and sustained performance. An example of this would be therapy that focuses on mediating impulses with "stop and think" verbal statements (ie, inhibitory control). Specific tutoring in organization and strategic problem solving may be warranted as Emily progresses in school, to promote a sense of control over her cognitive processing.

Empathy training for Emily is warranted to support her interpersonal development. Children with symptoms of bipolar disorder may often act in self-centered ways, resulting from inner feelings of being out of control and perceiving reality as vague or chaotic. This experience can prompt a child to want to simplify things, reduce unpredictable or novel events, and do things her way. The fostering of empathy (ie, a focus outward onto the experiences of others) may help reduce self-centered behavior. Further development of social skills training is also recommended and should be geared toward developing effective strategies for dealing with unexpected changes in routine. All this may be done as part of her individual therapy time.

Emily would benefit from learning self-soothing and self-regulating measures in moments of volatility, such as waking from a troubled sleep. Listening to music or playing with soft objects may serve to distract her from her thoughts and impulses. Teachers, therapists, and Emily's parents can collaborate in practicing and reinforcing these self-soothing techniques.

Emily's parents are encouraged to continue expressing their expectations of her by providing clear, short, and reasonable expectations. This imposed structure will ideally serve to compensate for Emily's present lack of inner structure and stability.

At school, Emily is most likely to grow and flourish in an environment with very clear boundaries, expectations, and outcomes. This will ideally foster "internal boundaries" for coping, managing her mood, and tolerating stress.

Emily's parents are involved, caring, and dedicated caregivers who have developed a keen insight into her issues. Ongoing family therapy may be instrumental in helping all parties cope with difficult moments. In addition, her parents are ideally positioned to form an active partnership with all of Emily's care providers and school staff. This home-school collaboration and communication is crucial in ensuring consistency across settings and generalization of acquired skills and coping mechanisms. Emily's parents are encouraged to share this report with her school-based team.

A HELPFUL TOOL—A DEVELOPMENTAL HISTORY FORM

I have included a sample developmental history form that I use in my practice, which I assembled on the basis of several others available in the field. Since my practice serves mostly children with pervasive developmental disorders, such as autism, Asperger syndrome, SPD, nonverbal learning disorder, and disorders affecting children's social functioning, the focus of this particular form is obtaining information that is most pertinent to these disorders.

However, I believe that thinking about the questions on this form is a great start for any family that may be seeing a neuropsychologist for testing. This form will provide a helpful framework for the information you may be asked about by the clinician regarding your pregnancy, your child's birth, developmental milestones, past and current levels of functioning, and family history.

Developmental History Form

Child's Name: _____

Date of Birth: _____

Instructions

Please read the following questions carefully and answer to the best of your ability and recollection. In doing so, you may wish to consult with family members, extended family, babysitters, and your child's baby book. You may also find that looking at your child's photo albums or videotapes may help you to recall some of the information requested below. If you do not know or remember the answer to a question, just indicate that it is so and move on to the next question.

This form will be helpful to me in two ways. The first is to obtain a complete record of the requested information ahead of time, which will help me prepare for your child's evaluation. The second is to help you think about and anticipate what areas of your child's development you may want to focus on in our initial intake meeting. Once you have completed the form, please do not hesitate to make a separate list of specific questions, concerns, and issues you wish to discuss during the intake meeting.

During the intake meeting, you will be asked similar questions and asked to clarify or elaborate on your responses, with discussion of more relevant issues for the evaluation. There will also be an opportunity to provide more detailed information and further explanations.

Thank you in advance for your attention and cooperation.

Today's Date: _____ Child's Name: _____

Sex: ☐ Female ☐ Male

Date of Birth: _____ Age: _____

Current Grade in School: _____

Hand Preference: ☐ Right ☐ Left ☐ Ambidextrous

Current Medications: _____

Current Diagnosis (if any): _____

Your Name: _____ Relationship to Child: _____

Family History—<u>Maternal</u> Side   **Is there any history of...**

Learning Disorders ☐ No ☐ Yes If yes, what and whom? _____

_____

Psychiatric Disorders ☐ No ☐ Yes If yes, what and whom? _____

_____

Mental Retardation ☐ No ☐ Yes If yes, what and whom? _____

_____

Pervasive Developmental Disorders (eg, autism, Asperger disorder, pervasive developmental disorder not otherwise specified)

☐ No ☐ Yes If yes, what and whom? _____

_____

Genetic/Chromosomal abnormalities? ☐ No ☐ Yes

If yes, what and in whom? _____

Other _____

_____

_____

Family History—<u>Paternal</u> Side   **Is there any history of...**

Learning Disorders   ☐ No ☐ Yes If yes, what and whom? _____

_____

Psychiatric Disorders ☐ No ☐ Yes If yes, what and whom? _____

_____

Mental Retardation   ☐ No ☐ Yes If yes, what and whom? _____

_____

Pervasive Developmental Disorders (eg, autism, Asperger disorder, pervasive developmental disorder not otherwise specified)

☐ No ☐ Yes If yes, what and whom? _____

_____

Genetic/Chromosomal abnormalities?   ☐ No ☐ Yes

If yes, what and in whom?_____

Other _____

_____

Perinatal History

Is this child... ☐ Adopted ☐ Foster ☐ Biological ☐ Other_____

Total no. of pregnancies: Live birth: ___ Birth order of this baby: _____

Mother's age during pregnancy: _____

Was the pregnancy healthy? ☐ Yes ☐ No Comments: _____

During pregnancy, did the child's mother:

Use drugs? ☐ Yes ☐ No If yes, what kind? _____

How much/often? _____

Use prescribed medications? ☐ No ☐ Yes If yes, what kind? _____

How much/often? _____

Use alcohol?   ☐ No ☐ Yes If yes, what kind? _____

How much/often? _____

Drink caffeine? ☐ No ☐ Yes If yes, what kind? _____

How much/often? _____

Smoke?   ☐ No ☐ Yes If yes, what kind? _____

How much/often? _____

Have a fever?   ☐ No ☐ Yes If yes, how high and for how long? ___

_____

Have high blood pressure?   ☐ Yes ☐ No

If yes, how high and for how long?

Get hurt, injured seriously, or hospitalized?   ☐ No ☐ Yes

If yes, how? _____

Have diabetes?   ☐ No ☐ Yes

Have toxemia (pregnancy-induced hypertension)?   ☐ No ☐ Yes

Have eclampsia (a toxic condition
characterized by convulsions)?   ☐ No ☐ Yes

Delivery History

Was the pregnancy: ☐ Full term ☐ Premature

If premature, at what week was your child born?_____

Please list any complications: _____

Was labor (indicate all that apply):

Normal: ☐ Yes ☐ No   If not, what problems? ___

☐ Spontaneous   ☐ Induced   ☐ Induced with Pitocin (syn-
                                             thetic hormone to start
                                             contraction)

☐ Breech (feet first)   ☐ Caesarian Section   ☐ Anesthesia, if yes,

                                                   what type? _____

☐ Less than 2 hours   ☐ More than 24 hours

Meconium-stained amniotic fluid delivery   ☐ No ☐ Yes

Newborn History (first month)

What was your child's: Apgar Score:_____   Birth Weight:_____

Did (or was) your child:

Have any birth injuries: ☐ No ☐ Yes If yes, please describe: _____

Have trouble starting
  to breathe?   ☐ No ☐ Yes If yes, for how long?_____

Need oxygen?:   ☐ No ☐ Yes If yes, for how long?_____

Born with the cord around his neck?   ☐ No ☐ Yes

Jaundiced?   ☐ No ☐ Yes If yes, for how long?_____

Anemic?   ☐ No ☐ Yes If yes, please describe:_____

Require transfusions?   ☐ No ☐ Yes If yes, how much?_____

Born with birth defects? ☐ No ☐ Yes If yes, what? _____

A twin   ☐ No ☐ Yes

Hospitalized more than 5 days? ☐ No ☐ Yes If yes, why? _____

Have trouble sucking?   ☐ No ☐ Yes If yes, for how long?_____

Have trouble with gagging, reflux, or vomiting?

                         ☐ No ☐ Yes If yes, please describe: _____

Have seizures?   ☐ No ☐ Yes If yes, please describe:_____

Have other problems in the first month?

                         ☐ No ☐ Yes If yes, please describe: _____

Medical Problems

Please describe any medical problems during:

First week of life:

First month:

First year:

Please list all medical procedures (surgeries, etc) and the age at which they occurred:

Did you ever suspect that your child
could have been deaf? ☐ No ☐ Yes

Did your child have a hearing test? ☐ No ☐ Yes

If yes, when and what was the result? _____

Did your child have an auditory processing evaluation? ☐ No ☐ Yes

If yes, when and what was the result?

Are there any significant current medical problems? ☐ No ☐ Yes

If yes, please explain. _____

Is there a history of any significant illnesses, surgeries,
head injuries, or falls? ☐ No ☐ Yes

If yes, please explain. _____

_____

_____

Has your child received a diagnosis
of seizure disorder or epilepsy? ☐ No ☐ Yes

If yes, when?

Are the seizures currently under control? ☐ No ☐ Yes

Please indicate if there are any other significant medical issues not listed

on this form._____

_____

Developmental History

Was your child breastfed? ☐ No ☐ Yes For how long?_____

Please rate the following areas as they apply:

	Normal	Adequate	Concern	Poor	Describe Problems
Sucking reflex	1	2	3	4	_____
Response to					
mother's cues	1	2	3	4	_____
Weight gain	1	2	3	4	_____
Eating habits	1	2	3	4	_____
Sleeping habits	1	2	3	4	_____
Startle reaction	1	2	3	4	_____

Please rate the child's temperament at the following ages:

	Easy	Slow to warm up	Difficult	Describe problems
Up to 6 weeks	1	2	3	_____
Up to 6 months	1	2	3	_____
6 to 12 months	1	2	3	_____
12 to 14 months	1	2	3	_____

Developmental Milestones—Gross Motor

When did your child first: Roll over: _____ Sit up independently: _____
Crawl: _____ Walk independently: _____

Was your child's gross motor activity:

☐ Normal ☐ Clumsy ☐ Robotic ☐ Other _____

Does (or did) your child have difficulty with any of the following tasks (child's age will be considered)

Hopping on one foot:	☐ No	☐ Yes
Climbing on play structures:	☐ No	☐ Yes
Walking up and down stairs:	☐ No	☐ Yes
Jumping over objects:	☐ No	☐ Yes
Running while changing directions:	☐ No	☐ Yes

At what age did your child learn to ride a bicycle independently? _____

If older than 6 years, please explain. _____

Please list anything unusual about the child's early gross motor activity:

_____

Motor Developmental Milestones—Fine Motor

Was your child's early fine motor ability:
☐ Normal ☐ Adequate ☐ Poor ☐ Other_____

Does (or did) your child have difficulty with any of the following tasks (child's age will be considered):

Building three-dimensional structures with blocks:	☐ No	☐ Yes
Using scissors to cut paper:	☐ No	☐ Yes
Completing puzzles:	☐ No	☐ Yes
Using erasers without tearing the paper:	☐ No	☐ Yes
Tying shoelaces:	☐ No	☐ Yes

Muscle Strength and Energy Level

Does (or did) your child have poor muscle tone (hypotonia)? ☐ No ☐ Yes

If yes, explain. _____

Have poor endurance and tire easily: ☐ No ☐ Yes

If yes, explain. _____

Always seem to need props or support when seated or standing
(eg, puts upper body or head on desk): ☐ No ☐ Yes

If yes, explain. _____

Have a weaker grasp compared with peers of the same age: ☐ No ☐ Yes

If yes, explain. _____

Have trouble using just his or her upper body strength to pull him- or
herself up (eg, using the arms and/or upper body to get out of the pool
in a push-up style): ☐ No ☐ Yes

If yes, explain. _____

Developmental Milestones—Speech, Language, Communication

Please rate the following areas as they best apply.

	Normal	Adequate	Concern	Poor	Describe problems/age delays
Smiling at 4–6 weeks	1	2	3	4	_____
Cooing at 3 mos	1	2	3	4	_____
Babbling at 6 mos	1	2	3	4	_____
Jargon at 10–14 mos	1	2	3	4	_____
First word at 12 mos	1	2	3	4	_____
First word was:					_____

Spoke three words other than Mama, Dada at 12 mos

                    1   2   3   4   _____

List words:._____

Spoke two-word combinations at 22 mos

                    1   2   3   4   _____

Spoke three-word combinations at 3 years

                    1   2   3   4   _____

Had or has speech problems or misarticulations   ☐ No ☐ Yes

If yes, describe: _____

Speech was: ☐ Normal ☐ Slow ☐ Rapid/pressured

                   ☐ Other _____

Inflection was   ☐ Normal ☐ Flat ☐ Monotonous ☐ Pedantic

                   ☐ Other _____

Quantity of Language

Did your child's language include:

Lack of cohesion in conversation

               ☐ No ☐ Yes If yes, please describe _____

Non sequiturs (starting a new topic before completing the first topic)

               ☐ No ☐ Yes

Idiosyncratic use of words

               ☐ No ☐ Yes If yes, please describe _____

Repetitive speech patterns

               ☐ No ☐ Yes If yes, please describe _____

Echolalia (repeating of words and phrases, either with or without delay)

               ☐ No ☐ Yes If yes, please describe _____

Does (or did) your child's conversational content of thought include:

Mimicking ☐ No ☐ Yes If yes, please describe _____

Logical sequence ☐ No ☐ Yes If no, please describe _____

Rapid digression from one idea to the next

☐ No ☐ Yes If yes, please describe _____

Loose associations, or was difficult to follow:

☐ No ☐ Yes If yes, please describe _____

Conversation with others on topics of mutual interest:

☐ No ☐ Yes If no, please describe _____

Initiation of conversations on topics of interest to peers:

☐ No ☐ Yes If no, please describe _____

Laughing or smiling appropriately in response to peers:

☐ No ☐ Yes If no, please describe _____

Nonverbal communication (facial expressions, gestures, body language)

Please rate the following abilities as they best apply:

	Normal	Adequate	Concern	Poor	Describe problems/age delays
Interpreting facial expressions	1	2	3	4	_____
Reading emotion from facial expressions	1	2	3	4	_____

Using facial expressions 1　　　2　　　3　　　4　　_____

Making eye contact　　1　　　2　　　3　　　4　　_____

Making an eye-to-eye gaze

　　　　　　　　　1　　　2　　　3　　　4　　_____

Giving messages with the eyes

　　　　　　　　　1　　　2　　　3　　　4　　_____

Using hand gestures　1　　　2　　　3　　　4　　_____

Cognizance of body in space

　　　　　　　　　1　　　2　　　3　　　4　　_____

Comes too close　　1　　　2　　　3　　　4　　_____

Maintains body posture 1　　　2　　　3　　　4　　_____

Responds to nonverbal cues in conversation

　　　　　　　　　1　　　2　　　3　　　4　　_____

Describe any regressions or loss of skills your child may have had in any of these areas:

_____

_____

_____

Do you suspect your child could read facial expressions and use body language if prompted, or do you feel he or she has a deficit in this ability?

_____

_____

_____

Type of Communication

Does you child understand:

Nonliteral speech ☐ Yes ☐ No If no, please describe:_____

Irony ☐ Yes ☐ No If no, please describe:_____

Sarcasm ☐ Yes ☐ No If no, please describe:_____

Joking ☐ Yes ☐ No If no, please describe:_____

Metaphors ☐ Yes ☐ No If no, please describe:_____

Inferential communication (recognition of intent in communication)

☐ Yes ☐ No If no, please describe:_____

Were any of these areas ever a problem: _____

Is your child's interpretation of language:

☐ Normal ☐ Literal ☐ Rigid ☐ Other_____

Did your child ever develop a skill and then regress, or lose the skill, and could not do it again? (Examples may include regressions from all areas of development, such as speaking several words and losing the ability to say them, walking and then going back to crawling, etc.) Explain: _____

_____

_____

Emotions/Feelings

Please rate the following as they relate to emotions.

Understanding of emotions:

☐ Full ☐ Only knows sad, happy, angry ☐ Difficulty with understanding range

Affect (immediate expressions of emotion):

☐ Full range ☐ Normal ☐ Flat ☐ Constricted or restricted

☐ Exhibits inappropriately (laughs when anxious)

Changes in affect ☐ Smooth ☐ Fixed ☐ Abrupt

☐ Other _____

Cognitive functioning:

Does your child understand relevant from nonrelevant information (judging what parts of a task are important to note and which can be ignored)

☐ Yes ☐ No

If no, please explain: _____

Does (or is) your child:

Good at details ☐ Yes ☐ No   If no, please describe: _____

See the whole picture ☐ Yes ☐ No   If no, please describe: _____

Understand cause and effect

☐ Yes ☐ No   If no, please describe: _____

Able to generate alternative solutions to problems

☐ Yes ☐ No   If no, please describe: _____

Understand consequential thinking

☐ Yes ☐ No   If no, please describe: _____

Were any of these ever a problem: _____

Social Functioning

Check all that apply to your child both past and present

	No	Yes	At what age	Describe
Takes care of personal needs	☐	☐	_____	_____
Has close friends	☐	☐	_____	_____
Avoids others	☐	☐	_____	_____
Has interest in friends	☐	☐	_____	_____

Wants desperately to interact ☐ ☐ _____ _____

Has the skills to interact with others

☐ ☐ _____ _____

Greets others in an appropriate manner

☐ ☐ _____ _____

Initiates conversations ☐ ☐ _____ _____

Continues conversations ☐ ☐ _____ _____

Reads cues to enter social groups

☐ ☐ _____ _____

Has difficulty with or a clumsy approach to group situations

☐ ☐ _____ _____

Ends conversations appropriately

☐ ☐ _____ _____

Does (or did) your child:

Usually share and take turns willingly? ☐ No ☐ Yes

Usually play well with two or more children ☐ No ☐ Yes

Willingly and cooperatively participate

in small groups, activities, or games? ☐ No ☐ Yes

Play pretend ☐ No ☐ Yes

Have a one-sided response to conversations ☐ No ☐ Yes

Have a one-sided response to peers ☐ No ☐ Yes

Does (or did) your child have difficulty

understanding the feelings of others? ☐ No ☐ Yes

Social Interactions (Adults and Peers)

Please describe your child's relatedness to the following

	Related	Marginal	Noninterest	Describe
Relatedness to adults	1	2	3	_____
Relatedness to peers	1	2	3	_____

Can your child share an adult's attention? ☐ No ☐ Yes

Explain: _____

Does your child feel anxious in situations involving new people?

☐ No ☐ Yes Explain: _____

Is your child preoccupied with his inner world or stays in his own world?

☐ No ☐ Yes Explain: _____

Does (or did) your child engage in mutual sharing of interests, activities, or emotions?

☐ No ☐ Yes Explain: _____

Cuddling:

Did your child have a snuggly object as an infant?

☐ No ☐ Yes Describe: _____

Does your child still have or need a snuggly object and use it to calm

down or fall asleep? ☐ No ☐ Yes Describe: _____

Interests

Were (or are) your child's preschool play interests

☐ Narrow ☐ Restricted ☐ Similar to peers the same age

In preschool: was (or is) your child's play

☐ Parallel (beside) ☐ Peripheral ☐ Interactive with peers (with)

☐ Cooperative

Does your child have a past or present preoccupation with the nonfunctional aspects of objects, such as

	No	Yes	At what age	Describe
Odor	☐	☐	_____	_____
Feel of the surface	☐	☐	_____	_____
Noise/Vibration generated	☐	☐	_____	_____
Spinning the object	☐	☐	_____	_____

Please rate your child's history with the following abilities

	Overdeveloped	Normal	Underdeveloped	Describe
Repetitive activities	1	2	3	_____
Savant skills	1	2	3	_____
Rote memory of facts	1	2	3	_____

Special interests or talents

Please check any special interests or talents your child may have:

☐ Dinosaurs ☐ Maps ☐ Weather ☐ Computers ☐ Video Games

☐ Weapons ☐ Vehicles ☐ Railroad Systems/Cars ☐ Electric fans

Other:_____

Collections or Hobbies:

Does your child collect things?   ☐ No ☐ Yes
If yes, explain: _____

Does your child save things?   ☐ No ☐ Yes
If yes, explain: _____

Is your child's range of interests:

☐ Nonexistent (child doesn't like anything)

☐ Restricted to one interest (child seems obsessed by one area of interest)

☐ Restricted to one or two interests

☐ Normal

☐ Other _____

Use of Toys

Please check all that describe your child's PRESCHOOL use of toys:

☐ Sequenced, lined up   ☐ Repetitive   ☐ Restrictive

☐ Demonstrates cognitive flexibility ☐ Is able to shift from one to another

☐ Is able to shift peers' interest ☐ Demonstrates symbolic use

☐ Demonstrates preoccupation with parts

Comments _____

_____

Sensory Integration and Sensory Processing

Does or did your child have sensory modulation, sensory discrimination, or sensory-based motor difficulties?   ☐ No ☐ Yes

If yes, explain: _____

Has your child ever received a diagnosis of sensory processing disorder (SPD)?   ☐ No ☐ Yes

Has your child ever been evaluated by an occupational therapist? If so, please attach report.

Please rate your child's reaction (past and present) to the following:

Touch arousal: ☐ Normal ☐ Underresponsive ☐ Overresponsive

Describe: _____

New clothes:　☐ Normal　☐ Underresponsive　☐ Overresponsive

Describe: _____

Does he or she flinch or tense up when touched or hugged?

☐ No　☐ Yes　If yes, describe: _____

Does he or she react as if "attacked" when unexpectedly bumped?

☐ No　☐ Yes　If yes, describe: _____

Does he or she blink or protect self from a ball even when trying to catch it?

☐ No　☐ Yes　If yes, describe: _____

Auditory arousal:　☐ Normal　☐ Underresponsive　☐ Overresponsive

Describe: _____

Loud noises:　☐ Normal　☐ Underresponsive　☐ Overresponsive

Describe: _____

Aversion to sounds:

　　　　　　　　　☐ Normal　☐ Underresponsive　☐ Overresponsive

Describe: _____

Does your child cover his or her ears in reaction to certain sounds?

　　　　　　　　　　　　　　　　　　　☐ No　☐ Yes

If yes, describe: _____

Olfactory arousal (smell):

　　　　　　　　　☐ Normal　☐ Underresponsive　☐ Overresponsive

Describe: _____

Oral arousal (taste):

　　　　　　　　　☐ Normal　☐ Underresponsive　☐ Overresponsive

Describe: _____

Reaction to food texture:

☐ Normal ☐ Underresponsive ☐ Overresponsive

Describe:_____

Picky eater? ☐ No ☐ Yes

What foods does your child tend to prefer? _____

What foods does your child tend to avoid? _____

Visual arousal: ☐ Normal ☐ Underresponsive ☐ Overresponsive

Stereotypes

Did or does your child have stereotypes or stereotyped (repetitive) behaviors, such as odd finger or body movements, running in circles, staring at the fan, spinning objects, or lining up objects?

☐ No ☐ Yes   If yes, at what age? _____

Please describe the stereotypes: _____

Self-Stimulation Behaviors

Does (or did) your child have any of the following:

			Age of onset	Age it stopped
Hand/Finger flapping	☐ No	☐ Yes	_____	_____
Hand movements	☐ No	☐ Yes	_____	_____
Pacing	☐ No	☐ Yes	_____	_____
Purposeless complex whole-body movements	☐ No	☐ Yes	_____	_____
Head banging	☐ No	☐ Yes	_____	_____
Rocking	☐ No	☐ Yes	_____	_____
Sifting materials	☐ No	☐ Yes	_____	_____
Other	☐ No	☐ Yes	_____	_____

Need for Sameness

Does (or did) your child have

Difficulty in transitions   ☐ No   ☐ Yes

Difficulty with temporal change (change in time schedule)

                                               ☐ No   ☐ Yes

Difficulty with small, nonfunctional changes in details   ☐ No   ☐ Yes

Difficulty with small, nonfunctional changes in routines   ☐ No   ☐ Yes

Please describe: _____

Rituals

Does (or did) your child have excessive repetitive
fears, worries, or rituals?   ☐ No   ☐ Yes

     When were they first noted, and have they stopped? _____

     Please describe the main fears/worries/obsessions: _____

     Please describe the rituals/compulsions: _____

Does (or did) your child have impulsive control?   ☐ No   ☐ Yes

Does (or did) your child treat people as objects?   ☐ No   ☐ Yes

Does (or did) your child live in a world of his or her own? ☐ No   ☐ Yes

Does (or did) your child live in our world when he or she can?

                                              ☐ No   ☐ Yes

Please describe: _____

     Thank you again for your time and care in filling out this form.
Please do not hesitate to contact me with any questions regarding this
questionnaire or other issues related to your child's evaluation.

APPENDIX A

TYPICAL DEVELOPMENTAL STAGES IN CHILDREN

At birth, an infant's brain is capable of "reading" very basic tactile (touch), vestibular (balance), and proprioceptive (movement) information. Each time an infant responds to sensory information, the pathway to that response is strengthened, making future sensory processing easier and quicker.

Although the bulk of our neural pathways are created during early childhood, some recent studies show us that a mature adult central nervous system may at times demonstrate plasticity (change),[1] although this process is not well understood.

Clinicians and scientists agree that sensory information acts as nourishment or "food" for the developing brain. The early years of childhood are filled with tremendous developmental growth, much of which is fueled by sensory experiences, such as crawling, grasping, walking, playing, and "mouthing" toys. A basic understanding of human development will help us in thinking about the way the sensory system develops, and how SPD could emerge.

Understanding Your Child's Development

There are many theories and approaches used to describe human development. Because we are focusing on SPD, it will be most helpful to view child development through two specific models. The first model involves a description of cognitive development and was created by Jean Piaget, the Swiss psychologist, researcher, scientist, and developmental theorist.

The second model we will reference is a developmental assessment[2] endorsed by the American Society of Pediatricians. This assessment has been adapted for parental use and is available as an interactive checklist.[3]

Piaget's Developmental Theory

Over the course of six decades, Jean Piaget (1896-1980) constructed a theory of human cognitive (thinking) development that has shaped educational curriculum and changed the way people think about human cognitive development. Piaget's basic point was that, as children develop physically, they construct their own cognitive frameworks through interacting with other people and their environment. These frameworks are ways of understanding the world, and have distinctive stages of development.

According to Piaget's model, there are four main stages of cognitive development that children work through:

- Sensorimotor
- Preoperational
- Concrete operational
- Formal operational

Children move through these stages by taking in new sensory input, which in turn modifies their cognitive frameworks by two complementary processes that Piaget called assimilation and accommodation.[4] Assimilation refers to the process of taking in new information by incorporating it into an existing framework. In other words, people assimilate experiences by relating them to things they already know. Accommodation is what happens when the framework itself changes to accommodate new knowledge.

According to Piaget, cognitive development involves an ongoing attempt to achieve a balance between assimilation and accommodation, which he termed "equilibrium." Let's look at Piaget's stages of cognitive development within the context of sensory development.

Sensorimotor Stage

This stage lasts from birth until age 2. At birth, infants' movements are mostly reflexive. They cry in response to changes in their physical state, such as hunger, cold, heat, and fatigue, but they don't yet babble or utter sounds as symbols for objects or thoughts. As the infant matures, it becomes clear to parents and caregivers that their baby is developing in leaps and bounds and is on his or her way to becoming a toddler. By the time children reach the age of 2, they have worked hard on coordinating their sensory experience with physical and motor activities.

Preoperational Stage

This stage lasts from about age 2 until age 7. During this stage, toddlers and preschoolers begin to represent the world with symbols and are able to think more symbolically. Children enjoy imaginary play during this stage and are eager to draw and create images about their world.

The Concrete Operational Stage

This third stage of cognitive development begins at around age 7 and ends when the child is about 11. Unlike the first two stages, the concrete operational stage is characterized by children developing the capacity for logical reasoning but being unable to apply those reasoning skills beyond a familiar or specific situation.

The key to this phase is that children become real problem solvers, as long as they can physically interact with the problem at hand. An example of concrete operational activity includes situations where children are active learners—such as classroom assignments that involve group-based, hands-on activities, in addition to traditional lecturing or lessons. For example, an interactive art project involving a diorama combines rich cognitive and sensory learning experiences.

How an Art Project Can Act as a Sensory Feast

Art projects offer a fun and creative medium for teaching a number of concepts and skills. For example, a diorama project depicting a moment in time from colonial America offers a variety of sensory and cognitive learning opportunities.

The classroom is filled with drawings, pictures, models, and replicas of objects from colonial America, and the teacher begins by reading aloud a story about an event from colonial times. After the teacher is done reading the story, the children break into small groups and brainstorm ideas about the scene they would like to create for the diorama.

After the children have discussed their ideas, they develop a list of materials they will need for their project. They get the materials, and time is allocated at school for the child to work with his or her group on the diorama. As the children design and build their dioramas, they work with the material and problem-solve structural and design issues.

While the children are "learning" about colonial America through the construction of their dioramas, the teacher offers ongoing technical support and modifies the environment to support active learning. This could include playing popular music from the colonial era or creating a lunch or snack assignment involving food reminiscent of colonial America.

This learning scenario is an example of how meaningful learning, or learning that is built upon previous knowledge, can take place in a classroom setting. Unlike memorization or decontextualized learning, meaningful learning is key to supporting cognitive development throughout one's life (including adulthood), but it is particularly important during the concrete operational stage because it provides the much-needed sensory input to support cognitive development and serves as the bedrock for future abstract thinking skills.

Formal Operations

This phase of cognitive development begins at the tail end of the concrete operational stage around age 11, and is completed around age 15. The most obvious component of this phase is that it occurs around the beginning of adolescence.

The formal operations phase is characterized by the ability to think abstractly and understand complex philosophical and moral issues. Similarly, during this phase, teenagers are able to apply general rules to specific situations and are more efficient in their thinking and planning skills. Piaget outlined four distinct ways in which adolescent cognitive development differs from the previous phases of development.[5]

They are:

1. **The Possibilities.** Teenagers who are actively engaged in the formal operations phase of cognitive development are consciously and unconsciously able to think

beyond the obvious or what they already know. They are able to think about what might be possible, what could be. This skill is supported further by creative activities, such as poetry, theater, art, and music.

2. **Abstract Ideas.** Adolescence brings the dawning of abstract cognitive abilities that enable teenagers to reason through a debate or ethical consideration. Their ability to apply higher-order mathematics and logic opens the door to more sophisticated problem solving, including applied engineering or community-planning projects (such as building a community farm). The ability to think abstractly enables the teenager to consider contemporary social, religious, and political issues.

3. **Metacognition.** Formal operations also give rise to the ability to think about thinking. This means that adolescents have honed their ability to think introspectively and consider their own theories, beliefs, and opinions about large, often complex issues. For example, an adolescent may become acutely aware of global warming and spend a fair amount of time thinking about the way he or she understands global warming from a scientific, political, and economic perspective.

4. **Multidimensional.** In contrast to the concrete-operational child, the adolescent's thinking is multi-faceted and complicated. Things are not just black or white. From the adolescent's perspective, issues or problems can be analyzed from several perspectives. The ability to view a situation from multiple viewpoints also plays out in the social arena. Adolescents who are able to think multidimensionally have the ability to understand that individuals are complex, and that personalities are not easily summed up in one word.

APPENDIX B

CDC DEVELOPMENT MILESTONES FOR CHILDREN

The U.S. Department of Health and Human Services Centers for Disease Control and Prevention, or CDC, has developed a helpful guide for tracking your child's social, emotional, physical, and cognitive development. Pediatricians use this assessment often, and the CDC even offers an interactive version of the checklist that is geared toward parental use.

I've included this model of describing your child's development in addition to the milestones in chapter 1 because it has the added benefit of assessing social, emotional, cognitive, and sensory development. You can also find these developmental milestones on the CDC's Web site at www.cdc.gov/ncbddd/autism/actearly/milestones_3months.html.

Important Milestones by the End of 3 Months

Social and Emotional

- Begins to develop a social smile
- Enjoys playing with other people and may cry when playing stops

- Becomes more expressive and communicates more with face and body
- Imitates some movements and facial expressions

Movement

- Raises head and chest when lying on stomach
- Supports upper body with arms when lying on stomach
- Stretches legs out and kicks when lying on stomach or back
- Opens and shuts hands
- Pushes down on legs when feet are placed on a firm surface
- Brings hand to mouth
- Takes swipes at dangling objects with hands
- Grasps and shakes hand toys

Vision

- Watches faces intently
- Follows moving objects
- Recognizes familiar objects and people at a distance
- Starts using hands and eyes in coordination

Hearing and Speech

- Smiles at the sound of your voice
- Begins to babble
- Begins to imitate some sounds
- Turns head toward direction of sound

Developmental Health Watch

Alert your child's doctor or nurse if your child displays any of the following signs of possible developmental delay for this age range.

- Does not seem to respond to loud noises

- Does not notice hands by 2 months

- Does not follow moving objects with eyes by 2 to 3 months

- Does not grasp and hold objects by 3 months

- Does not smile at people by 3 months

- Cannot support head well by 3 months

- Does not reach for and grasp toys by 3 to 4 months

- Does not babble by 3 to 4 months

- Does not bring objects to mouth by 4 months

- Begins babbling, but does not try to imitate any of your sounds by 4 months

- Does not push down with legs when feet are placed on a firm surface by 4 months

- Has difficulty moving one or both eyes in all directions

- Crosses eyes most of the time (occasional crossing of the eyes is normal in these first months)

- Does not pay attention to new faces, or seems very frightened by new faces or surroundings

- Experiences a dramatic loss of skills he or she once had

Important Milestones by the End of 7 Months

Social and Emotional

- Enjoys social play
- Is interested in mirror images
- Responds to other people's expressions of emotion and appears joyful often

Cognitive

- Finds partially hidden objects
- Explores with hands and mouth
- Struggles to get objects that are out of reach

Language

- Responds to own name
- Begins to respond to "no"
- Can tell emotions by tone of voice
- Responds to sound by making sounds
- Uses voice to express joy and displeasure
- Babbles chains of sounds

Movement

- Rolls both ways (front to back, back to front)
- Sits with, and then without, support on hands
- Supports whole weight on legs
- Reaches with one hand

- Transfers object from hand to hand
- Uses hand to rake objects

Vision

- Develops full-color vision
- Shows maturing distance vision
- Shows increased ability to track moving objects

Developmental Health Watch

Alert your child's doctor or nurse if your child displays any of the following signs of possible developmental delay for this age range.

- Seems very stiff, with tight muscles
- Seems very floppy, like a rag doll
- Has difficulty with neck stability (head flops back when body is pulled to a sitting position)
- Reaches with one hand only
- Refuses to cuddle
- Shows no affection for the person who cares for him or her
- Doesn't seem to enjoy being around people
- One or both eyes consistently turn in or out
- Has persistent tearing, eye drainage, or sensitivity to light
- Does not respond to sounds around him or her
- Has difficulty getting objects to the mouth
- Does not turn head to locate sounds by 4 months

- Does not roll over in either direction (front to back or back to front) by 5 months
- Seems impossible to comfort at night after 5 months
- Does not smile on his or her own by 5 months
- Cannot sit with help by 6 months
- Does not laugh or make squealing sounds by 6 months
- Does not actively reach for objects by 6 to 7 months
- Does not follow objects with both eyes at near (1 foot) and far (6 feet) ranges by 7 months
- Does not bear weight on legs by 7 months
- Does not try to attract attention through actions by 7 months
- Does not babble by 8 months
- Shows no interest in games of peek-a-boo by 8 months
- Experiences a dramatic loss of skills he or she once had

Important Milestones by the End of 12 Months

Social and Emotional

- Is shy or anxious with strangers
- Cries when mother or father leaves
- Enjoys imitating people in play
- Shows specific preferences for certain people and toys

- Tests parental responses to his or her actions during feedings
- Tests parental responses to his or her behavior
- May be fearful in some situations
- Prefers mother and/or regular caregiver over all others
- Repeats sounds or gestures to get attention
- Feeds self with fingers
- Extends arm or leg to help when being dressed

Cognitive

- Explores objects in many different ways (shaking, banging, throwing, dropping)
- Finds hidden objects easily
- Looks at the correct picture when an image is named
- Imitates gestures
- Begins to use objects correctly (drinking from a cup, brushing hair, dialing a phone, listening to the receiver)

Language

- Pays increasing attention to speech
- Responds to simple verbal requests
- Responds to "no"
- Uses simple gestures, such as shaking head for "no"
- Babbles with inflection (changes in tone)
- Says "dada" and "mama"
- Uses exclamations, such as "Oh-oh!"
- Tries to imitate words

Movement

- Reaches sitting position without assistance
- Crawls forward on belly
- Assumes hands-and-knees position
- Creeps on hands and knees
- Gets from sitting to crawling or prone (lying on stomach) position
- Pulls self up to stand
- Walks by holding on to furniture
- Stands momentarily without support
- May walk two or three steps without support

Hand and Finger Skills

- Uses pincer grasp
- Bangs two objects together
- Puts objects into container
- Takes objects out of container
- Lets objects go voluntarily
- Pokes with index finger
- Tries to imitate scribbling

Developmental Health Watch

Alert your child's doctor or nurse if your child displays any of the following signs of possible developmental delay for this age range.

- Does not crawl
- Drags one side of body while crawling (for more than 1 month)

- Cannot stand when supported
- Does not search for objects that are hidden while he or she watches
- Says no single words ("mama" or "dada")
- Does not learn to use gestures, such as waving or shaking head
- Does not point to objects or pictures
- Experiences a dramatic loss of skills he or she once had

Important Milestones by the End of 2 Years

Social

- Imitates behavior of others, especially adults and older children
- Is more aware of self as separate from others
- Is more excited about the company of other children

Emotional

- Demonstrates increasing independence
- Begins to show defiant behavior
- Separation anxiety increases toward midyear then fades

Cognitive

- Finds objects even when hidden under two or three covers
- Begins to sort items by shape and color
- Begins make-believe play

Language

- Points to an object or picture when named for him or her
- Recognizes names of familiar people, objects, and body parts
- Says several single words (by 15 to 18 months)
- Uses simple phrases (by 18 to 24 months)
- Uses two- to four-word sentences
- Follows simple instructions
- Repeats words overheard in conversation

Movement

- Walks alone
- Pulls toys behind him or her while walking
- Carries a large toy or several toys while walking
- Begins to run
- Stands on tiptoe
- Kicks a ball
- Climbs onto and down from furniture unassisted
- Walks up and down stairs by holding on to a support

Hand and Finger Skills

- Scribbles on his or her own
- Turns over a container to pour out contents
- Builds a tower of four blocks or more
- Might use one hand more often than the other

Developmental Health Watch

Alert your child's doctor or nurse if your child displays any of the following signs of possible developmental delay for this age range.

- Cannot walk by 18 months

- Fails to develop a mature heel-toe walking pattern after several months of walking, or walks only on his or her toes

- Does not speak at least 15 words

- Does not use two-word sentences by age 2

- By 15 months, does not seem to know the function of common household objects (such as a brush, telephone, bell, fork, or spoon)

- Does not imitate actions or words by the end of this period

- Does not follow simple instructions by age 2

- Cannot push a wheeled toy by age 2

- Experiences a dramatic loss of skills he or she once had

Important Milestones by the End of 3 Years

Social

- Imitates adults and playmates

- Spontaneously shows affection for familiar playmates

- Can take turns in games

- Understands concept of "mine" and "his or hers"

Emotional

- Expresses affection openly
- Expresses a wide range of emotions
- Separates easily from parents
- Objects to major changes in routine

Cognitive

- Makes mechanical toys work
- Matches an object in his or her hand or room to a picture in a book
- Plays make-believe with dolls, animals, and people
- Sorts objects by shape and color
- Completes puzzles with three or four pieces
- Understands concept of "two"

Language

- Follows a two- or three-part command
- Recognizes and identifies almost all common objects and pictures
- Understands most sentences
- Understands placement in space ("on," "in," "under")
- Uses four- to five-word sentences
- Can say name, age, and sex
- Uses pronouns (I, you, me, we, they) and some plurals (cars, dogs, cats)
- Is mostly understandable (strangers can understand most of his or her words)

Movement

- Climbs well
- Walks up and down stairs, alternating feet (one foot per stairstep)
- Kicks a ball
- Runs easily
- Pedals a tricycle
- Bends over easily without falling

Hand and Finger Skills

- Makes up-and-down, side-to-side, and circular lines with a pencil or crayon
- Turns book pages one at a time
- Builds a tower of more than six blocks
- Holds a pencil in writing position
- Screws and unscrews jar lids, nuts, and bolts
- Turns rotating handles

Developmental Health Watch

Alert your child's doctor or nurse if your child displays any of the following signs of possible developmental delay for this age range.

- Frequently falls and has difficulty with stairs
- Persistently drools or has very unclear speech
- Cannot build a tower of more than four blocks
- Has difficulty manipulating small objects
- Cannot copy a circle by age 3

- Cannot communicate in short phrases
- Has no involvement in "pretend" play
- Does not understand simple instructions
- Takes little interest in other children
- Has extreme difficulty separating from mother or primary caregiver
- Demonstrates poor eye contact
- Has limited interest in toys
- Experiences a dramatic loss of skills he or she once had

Important Milestones by the End of 4 Years

Social

- Is interested in new experiences
- Cooperates with other children
- Plays "Mom" or "Dad"
- Is increasingly inventive in fantasy play
- Dresses and undresses self
- Negotiates solutions to conflicts
- Is more independent

Emotional

- Has a rich imagination and may believe that many unfamiliar images may be "monsters"
- Views self as a whole person involving body, mind, and feelings

- Begins to be able to tell the difference between fantasy and reality

Cognitive

- Correctly names some colors
- Understands the concept of counting and may know a few numbers
- Tries to solve problems from a single point of view
- Begins to have a clearer sense of time
- Follows three-part commands
- Recalls parts of a story
- Understands the concepts of "same" and "different"
- Engages in fantasy play

Language

- Has mastered some basic rules of grammar
- Speaks in sentences of five to six words
- Speaks clearly enough for strangers to understand
- Tells stories

Movement

- Hops and stands on one foot up to 5 seconds
- Goes upstairs and downstairs without support
- Kicks a ball forward
- Throws a ball overhand
- Catches a bounced ball most of the time
- Moves forward and backward with agility

Hand and Finger Skills

- Copies square shapes
- Draws a person with two to four body parts
- Uses scissors
- Draws circles and squares
- Begins to copy some capital letters

Developmental Health Watch

Alert your child's doctor or nurse if your child displays any of the following signs of possible developmental delay for this age range.

- Cannot throw a ball overhand
- Cannot jump in place
- Cannot ride a tricycle
- Cannot grasp a crayon between thumb and fingers
- Has difficulty scribbling
- Cannot stack four blocks
- Still clings or cries whenever parents leave
- Shows no interest in interactive games
- Ignores other children
- Doesn't respond to people outside the family
- Doesn't engage in fantasy play
- Resists dressing, sleeping, using the toilet
- Lashes out without any self-control when angry or upset
- Cannot copy a circle

- Doesn't use sentences of more than three words
- Doesn't use "me" and "you" correctly
- Experiences a dramatic loss of skills he or she once had

Important Milestones by the End of 5 Years

Social

- Wants to please friends
- Wants to be like his or her friends
- Is more likely to agree to rules
- Likes to sing, dance, and act
- Shows more independence and may even visit a next-door neighbor by him- or herself

Emotional Milestones

- Is aware of gender
- Is able to distinguish fantasy from reality
- Is sometimes demanding, sometimes eagerly cooperative

Cognitive Milestones

- Can count 10 or more objects
- Correctly names at least four colors
- Better understands the concept of time
- Knows about things used every day in the home (money, food, appliances)

Language

- Recalls part of a story
- Speaks sentences of more than five words
- Uses future tense
- Tells longer stories
- Says own name and address

Movement

- Stands on one foot for 10 seconds or longer
- Hops, somersaults
- Swings, climbs
- May be able to skip

Hand and Finger Skills

- Copies triangles and other shapes
- Draws a person with a body
- Prints some letters
- Dresses and undresses without help
- Uses a fork, a spoon, and (sometimes) a table knife
- Usually cares for own toilet needs

Developmental Health Watch

Alert your child's doctor or nurse if your child displays any of the following signs of possible developmental delay for this age range.

- Acts extremely fearful or timid

- Acts extremely aggressively

- Is unable to separate from parents without major protest

- Is easily distracted and unable to concentrate on any single activity for more than 5 minutes

- Shows little interest in playing with other children

- Refuses to respond to people in general, or responds only superficially

- Rarely uses fantasy or imitation in play

- Seems unhappy or sad much of the time

- Doesn't engage in a variety of activities

- Avoids or seems aloof with other children and adults

- Doesn't express a wide range of emotions

- Has trouble eating, sleeping, or using the toilet

- Can't tell the difference between fantasy and reality

- Seems unusually passive

- Cannot understand two-part commands with prepositions ("Put the doll on the bed, and get the ball under the couch.")

- Can't correctly give his or her first and last name

- Doesn't use plurals or past tense properly when speaking

- Doesn't talk about his or her daily activities and experiences

- Cannot build a tower of six to eight blocks

- Seems uncomfortable holding a crayon

- Has trouble taking off clothing
- Cannot brush his or her teeth efficiently
- Cannot wash and dry his or her hands
- Experiences a dramatic loss of skills he or she once had

NOTES

Introduction and Chapter 1

1. Auer CR, Blumberg SL. *Parenting a Child with Sensory Processing Disorder*. Oakland, CA: New Harbinger Publications Inc; 2006.

2. Mennella JA, Pepino MY, Reed DR. Genetic and environmental determinants of bitter perception and sweet preferences. *Pediatrics*. 2005; 115(2):e216–222.

3. Ramos Da Conceicao Neta ER, Johanningsmeier SD, McFeeters RF. The chemistry and physiology of sour taste—a review. *J Food Sci*. 2007; 72(2):R33–38.

4. Jarup L, Babisch W, Houthuijs E, et al. Hypertension and exposure to noise near airports: the HYENA study. *Environ Health Perspect*. 2008; 116:329–333.

5. Proust M. *Remembrance of Things Past*. New York, NY: Random House; 1924.

Chapter 2

No references

Chapter 3

1. Levine S. Stress: an historical perspective. In: Steckler T, Kalin NH, Reul JMHM, eds. *Handbook of Stress and the Brain: Part 1 The Neurobiology of Stress*. The Netherlands: Elsevier BV; 2005.

2. Fulford A, Harbuz M. An introduction to the HPA axis. In: Steckler T, Kalin NH, Reul JMHM, eds. *Handbook of Stress and the Brain: Part 1 The Neurobiology of Stress*. The Netherlands: Elsevier BV; 2005.

3. National Center for Complementary and Alternative Medicine page. National Institutes of Health Web site. Available at: http://nccam.nih .gov/. Accessed July 12, 2008.

4. Van der Kolk B. The body keeps score: approaches to the psychobiology of posttraumatic stress disorder. In: Van der Kolk B, McFarlane AC, Weisaeth L, eds. *Traumatic Stress: The Effects of Overwhelming Experiences on Mind, Body, and Society*. New York, NY; 1996.

5. Ljungberg J, Neely G. Stress, subjective experience and cognitive performance during exposure to noise and vibration. *J Environ Psychol.* 2007; 44–54.

6. Segerstrom S, Miller G. Psychological stress and the human immune system: a meta-analytic study of 30 years of inquiry. *Psychol Bull.* 2004; 130:601–630.

7. Gurvits T, Metzger LJ, Lasko NB, et al. Subtle neurologic compromise as a vulnerability factor for combat-related posttraumatic stress disorder. *Arch Gen Psych.* 2006; 63:571–576.

8. Kremen WS, Koenen KC, Boake C, et al. Pretrauma cognitive ability and risk for posttraumatic stress disorder. *Arch Gen Psych.* 2007; 64:361–368.

9. Schafer A, Braver TS, Reynolds JR, Burgess GC, Yarkoni T, Gray JR. Individual differences in amygdala activity predict response speed during working memory. *J Neurosci.* 2006; 26:10120–10128.

10. Ziv Y, Schwartz M. Immune-based regulation of adult neurogenesis: implications for learning and memory. *Brain Behav Immun.* 2008; 22:167–176.

11. Newcomer JW, Selke G, Melson AK, Hershey T, Craft S, Richards K. Decreased memory performance in healthy humans induced by stress-level cortisol treatment. *Arch Gen Psych.* 1999; 56:527-533.

Chapter 4

1. Gazell H, Rudolph KD. Moving toward and away from the world: social approach and avoidance trajectories in anxious solitary youth. *Child Dev.* 2004; 75:829–849.

2. Kranowitz CS. *The Out-of-Sync Child Has Fun: Activities for Kids with Sensory Processing Disorder*. New York, NY: Penguin Group, 2003.

Chapter 5

1. American Occupational Therapy Association Web site. Available at: http://www.aota.org.

2. Parham D, et al. Fidelity in sensory integration intervention reserach. *Am J Occup Ther.* 2007; 61:216-227.

Chapter 6

No references

Chapter 7

1. *Diagnostic and Statistical Manual of Mental Disorders.* 4th ed. Text Revision; DSM-IV-TR. Arlington, VA: American Psychiatric Association; 2000.

2. Long B. Autistic psychopathy in childhood, his (Hans Asperger) 1944 Article. 2007.

3. Robins, Fein, and Barton. Modified Checklist for Autism in Toddlers (M-CHAT). 2001. Available at: http://firstsigns.org.

4. Rourke BP, ed. Syndrome of Nonverbal Learning Disabilities: Neurodevelopmental Manifestations. New York, NY: Guilford Press; 1995.

Appendix A: Typical Developmental Stages in Children

1. Duan X, Kang E, Liu CY, Ming GL, Song H. Development of neural stem cell in adult brain. *Curr Opin Neurobiol.* 2008; 18:1108-1115.

2. Learn the signs. Act early. National Center on Birth Defects and Developmental Disabilities page. Department of Health and Human

Services Centers for Disease Control and Prevention Web site. http://www.cdc.gov/ncbddd/autism/actearly/milestones_3months.html. Accessed July 11, 2008.

3. Learn the signs. Act early. National Center on Birth Defects and Developmental Disabilities page. Department of Health and Human Services Centers for Disease Control and Prevention Web site. http://www.cdc.gov/ncbddd/autism/actearly/interactive/index.html. Accessed July 11, 2008.

4. Piaget J. *The Construction of Reality in the Child.* New York, NY: Basic Books Inc; 1954.

5. Santrock JW. *Adolescence.* 7th ed. New York, NY: McGraw-Hill; 1998.

RESOURCES

Books

Answers to Questions Teachers Ask about Sensory Integration
Carol Stock Kranowitz, MA; Stacy Szklut, MS, OTR/L; Lynn Balzer-Martin, PhD, OTR; Jane Koomar, PhD, OTR/L (2001)

Asperger's Syndrome and Other Sensory Issues: Practical Solutions for Making Sense of the World
Brenda Smith Myles, et al (2001)

Building Bridges through Sensory Integration
Ellen Yack, MEd, OT; Paula Aquilla, OT; Shirley Sutton, OT (2003)

Combining Neuro-developmental Treatment and Sensory Integration Principles: An Approach to Pediatric Therapy
Erna Blanche, MA, MOT; Tina Botticelli, MS, PT; Mary Hallway, OTR (1998)

Love, Jean: Inspiration for Families Living with Dysfunction of Sensory Integration
A. Jean Ayres, PhD, OTR (2004)

The Mislabeled Child: How Understanding Your Child's Unique Learning Style Can Open the Door to Success
Brock Eide, MD, MA; Fernette Eide, MD (2006)

Occupational Therapy for Children
Jane Case-Smith, PhD, OTR (Editor) (Third edition, 1996)

The Out-of-Sync Child: Recognizing and Coping with Sensory Processing Disorder. 2nd ed.
Carol Stock Kranowitz, MA (2005)

Parenting a Child with Sensory Processing Disorder: A Family Guide to Understanding & Supporting Your Sensory-Sensitive Child
Christopher R. Auer, MA; Susan L. Blumberg, PhD (2006)

Pediatric Occupational Therapy and Early Intervention
Jane Case-Smith, PhD, OTR (Second edition, 1997)

Raising a Sensory Smart Child: The Definitive Handbook for Helping Your Child with Sensory Integration Issues
Lindsey Biel, MA, OTR/L; Nancy Peske (2005)

Sense Abilities: Understanding Sensory Integration
Maryann Colby Trott, MA; Marci Laurel, MA, CCC-SLP; Susan Windeck, MS, OTR/L (1993)

Sensational Kids: Hope and Help for Children with Sensory Processing Disorder (SPD)
Lucy Jane Miller, PhD, OTR (2006)

Sensory Integration and Learning Disorders. 25th anniversary ed.
A. Jean Ayres, PhD, OTR; Zoe Mailloux, ed

Sensory Integration: Theory and Practice
Anita A. Bundy, et al (2002)

Sensory Motor Handbook: A Guide to Implementing and Modifying Activities in the Classroom
Jean Bissell, MA, OTR; Jean Fisher, MA, OTR; Carol Owens, OTR; Patricia Polcyn, OTR (Second edition, 1998)

The Sensory-Sensitive Child: Practical Solutions for Out-of-Bounds Behavior
Karen A. Smith, Karen A. Gouze (2004)

Too Loud, Too Bright, Too Fast, Too Tight: What to Do If You Are Sensory Defensive in an Overstimulating World
Sharon Heller, PhD (2003)

Tools for Teachers
Diana Henry, MS, OTR (1996)

Understanding Sensory Dysfunction: Learning, Development, and Sensory Dysfunction in Autism Spectrum Disorders, ADHD, Learning Disabilities, and Bipolar Disorder
Polly Godwin Emmons, Liz McKendry Anderson (2005)

Understanding the Nature of Sensory Integration with Diverse Populations
Roseann C. Schaef, Susanne Smith Roley (ed), Erna I. Blanche (ed) (2001)

Videos

Sensory Processing for Parents: From Roots to Wings
Judy Reisman, OTR, PhD (1996); Length, 28 minutes

Learning about Learning Disabilities
Judy Reisman, OTR, PhD; Nancy Scott, OTR (1991); Length, 30 minutes

Seizing the Moment
Center for Neurodevelopmental Studies (1998); Length, 30 minutes

Making Contact: Sensory Integration and Autism
Lorna Jean King, OTR, FAOTA; Judy Reisman, OTR, PhD (1993); Length, 30 minutes

Sensory Defensiveness
Patricia Wilbarger, MEd, OTR (1993); Length, 60 minutes

Web Sites

Autism Research Institute
www.autism.com

Kid Power: Sensory Integration Dysfunction
www.kid-power.org

New England Index: A database for special education and disability information
www.disabilityinfo.org

Occupational Therapy Associates–Watertown
www.otawatertown.com

Roya Ostovar
www.royaostovar.com

Sensory Processing Disorder
www.sensory-processing-disorder.com

Sensory Processing Disorder Foundation
www.SPDfoundation.net

Sensory Smarts
www.sensorysmarts.com

Temple Grandin's site for Asperger disorder and sensory integration disorder
www.templegrandin.com

The Out-of-Sync Child: Sensory Processing Disorder
www.out-of-sync-child.com

The Spiral Foundation (Sensory Processing Institute for Research and Learning)
www.thespiralfoundation.org

Tony Atwood's site for information regarding Asperger disorder
www.tonyattwood.com/au

Organizations

Asperger's Association of New England (AANE)
182 Main St
Watertown, MA 02472
(617) 393-3824
info@aane.org
www.aane.org

Autism Support Center (northeastern region of Massachusetts)
North Shore Arc
Susan Gilroy, Coordinator
(978) 777-9135 or 800-7-AUTISM for general information
Spotlight Program: This is a social pragmatics group for ages 9-18 that focuses on learning skills through improvisation games and dramatics. Sensory integration is also part of the curriculum of this program.
North Shore Arc
Michael Culp, Program Coordinator
(978) 762-8352
www.nsarc.org

LADDERS/MGH
(781) 449-6074
info@ladders.org
www.ladders.org

Sensory Processing Disorder Foundation
5655 S Yosemite, Suite 305
Greenwood Village, CO 80111
(303) 794-1182 phone
(303) 322-5550 fax
www.SPDfoundation.net

INDEX

Abuse, 84
Abuse, survivors of, 87
Academic performance,
    219–221
Accommodations for SPD
    students
    at school, 177–179, 189,
        191–192, 194, 203, 205,
        241
    at special events, 98, 104–
        105, 109
Accommodations for vaca-
    tions, 109
Acting out, 187–189
Acute stress, 85–86
Adaptive behaviors, 233–234
ADHD. *See* Attention-deficit/
    hyperactivity disorder
    (ADHD)
Adults with SPD, 21, 71
Adults, involving, 94
After events, 99–100
After sports events, 114–115
After weddings, 105
Aggressive depression, 239
Alarms, 179–180
Ali (case study), 190–191
Allowing movement, 203–205
Alternative assignments, 79
Alternative behaviors, 163

Alternatives, providing, 95
Alzheimer disease, 46
American Occupational Ther-
    apy Association, 168
American Psychiatric Asso-
    ciation, 17–18
Anecdotal references, 20
Anxiety, 215–218, 234
Applied behavioral analysis
    (ABA), 146
Appointment with teacher,
    193–194
Ariel (case study), 144–162
Arrival ahead of time, 180
Arya (case study), 77
Asperger disorder or syndrome,
    4, 70, 136, 187,
    215–216
Assessing need for therapy,
    139–141
Assessment process, 143–144
Assignment changes, 192
Assignment lists, 180
Assignment of teacher, 194
Assisting children, 213
Asymmetrical tonic neck
    reflex (ATNR), 155
Attention-deficit/hyperactivity
    disorder (ADHD), 17,
    55, 221–225

and bipolar disorder, 239
and sensory-seeking
  responses, 28
and SPDs, 224
Attention-getting, 185
Auditory issues. *See also*
  Hearing
  activities, 165–166
  impulses, 14
  nucleus, 152–153
  processing difficulties, 151
  processing evaluation, 59
  sense difficulties, 128–129
  system, 17, 27–29, 59–60,
    122, 132
Author's background, 4–7
Autism, 5, 20, 136, 177,
  213–216
Autism spectrum disorders,
  135, 145
Avoiding embarrassment,
  187–189
Awareness of body position.
  See Proprioceptive
  system
Awareness of stress effects,
  83
Ayres, A. Jean, 4, 21, 138

Baby crying, 185–186
Background music, 206
Background sounds, 59, 132
Balance, 52
Balance and movement. *See*
  Vestibular sense and
  system
Before events, 96–98
Beginning of school year, 193

Behavior as communication,
  184–191
Behavior as sign language,
  185
Behavior, part of stress, 84–85
Behavioral challenges,
  230–231
"Behavioral" child, 42–43,
  188–189, 230
Behavioral clues to SPD, 33
Behavioral intervention plan,
  242
Behavioral intervention plan,
  developing, 185–186
Behavioral management, 242
Behavioral observations sam-
  ple, 147–148
Behaviors, difficult, 123–134
Bells, school, 180
Better organization, 179–184
Big picture in education, 176
Bins, plastic, 182
Biological systems, 81
Bipolar disorder, 229–230
Birthday parties, 115–118,
  217–218
BlackBerries (digital), 183
Blame, taking, 141–142
Blended families, 227
Blood pressure and noise pol-
  lution, 14
Bodily space needs, 207
Body language, 68
Boundaries, 74, 209, 244
Brain. *See also* Central ner-
  vous system
  architecture, 47
  imaging technology, 42

maps, 46
neurodevelopment, 45–46
stem, 14
Bread baking analogy, 12,
16–17
Breaks
classroom, 192, 197
movement, 167
sensory integration, 62,
201, 216
stretch, 73
Bullies, 163

Calendars of events, 111
Caregivers. *See* Parents
Carrey, Benedict, 19
Case examples, description
of, 5
Case studies, 32
Ali, 190–191
Ariel, 144–162
Arya, 77
Emily, 231–244
Oliver, 64–74
Omid, 9–10, 18–19
Ray, 187–189
Samantha, 54–63, 213
Caskets, 107
Causes of SPD, 50–51
Central nervous system, 152,
158–159, 265
Cerebellum, 152–154
Cerebral cortex, 14, 152–153,
155
Cerebral palsy, 37
Certification, 138
Chalkboards, 206
Challenges, 102

Checklists before classroom,
180–181
Child development mile-
stones, 273–292
Child psychiatrist, 240
Child psychologist, 242
Children's Hospital Boston,
46–47
Child's shoes, stepping into,
51–53
Choice of teacher, 194
Choices for wedding partici-
pation, 103–104
Choosing tasks, 196, 201–202
Chronic stress, 86
Classes, special arrange-
ments, 191–192
Classical music, 200
Classmates. *See* Peers
Classrooms, 173–210
Classroom treatment, 60
Clinical examples, 53–74
Clinicians, 76
Clothing, 1, 58, 123–124
setting aside for next day,
180
Clutter, 200
Cognition, interferences by
stress, 84
Cognition skills, 37–38
Cognitive ability and PTSD,
91
Cognitive developmental
stages, 267–272
Cognitive frameworks,
268–272
Cognitive tests, 42
Colds, 82

Combat, 84
Commonalities, 18
Communication by behavior, 184–191
Community support, 141–142
Comparative shopping, 111–112
Competing stimuli, 58
Compression activities, 164
Computers, 182, 183
Concerns list, 120–121
Confidentiality, 227
Congenital heart condition, 37
Connecting with others, 141–142
Consequences of behavior, 204
Constant movement, 237
Controllability, lack of, 80
Coping mechanisms, 78–79
Core muscles, 154, 159
Core strengthening activities, 161
Correct diagnoses, 138
Cortex of brain, 47
Cost of not making accommodations, 179
Counseling services, 57
Counselors, nonacademic, 198
Creative teaching, 202–203
Criticism from others, 142
Culinary arts class, 190–191
Cultural influences on taste, 13
Curiosity, 147–148, 215
Current knowledge about SPD, 4–5
Curtains, 206

Daily planners, 181
Dancing, 127, 166–168
Death, discussions of, 106
Defiance, 235
DeGangi-Berk Test of Sensory Integration (TSI), 138–139
Degree requirement modifications, 192
Delivery history (on history form), 248–249
Depression, 80
Depression, contribution to by stress, 84
Depression, vulnerability to, 93
Destinations for vacations, 109
Developmental history (on history form), 251
Developmental history form, 245–265
Developmental milestones, 34–41
Developmental milestones, motor (on history form), 251
Developmental pediatricians, 135
Developmental stages, 267–272
Developmental therapy referral, 35–41
Devil, 235
Diabetes, 195
Diagnostic and Statistical Manual of Mental Disorders, 18, 76, 212–214, 219, 221–222

Difference from others, 195–196

Differences in taste preferences, 13

Digital timers, 182–183

Dimmers, 206

Dioramas, 202

Directions, 61, 73, 146–149, 207–208

Disabilities, students with, 191

Disability laws, 192

Discipline by parents, 49

Discipline in classrooms, 204

Discomfort levels, 21

Disconcerting behaviors, 234–235

Discrimination between inputs, 88

Discussing SPD with child, 101–102

Discussion after events, 100

Disruptive behavior disorder, 221–223

Dissociation, 84

Divorces, 227

Dizziness, 16

Dopamine, 44–45

Down syndrome, 36–37

Drapes, 206

Dreams, 15

Drooling, 130

During events, 98–99

Dyslexia, 220, 232–233

Dyspraxia, 30–31

Early detection, 139

Early diagnosis, 139–141

Early intervention programs, 135, 145

Early intervention referral, 35–41

Early intervention services, 64–66

Early onset bipolar disorder. *See* Bipolar disorder

Earplugs, 206

Educating about SPD
family and friends, 80
self, 136–137
students and teachers, 177–178

Eggs, 190–191

Electrical system analogy, 3

Embarrassment, avoiding, 187–189

Emily (case study), 231–244

Emotional regulation, 214

Emotions
on history form, 257–258
link to smell, 15

Emotions and feelings, 102–109

Empathy training, 243

Endurance, 159

Environment, 46–47

Evaluation, 143–144, 225–228

Evaluation, first line of, 41–43

Evaluation process, 34, 227–228

Evaluation sample, 144–162

Events participation, 98–99

Events preparation, 96–98

Events summary checklist, 94–95

Executive function tasks, 199

Exhaustion, 53
Exit strategies, 95, 117
Expectations from treatment, 167–171
Explaining rules, 209
Eye contact, 38–40, 56–57, 66, 146–147, 152, 154, 160
Eye movements, 154
Eyes, 15

Fabrics, 123
Facial expressions, 68
Familial vulnerability to PTSD, 91
Families, 109–110
Family histories, 55, 227
    on history form, 246
Family issues, 75
Family support, 142
Family therapy, 244
FBA. See Functional behavioral assessments (FBA)
Fears, 26, 77, 125, 129
Feedback to parents, 151
Financial aid, 192
Financial stress, 75
Fine motor skills, description, 36–37
First thing in the morning, 180
Five senses, 12–17
Five W's of events, 96
Fleeing, 84, 175
Flexibility in the classroom, 195
Floor treatment, 200
Fluorescent lights vs incandescent, 200, 206
Focusing, 131

Folders, 181
Following events, 99–100
Follow-up to weddings, 105
Food, 12–13
Friends
    child's interaction with, 21–22, 24, 54, 57, 62, 67–70
    parents' support from, 95, 98, 100
    understanding of SPD, 22, 80
Friendships, 67–68
Fringe disorder, 19
Frustration, 133
Fun, 205, 210
Functional behavioral assessments (FBA), 62–64, 72, 185–186, 230–231, 242
Functional clues, 32
Funding for research, 19, 76
Funerals, 105–109. See also Weddings
    alternatives to, 108

Gaining from behavior, 185
Games, 22, 210. See also Sports events
Gene expression, 46–47
Generalization of skills, 149, 171
Genetic component of taste, 13
Genetic mutations, 47
Genetically based disorders, 20
Ghosts, 237
Goal-directed activity clues, 32
Grades, 192

Graphomotor abilities, 184
Gravity, 16, 125, 152, 157–158
Grief process, 108–109
Grooming activities, 39, 71, 77, 123
Gross motor skills, description, 35–36
Group projects, 202
Guide for conducting SPD research, 17
Gustatory sense, 12–13
Gym classes. See Physical education classes
Gymnasiums, 208–209

Handwriting, 31
Hard-to-control impulses, 238
Harvard Medical School, 46–47
Health insurance, 19, 76
Health psychology, 75
Hearing, 14. See also Auditory issues
    problems, 39, 128–129
Heavy-work activities, 164
Help
    from parents and teachers, 79–81
    from schools, 177–178
History, 227
History sample, 145–147
Hitting siblings, 55–56
Holidays, 95–100
Home, differences from school, 174–176, 191
Home-school communication and collaboration, 63, 72, 149–150, 192–194, 240, 244

Honesty, 227
Hormones, changes in, 83
Human genome, 46–47
Humiliation, 87, 189
Humor, 205
Hyperactivity, 221–223, 229
Hyperalertness, 53, 77
Hypervigilance, 207
Hypothalamus-pituitary-adrenal axis (HPA axis), 82, 89
Hypotonia, 126, 153, 160, 161. See also Poor muscle tone
Hypotonic, 38

Identifying voices, 132
Immune system, effects of stress on, 89
Impulses, hard to control, 238
Impulsivity, 222–223, 238
In utero, 13
In-school support, 198
Incandescent lights vs fluorescent, 200, 206
Inconsistent performance, 196
Independence, 182
Independent living skills, 149
Independent providers, 146
Indiana University, 47
Individualized sensory diet. See Sensory diet
Individuals with Disabilities Education Act (2004), 185, 191–192, 231
Infant's brain, 265
Inner ear, 14, 151–153, 166
Inner skin linings, 164–165

Insurance companies, 41, 135, 225
Integration of senses, 14
Intelligence quotient (IQ), 42–43
Intense moods, 232
Intensity of symptoms, 140
Interference of behaviors with life, 139–141
Interference with thinking, 84
Internal regulation, 134
Internet. See Web sites
Interoceptive sense, 122, 134
Interrupting, 238
Interviewing evaluators, 226
Investigating teachers, 194
Invitations to birthday parties, 115–117
Isolation, 21, 80
Isometric resistance, 161

Job-related stress, 75
Joints. See Muscles and joints
Jokes, playing on others, 238

Kaveh, 1–3
Kevin, 86–87
Kranowitz, Carol Stock, 22
Kremen, William S., 91

Labeling, 141
Language, 59–60, 68–70, 132, 145–149, 213–216
Laptops, 182–183
Laughter, 205
Law and special education, 191–192
Learning disorders, 219–221

Leaving students behind, 176
Leaving the classroom, 201
Levels of discomfort, 21
Light, 52, 131
Light waves, 15
Limbic system, 15
Listening to child, 94
List of concerns, 120–121
Local sports, 113
Long-term stress, 86, 90
Look-alike disorders, 211–265
Loss of self-control, 3
Lower brainstem, 158
Lunch packing, 180

Magnetic resonance imaging (MRI), 42
Mainstream medicine, 19, 79, 85
Making changes at school, 177–178
Maladaptive, 223
Managing time, 182–183
Manic episodes, 229
Manic-depressive. See Bipolar disorder
Manifestations, 49–50
Map of neural wiring, 47
Marker boards, 206
Massachusetts General Hospital, 90–91
Mathematics disorder, 220–221
Math skills, 112
McLean Hospital's Center for Neurodevelopmental Services, 5
Medical necessity, 41

Medical problems (on history form), 249–250
Meeting with teacher, 193–194
Meltdowns, 140, 174–175, 196, 201
Mental health professionals, 17
Mental illness history, 232–233
Mental retardation, 55, 213
Meta-analysis, 90
Middle ear, 15–16
Migraine headaches, 205
Milestones for child development, 273–292
Miller, Gregory, 89–90
Miller, Lucy Jane, 17
Minor-league sports, 113
Misbehavior, 44
Misdiagnoses, potential consequences, 18
Misinterpreting refusals, 202
Misinterpreting sensory information, 71
Modified Checklist for Autism in Toddlers (M-CHAT), 214–215
Modifying classroom, 199–201
Modulation section, 158–159
Monkeys, experiments on, 44–45
Mood disorders, 229–230, 239
Mood swings, 133, 229
Morning routines, 179–180
Motion, excess, 126
Motion planning, 158

Motor developmental milestones, speech, language, communication (on history form), 251–255
Mouth, 12, 17, 25, 28, 122–130, 158, 163–165, 195, 197
Movement
   allowing, 203–205
   constant, 237
Movement and balance. See Vestibular sense and system
Multisensory processing, 156–158
Muscle-joint awareness. See Proprioceptive sense
Muscles and joints, 16
Muscle tone. See Poor muscle tone
Music listening, 165

National Institute of Mental Health, U.S. Child Psychiatry Branch, 46
Natural sounds, 165–166
Need for therapy, assessing, 139–141
Negotiating, 133
Nervous system, 175
Networks, 142
Neural pathways, 47–48
Neurological disorders, 47
Neuropsychiatric Institute and Hospital, University of California, Los Angeles, 4

Neuropsychological assessments, 144, 225, 226
Neuropsychological evaluations, 41, 64–74, 143, 145–151, 225–228
sample, 231–244
Neuropsychological testing, 69–70
Neuropsychologists, 41–43, 54, 227
Neurotransmitters, 44–45
New York Times, 19
Newborn history (on history form), 248–249
Newborns, 135
Nightmares, 232, 236
Noise, 52, 63, 67, 129, 195, 205–206
Noise levels, 63, 149, 200, 205
Noise pollution and blood pressure, 14
Nonacademic counselors, 198
Nonprofit organizations, 136
Nonverbal learning disorder (NLD), 217–219
Noses, 14–15
Nutrition, 46–47
Nystagmus, 155

Occupational therapists, 2, 5, 42, 54, 61, 72, 93, 134–136, 197–198, 242
finding, 137–139
Occupational therapy, 2, 57, 61, 74, 135, 150, 161, 168–172, 241
compared to physical therapy, 169
definition, 168

Occupational therapy sensory evaluation sample, 151–162
Ocular nuclei, 152–154
Odd motor mannerisms, 215
Odors, 207. *See also* Olfactory system
Olfactory system, 14–16, 27–29
difficulties, 130–131
Oliver (case study), 64–74
Omid (case study), 9–10, 18–19
Online resources, 142
Oral difficulties, 130
Organizational skills, 179–184, 199
Organizations, 141–142
Orienting sounds, 132
Other families, 141–142
Other parents, 184, 194
Outsiders, feeling like, 93
Outward behavior, 188–189
Overactivity, 221–223
Overexcitability, 66, 71
Overindulgence, 28
Overlapping symptoms (SPD, ADHD, and mood disorders), 229
Overprotection, 95
Overreacting, 133
Overresponsivity, 26–27, 58–59, 64, 66, 71, 76, 196
Overstimulation, 53, 57

Packing a lunch, 180
Pain, 26
Pain tolerance, 124, 160
Panic, 58
Paperwork, 182

Parents, 6–8, 43, 49–56,
    79–81, 93–144,
    231–244
Participation in events, 98–99
Paternal histories, 232–233
Patience, 134, 171
Patient compliance, 171
Pediatricians, 41, 134–135, 226
Peers, 56–58, 65–69, 74,
    79–80, 115–118, 133,
    146, 150, 163, 188–189,
    196–197
Perception of stress, 89
Perfectionists, 160–161
Perinatal history (on history
    form), 247–248
Personalized programs, 18–19
Pervasive developmental dis-
    orders, 212–216
Phenomonology, 83
Phonemes, 69
Physical development, 22
Physical education classes,
    208–210
Physical therapy compared to
    occupational therapy,
    169
Physical therapy evaluations,
    161
Piaget, Jean, 266
Piaget's developmental the-
    ory, 268–272
Picky eating, 38, 124, 130
Pitman, Roger K., 90–91
Planners, daily, 181
Planning. See also Preparation
    holiday celebrations, 111
    of motions, 158
    trips to stores, 111

Planning ahead, 94–95
Plastic bins, 182
Play as therapy, 170–172
Playgrounds, 166
Play therapy, 242
Poor muscle tone, 9, 10, 24,
    64, 126, 150, 153, 155–
    156, 159, 161
Position. See Proprioceptive
    system
Posttraumatic stress disorder
    (PTSD), 82, 87–88,
    90–92
Postural disorder, 30
Potter, Harry, 31
Practice, 96–98
Practicing, 94, 98, 104,
    171–172, 179, 183
Predisposing variables, 92
Predisposition for stress and
    SPD, 90
Preferences in taste, 13
Preferential seating, 191
Pregnancy, stress during,
    44–45
Premature birth, 64
Prenatal alcohol exposure,
    44–45
Prenatal stress, 44–45
Preoperational stage, 267
Preparation
    for birthday parties,
        115–118
    for funerals, 106–107
    for holidays, 96–98
    for shopping, 110–111
    for sports events, 112–114
    for weddings, 103–105
Preteaching, 182

Principals, 177
Private-payment arrangements, 135
Problem-solving skills, 37–38
Professional help
  for early diagnosis, 139–140
  in grief, 109
Progressive Academic Learning System (PALS), 146
Pronunciation, 31, 56, 69–70
Proprioceptive input, 166
Proprioceptive processing, 156–158
Proprioceptive sense and system, 16–17, 27–29
  difficulties, 127–128
Proprioceptive system, 204
Proust, Marcel, 15
Psychiatric medicine, 240–241
Psychological
  evaluation, 67
  functioning, 81
  processes, 79
Psychology of stress, 83
Psychoneuroimmunological (PNI), 79, 81, 90
Psychophysiological, 88
Psychosocial stressors, 75
Public health issue, stress as, 76
Pushing, 127–128

Questionnaires, 5, 144
Questions about SPD from child, 101–102

Radcliffe, Daniel, 31
Rapid speech, 237
Ray (case study), 187–189

Reading disorders, 219–221
Reality checks, 95, 105
Real stories, 53–74
Reasons for behavior, 184–191
Receptors, 13
Recommendations, 63, 69–70, 161–162
  sample, 148–151
Red flags, 35
Reducing family's stress, 2
References, 42
Referrals, 35–36, 53, 134–136, 144, 225–226, 240
Rehearsing, 182–183
Reimbursable expenses, 76
Reimbursement, 19, 225
Relating with teachers, 178
Reliving events, 87–88
Remembrance of Things Past (Proust), 15
Replacement of undesirable activities, 163
Research, 79, 240
Researchers, 76
Research funding, 19
Resources, 34
Response to movement, 151–156
Restrooms, 113
Rethinking behavioral disorders, 19
Retinas, 15
Rhythm, 22–23, 152, 155, 167
Risks, at sports events, 114
Risky behaviors, 239
Rituals (on history form), 262
Rules, explaining, 209

Saccule, 152
Safety awareness, 159–160
Samantha (case study), 54–63, 213
Sameness, need for (on history form), 262
Sample evaluation, 144–162
Scary feelings, 3
Schedules, 182
Schizophrenia, 46, 233
School
    assignments, 180
    bells, 180
    counselors and psychologists, 44, 63, 226, 242
    differences from home, 174–176, 191
    principals, 44, 177
    subjects, separation of, 181
    year beginning, 193
School-home communication and collaboration, 63, 72, 149–150, 192–194, 240, 244
Schools, 57, 62–63, 77, 79, 173–210
Screening tools, 214–215
Seatwork, 166
Security guard, 158
Seeing, 15
Segerstron, Suzanne, 89–90
Self-education, 136–137
Self-esteem
    boosting, 204
    inflated, 229
    and look-alike disorders, 221, 229
    loss as result of social isolation, 21
    loss as result of stress, 84
    loss from misdiagnosis, 18, 27, 80
    promoting, 22, 93, 105, 110, 115
    and school, 179, 193, 204
Self-isolation, 52, 64, 77
Self-management, 182–183
Self-stimulation behaviors (on history form), 262
Sensation-seeking, 71
Senses
    descriptions, 12–17
    reponses by SPD systems, 26–29
Sensorimotor, 70–72
Sensorimotor stage, 269
Sensory-based motor disorder, 30–31
Sensory deficit, 220
Sensory diets, 62, 143, 150, 162–167, 197–198, 216, 238, 242
    definition, 162–163
Sensory discrimination disorder, 29–30
Sensory-friendly classrooms, 176
Sensory input recommendations, 206–207
Sensory integration
    breaks, 62, 201, 216
    course, 138
    difficulties, 64
    dysfunction, 20
    evaluation, 72, 238
    intervention, 216

and sensory processing (on history form), 260–262
therapy, 63, 169–171, 216, 218, 230
Sensory Integration and Praxis Tests (SIPTs), 138
Sensory modulation, 158–159
Sensory modulation disorder, 26–29
Sensory overload, 200
Sensory processing disorder (SPD)
 causes, 50–51
 compared with typical development, 25
 definition, 2, 20
 diagnosis, 70–74
 distinguishing from ADHD, 223–224
 glossing over or misunderstanding, 76
 research results, 44–48
 as spectrum disorder, 32
 as types of stress, 75–76
Sensory Processing Disorder Foundation, 17, 21
Sensory Processing Disorder Resource Center Web site, 34
Sensory processing, meaning of, 11–17
Sensory-seeking response, 27–28
Sensory skills, 38–39
Sensory tools, 162
Separating out different sensory input, 29

Separating school subjects, 181
Separation of things, 182
Setting up classroom, 203–205
Seven senses, 12–17
Seyle, Hans, 83
Shades, 206
Sharing examples, 81
Sharing information with teachers and schools, 192–193
Shifting visual focus, 31
Shoelaces, 31
Shopping, comparative, 111–112
Short-term stress, 85–86, 90
Shutting down emotionally, 84
Siblings, 22, 55–56, 109–110, 114, 117
Sight, 15, 27–29
Simplifying classroom, 199–201
Simulation exercises, 51–53
SIPT test, 155
Sitting quietly, 204
Skill generalization, 171
Skin, 13, 123–124, 156
Sleeping, 133
Small-group therapy, 60, 149
Smell(s), 207. See also Olfactory system
 link to emotions, 15
Snacks, 167, 178
Social-emotional difficulties, 132–134
Social functioning (on history form), 258–259

Social interactions, 150
  on history form, 260
Social isolation, 21
Social pragmatics, 215–216
Social pragmatics groups, 241
Social skills training, 62, 73
Soldiering on, 84
Somatosensory sense. *See* Touch
Somatosensory system, 164
Sound, 52. *See also* Auditory
Sound therapy, 161
Sound waves, 14
Space in classroom, 203–205
SPD. *See* Sensory processing disorder (SPD)
Speakers, 137, 177
Special accommodations in classrooms, 191–192
Special education and the law, 191–192
Special education services, 241
Special interests, 196, 202
Spectrum disorder, SPD as, 32
Speech and language therapy, 59–60, 149
Speech evaluation, 65
Spiritual guidance, 106
Spoiling kids, 49
Sports events, 112–115
Sports, school, 86–87
Squeezing, 127–128
Stadiums, 112
Standardized tests, 219–220
Standard neurological tests, 42
Stereotyped (repetitive) behavior, 212–213

Stereotypes (on history form), 260–262
Stigmatization, 141
Stores, 110–112
Strategies for events, 97–98, 113–114
Strategies for parents, 6–8
Strengths, building on, 196
Stress, 75–92
  on family, 141
  during pregnancy, 44–45
  studies about, 88–92
Stress model, 6–8, 75–92
Stress psychology, 83
Stress-related disorders, 76
"Stuff," reducing, 199
"Stupid," 79, 188–189
Supplementary aids and services, 191–192
Support, 142
Surprise due dates, 181
Sweden, research in, 88–89
Swimming, 161
Switchboard, 13
Symbolic thinking, 269
Symptoms checklist, 120–122
Symptom *vs* syndrome (definitions), 121, 212, 224
Syndromes. *See* Asperger syndrome; Down syndrome

Tactile. *See also* Touch
  activities, 164–165
  overresponsivity, 51–52
  sense difficulties, 123–124
  sensitivity experiments, 44–45

Talking about SPD with child, 101–102

Talking after events, 100

Tantrums, 55, 67, 133, 213, 232–235

Taste, 12–13, 27–29, 52

Teacher, choice of, 194

Teachers, 43, 57–62, 67, 73–74, 79–81, 97, 144–148, 174–210

availability before school, 180

Teachers, investigating, 194

Teaching aids, 192

Teaching, creative, 202–203

Technology, 183

Temperature sensing, 134

Test format changes, 192

Testing of senses and sensory input, 138–139

Thalamus, 152–153

The Out-of-Sync-Child Has Fun: Activities for Kids with Sensory Process- ing Disorder, 22

Therapeutic items, 171

Therapy ball, 201

Thinking, interference by stress, 84

Three types of SPD, 26–31

Thrill-seeking behaviors, 27–28

Timed work, 133, 201

Time management, 182–183

Timers, digital, 182–183

Timing of treatments, 135

Tips for holidays, 96–100

Tips for planning outings, 94–118

Tips on classroom friendli- ness, 194–210

Tongue, 12–13, 158

Torture, 53

Touch, 13–14, 27–29, 51–52, 66, 156, 164. *See also* Tactile

Touch sensitivity, 184–185

Toy and game shopping, 112

Toys, 96–98

on history form, 262

Traffic jam, 20

Tra la trampoline game, 22–24

Traveling, 109

Treatment

differences (SPD, ADHD, and mood disorders), 229

expectations, 167–171

planning, 138

plans, 54, 59–63, 162–163

Triggering behavior, 185

TV, watching professional sports, 113

Twin brothers, 90–91

Unconscious processes, 11–12

Underresponsivitiy, 27

Understanding child's behav- ior, 3

Understanding sensory expe- rience, 29

Universal accommodations, 203

University of California, San Diego, Department of Psychiatry and Center for Behavioral Genomics, 91
University of Lausanne (Switzerland), 47
University of Wisconsin-Madison, 44–45
Unpredictable touching, 185
Utricule, 152

Vacations, 109–110
Vestibular processing, 151–156
Vestibular sense and system, 15–16, 161, 165–167
difficulties, 125–127
Veterans of wars, 87
Vibrating pens, 197
Vietnam veterans, 90–91
Visiting venues, 97
Visual aids, 61
Visual difficulties, 131–132
Visual sense. See Sight
Visual sensory overload, 199
Visuospatial functioning, 69–70, 73, 139, 218
Voices, 235–237
Voices, hearing, 232

Voices, identifying, 132
Volume, 52, 205–206
Volunteering in schools, 178

Wait-and-see periods, 139–140
Waiting lists, 136
Wall treatment, 200
War, 53
Warm-up times, 179–180
Weak muscle tone. See Poor muscle tone
Web sites, 34, 137–138, 142
Weddings, 102–105. See also Funerals
Weights, 158
Western Psychological Services Publishing, 138
Where's Waldo?, 29
White noise, 200. See also Noise
Willpower, 49–50
Window coverings, 206
Withdrawal, 57
Word approximations, 146–147
Word retrieval, 56
W-position definition, 166
Writing, 31
Written expression disorder, 220